God's Word, My Voice

A Lectionary for Children

Lyn Zill Briggs

Church Publishing
NEW YORK

Church Publishing, Incorporated.
19 East 34th Street
New York, New York 10016
www.churchpublishing.org

Cover design by Laurie Klein Westhafer
Typeset by: Rose Design

Library of Congress Cataloging-in-Publication Data
Briggs, Lyn Zill.
God's word, my voice : a lectionary for children / Lyn Zill Briggs.
pages cm
Includes index.
ISBN 978-0-89869-929-6 (perfect bound)—ISBN 978-0-89869-930-2 (ebook)
1. Lectionaries—Texts—Juvenile literature. 2. Episcopal Church.—Liturgy. I. Episcopal Church. Book of common prayer (2013). Selections. II. Common lectionary (1992) III. Bible. English. Selections. New Revised Standard. 2015. IV. Title.

BX5947.L4B75 2015
264'.032—dc23

2014034107

Printed in the Canada

To the glory of God with thanksgiving for
The children of the Church of the Resurrection
And my parents who taught me to love God's Word

Contents

Introduction

On the first Pentecost, the presence of the Holy Spirit empowered people to understand what was being said and heard. Understanding led to transformation. And transformation led to growth of the Body of Christ. Since that time, the scriptures have been translated for the purpose of transformation.

According to Wikipedia, the entire Bible has been translated into 518 languages, and portions of the Holy Scriptures have been translated into 2,798 different languages. Children use and understand language in different ways than adults do. We are responsible for helping them understand what God is saying to them through God's Word, so that the Spirit can transform them.

This collection of paraphrases is another tool to enable transformation. This book is intended to support children in reading Holy Scriptures aloud in church to the whole assembly of people. Adults love to hear God's Word spoken in a child's voice, and may come to understand God's Word in a whole new way. Incorporating the children more fully into the worshipping assembly strengthens all of us as God's people.

This resource does not contain scriptural translation, but biblical paraphrase. To that end, some details (like names of geographical places or difficult names of people) have been left out of the text. I've filled in some blanks (catching up with what happened previously, etc.) and fleshed out some details. But not much. Paraphrased readings correspond to each of the Sundays in the three-year lectionary cycle, along with Holy Week/Triduum readings and Christmas Day.

Reading aloud is incarnational activity! When you read aloud, you also hear yourself reading and are doubly impacted by God's Word. Adult readers know this.

Incorporating children in the liturgy can be challenging in some congregations. If there hasn't been a tradition of children being present or having any "kid" time, it may be difficult getting kids to come. Honoring children's place in the worshipping community shows that the message of God's love and the challenge of a faithful life are important to all generations. It's even difficult to bring God's Word alive for adults who have sixty years' experience of listening to the lectionary! Most of all, intergenerational worship brings a congregation together to experience the message of God's love offered to us all.

There are many benefits for including all ages in worship and having children read the lections. Incorporating children and their voices into the reading rota encourages parents to bring them and their extended families to church. Children will feel more fully part of their church and will become more comfortable in the "sacred" space of the chancel as they actively participate in their readings. An extra bonus is that reading aloud in church will help your children (and any reader) grow in confidence. Remember that children want to do a good job. Train them to read slowly and distinctly. Teach them how to introduce the reading properly and conclude with "The Word of the Lord."

Here are some suggestions for using this resource:

- Be creative in presenting these paraphrases, remembering that they are not performance pieces but God's Word. Use props as necessary, making sure the understanding of the word doesn't get upstaged.
- Have children read them exactly "as is." Or work with them to fit your context so that they are understood.
- When the children read from the Epistles, help them remember that they are letters. Have a child run up to the ambo or lectern just as someone is ready to read, with a scroll in hand, saying "Here's a letter we just got from Paul. Read it!" Have a group of children surround the reader with scroll in hand, anxiously awaiting Paul's words.
- Children enjoy leading the congregation in the psalms. A congregational refrain is included when appropriate in bold.
- Rework the lessons that contain lots of dialogue, dividing the speaking parts between several kids.
- If possible, print the readings in the bulletin in their entirety. Children may not be the best readers, but that doesn't mean they can't read aloud while we follow along. You'll be amazed at their improved reading skills and confidence over time.
- Introduce the children to the ambo/lectern before they are scheduled to read. Practice with them using the microphone or the stool they might need.
- E-mail the parents or the children themselves the lessons ahead of time with copies of what their child will be reading.
- The first time a child reads in church, send him or her a note of thanks and an invitation to read again.
- You can use all three readings at a service, or just one, whichever suits your congregation and the children who are reading.

- Involve groups of kids by dividing up the reading into discrete parts. Kids can alternate paragraphs, standing at the ambo together.
- It can be intimidating to stand and read before a room full of adults. Having a parent standing close by can give a child the confidence he or she needs.
- Engage the children in proclaiming the gospel. There is lots of dialogue in some lessons. Have a child read along with the gospeller perhaps being the voice of Jesus. It's *awesome* to hear Jesus' words from the mouth of a child.
- Encourage the use of this lectionary at home. If possible, e-mail the readings to the parents of all the children so they can read them together aloud as a family. Or give this book as a gift to families at special times.
- Read aloud in Sunday school classes or children's church.
- After church, invite the kids to re-phrase and tell you what they heard and read.
- Use your discretion in assigning readings. Some readings are more appropriate for younger children. All are appropriate for older children and adults.

Hear and read God's Word in as many ways as you can to as many people as you can. May God bless your hearing, reading, and understanding of the Holy Scriptures. I would love to hear your experience of *God's Word, My Voice*.

Lyn Zill Briggs
LynZBriggs@gmail.com
Pentecost, 2014

Thank you, Sharon Ely Pearson, for recognizing the power of the Spirit in the voice of a child and bringing this project to print. I deeply appreciate your encouragement and partnership.

Year A

The First Sunday of Advent

A Reading from Isaiah [2:1–5]

Here's what Isaiah sees for the future of Judah and Jerusalem:

God's house will be on the highest mountain of them all. And everyone will see it and want to come to it. Because they'll say to themselves, "Let's go see what good things God has to teach us so that we can become better people and follow the good path God has for us."

That's where you'll find some good ideas about living and loving—in God's house. God's ways to live are good ways to live.

In the future, when things go God's way, people who are different from each other will get along. Countries won't fight each other. They'll use their weapons as garden tools to grow good things to eat instead of using them to hurt each other. Let's walk on God's path together.

The Word of the Lord.

Psalm 122

It made me so happy when someone suggested we go to God's house!
Because my feet always want to take me there, to Jerusalem, where all the people praise God.

Pray for the peace of Jerusalem.
May good things happen to those who love God's house.

That's where decisions have been made, and kings have been crowned, and people thank God.
I think we should all pray for the peace of Jerusalem: May they prosper who love you.
May there be peace be within your walls, and security within your towers.
Let's do everything we can to make sure there is peace in Jerusalem, and see that those who live there are safe and happy.

Pray for the peace of Jerusalem.
May good things happen to those who love God's house.

A Reading from Romans [13:11–14]

The time has come. We need to wake up! Wipe the sleep from your eyes, because we are closer than ever to God's salvation. The rough times are almost over, and the sun is about to come up. We should put aside our dark thinking, and instead put on the armor made of light. We should act like we act when people are watching us, because they are. Don't do the things that would bring us shame: being drunk, messing around with people we shouldn't be messing with, being jealous, and sniping at each other. Rather, clothe yourselves with the Lord Jesus Christ, and don't even bother trying to make yourselves happy with other things.

The Word of the Lord.

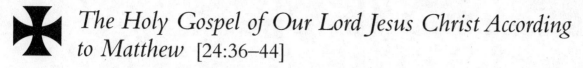

✠ *The Holy Gospel of Our Lord Jesus Christ According to Matthew* [24:36–44]

Nobody knows when the last day will come. Not the angels in heaven, or Jesus himself—only the Father knows. It will come all of a sudden. People go about their everyday lives, like at the time of the Flood, and then all of a sudden they're floating in water. The end will be sudden, just like that. Two men will be standing together, and one is taken, and the other is not. Surprise! So pay attention, because you don't know when that day will be. Just know you need to be ready for anything, because Jesus will return when you least expect it.

The Gospel of the Lord.

The Second Sunday of Advent

A Reading from Isaiah [11:1–10]

In an old stump of a tree, like the family tree of Jesse, there will be a new green shoot, and the shoot will grow into a branch. The branch will be the Messiah, and the Spirit of the Lord will rest on him. He will be wise and understanding. He will be strong and confident and know and love the ways of God. He won't judge a person by what he hears about them or by what they look like. He will see poor people through God's eyes, and will always be on the side of the powerless people. The wicked people had better watch out when he's around. He'll wear goodness and faithfulness like we wear coats and hats. Amazing things will happen—wolves will be friends with little lambs. Leopards will get along with the goats. Calves and lions will play together. And a little child will be in charge of them all. Cows and bears will share the pasture. And their babies will take naps side by side. Lions will eat hay like oxen do. Babies will play with snakes and the snakes won't bite them. There won't be any pain anymore, and all the earth will be covered with knowing God, just like the waters of the sea cover the earth. And that branch from Jesse's family tree will be a hero to all the people of the earth. Kings will wonder who he is, and wherever the Messiah is, that place will be beautiful.

The Word of the Lord.

Psalm 72:1–7, 18–19

Share your justice and goodness with the people in charge
    and with their children, God.
So that they may treat people right, and take care of poor people.

We say, Amen. And again we say, Amen.

So that the mountains can give people all good things and the little hills be examples of goodness.
Let the king be on the side of poor people, and rescue them from anyone who wants to hurt them even more.

We say, Amen. And again we say, Amen.

May good kings always be with us, as long as there is a sun and a moon.
A good king is like rain when rain is needed; a shower for the whole thirsty world.

We say, Amen. And again we say, Amen.

When there is a good king, there are plenty of good people, and peace will be on earth for as long as there is a moon in the sky.
We bless you, God; you are the only one who can make these good things happen. We will always bless your name. May all the earth be filled with your glory.

We say, Amen. And again we say, Amen.

A Reading from the Letter of Paul to the Romans [15:4–13]

The words written by people long ago were written to keep our spirits up. I pray that God who gives us encouragement can help you live peacefully with each other, like Jesus would want you to. I pray that all of us can someday sing one happy song to God, who is Jesus' father and father of us all. Be kind and welcome each other, just as Jesus welcomed you. Jesus became a servant of all of us, so that each of us could see who he is. Not all of us were born into the faith, but all of us are welcomed into it. Everyone is welcome—people who have believed a long time, as well as you newcomers. I pray that God fills you full of joy and peace as you believe more and more, so that you are drenched in hope by the power of the Holy Spirit.

The Word of the Lord.

✠ *The Holy Gospel of Our Lord Jesus Christ According to Matthew* [3:1–12]

A long time ago, John the Baptist, Jesus' cousin, showed up in the desert, shouting, "You had better change your ways, people. For God is very near." The prophet Isaiah wrote about John when he said, "There is someone out in the desert telling people to make way for the Lord because he's coming." John was a funny kind of guy. He wore camel skins with a leather belt, and he ate bugs and wild honey. He attracted a lot of attention and people came from the cities to check him out. They asked him to baptize them, knowing they needed to change. John saw people he thought were hypocrites because they thought they were God's special people who did no wrong. When he saw them he yelled at them, "You are a big pile of snakes. You'd better change your ways too. Don't think just because Abraham was your ancestor that you're going to get by with things. God could make all of these rocks here children of Abraham just like you if he wanted to. If you don't listen to God now, deep in your heart, you might as well be a chopped down tree that's thrown into the fire. I'll baptize you with water, but someone much, much greater than me is coming soon, and he will pour the Holy Spirit on you and light your souls on fire for God. He is ready to make everything new for God."

The Gospel of the Lord.

The Third Sunday of Advent

A Reading from the Book of Isaiah [35:1–10]

Someday, the desert will be so happy that it will break out in flowers! There will be yellow and purple and white crocuses all over and they'll be singing! The wilderness will look like the most beautiful part of Lebanon. Someday, we'll be so excited because we will see God in all God's glory. And those whose hands don't work will be strengthened, and if your knees creak and ache, they'll be like they're brand new. If you're scared, let me say to you, "Be strong. Don't be afraid. God has everything under control. God will come and save you." And then, blind people will be able to see and deaf people will hear. People who had trouble walking will jump around just like deer, and if you couldn't talk before, you won't be able to stop singing for joy. Water will rush through the wilderness and streams up from the desert. Instead of burning sand, there will be a swimming pool. The desert sands won't be thirsty anymore.

And there will be a highway running right through the desert, in the middle of nowhere, and we'll call it God's Highway. It will be for the people of God to walk. And no one who walks on it will get lost. You won't have to worry about dangerous animals coming after you when you're on God's Highway. Everyone who has walked away from God can come back singing. And nothing will make them sad anymore.

The Word of the Lord.

Canticle 15

My soul is so happy. I can't stop singing about God's kindness
  to me, a lowly servant.
From now on, everyone will know that I have been blessed.
God has done great things for me and God's name is holy.

God's heart goes out to those who walk the right way, in every generation, young and old.
God is strong enough to scatter proud people in every direction.
God picks up those who think they're better than anyone else, and flings them off their fancy chairs, but he picks up those who are sad and lifts up their chins so they can hold their heads high again.

God has done great things for me and God's name is holy.

God feeds hungry people the best food they've ever eaten. And when people with too much get in line, God says, "Enough already."
God remembers his promise of mercy and has come to help out the people in Israel.
God promised mercy to our ancestors, to all of Father Abraham's children forever.

God has done great things for me and God's name is holy.

A Reading from the Letter of James [5:7–10]

I know it's hard to wait, my friends, until the Lord comes again. Just like the farmer has to wait for his seeds to grow. He can't hurry them up. He has to be patient too, and wait for the rain. So be patient like the farmer. Make your hearts strong, for the Lord is coming again. Soon. Friends, please don't grumble about each other or to each other. When people hear you grumble, it's hard for them to believe that you follow Jesus. Believe me, I know it's tough to wait. The prophets before us who spoke in the Lord's name when no one would listen to them, they got discouraged in their waiting too. Look to them and their example when you get tired of waiting.

The Word of the Lord.

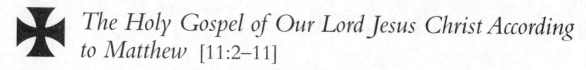

✠ *The Holy Gospel of Our Lord Jesus Christ According to Matthew* [11:2–11]

John the Baptist, Jesus' cousin, was in prison. Somehow he heard about what Jesus was doing, so he sent Jesus a message with some of his friends. "Tell me, Jesus, are you the one we've been waiting for? Or should we keep waiting for the right one to come?"

Jesus thought about this question. And he said, "Go tell John about what you see and hear: that blind people can see again, that people who couldn't walk are now jumping up and down, that people with diseases are healed, that people whose ears didn't work can hear, and that dead people are alive. And that poor people are hearing good news for the first time in their lives. Blessed are people who find nothing wrong with these things I'm doing in God's name."

So the disciples took that message to John. While they were gone, Jesus began to talk to the crowds of people about his cousin John.

"John's not quite what you expected, is he?" Jesus said. "Who did you think he'd be, someone in fancy, soft clothing? People who dress like that live in palaces, not in the desert like John. Did you expect him to be a prophet? Yes, John is a prophet because he tells the truth, even if it's difficult to hear. He is the one the prophets wrote about: 'A messenger will come ahead of you, and make the people ready for you.' John is closer to God and the truth than anyone ever has been; yet he is no better than anyone else in God's kingdom."

The Gospel of the Lord.

The Fourth Sunday of Advent

A Reading from the Book of Isaiah [7:10–16]

God spoke to Ahaz again. This time God said, "Ask me to do anything you want as a sign; anything as high as the highest heaven or as deep as the deepest sea. Go ahead ask me for a sign so I can prove myself to you."

But Ahaz didn't feel good about that. "I'm not going to ask you to prove yourself, God. I won't give you a test."

Isaiah said, "Listen to me, people of the house of David. Is it not enough for you to wear out human beings, do you have to pester God as well? God will give you a sign. Here's what it will be: A young girl will have a baby, and she will name him Immanuel. By the time he starts walking he'll have figured out the right way to live, and how to turn away from bad choices. And by the time that happens, the land ruled by the two kings you are scared of will be empty."

The Word of the Lord.

Psalm 80:1–7, 16–18

You are like the Shepherd of Israel, and we are like your sheep.
Glow brightly, because the angels are surrounding you on
your throne.
As you stand before your people, stir up your strength and come
to help us.

Make us whole again, O God of all the angels in heaven.
Just show us your shining face and we will be saved.

God, we cry out our prayers to you day and night. How long will
you be angry with us?

You give us bread made of tears, and bowls filled with tears
to drink.
All our neighbors make fun of us.

Make us whole again, O God of all the angels in heaven.
Just show us your shining face and we will be saved.

Rest your hand on the shoulder of your helper, the one you
picked to lead us back to you.
And we will never turn away from you again. Give us life, so that
we can come before you and speak your name.

Make us whole again, O God of all the angels in heaven.
Just show us your shining face and we will be saved.

A Reading from the Letter of Paul to the Romans [1:1–7]

We got a letter from Paul, and this is what it says:

I'm Paul, and I serve Jesus Christ himself. I was called to be an apostle and God gave me special instructions to spread the Good News. The prophets have been talking about this for centuries, the Good News about Jesus, God's son. King David was one of Jesus' great-great-grandfathers. Jesus was also proclaimed Son of God by his holiness, through his resurrection. Through Jesus we all have been given a second chance, and have been sent out to tell people the Good News about God's love for them. I send this letter in Jesus' name, and along with this letter, I send you grace and peace from God and God's Son Jesus.

The Word of the Lord.

✠ *The Holy Gospel of Our Lord Jesus Christ According to Matthew* [1:18–25]

Here's the story of when Jesus was born. Mary, his mother, was engaged to Joseph. But before they were married, Mary found out she was going to have a baby. The Holy Spirit made that happen! Joseph knew people would talk about Mary behind her back because she wasn't married, and he didn't want that to happen to her. So he planned to stop the engagement quietly and no one need know about this baby. That sounded like a good plan to Joseph. But then one night a messenger from God came to him while he was sleeping and said, "Joseph, don't worry about taking Mary as your wife, even though that baby isn't yours. This baby is very special and the Holy Spirit is the reason he will be born. When the baby is born, name him Jesus; he's the one who will save his people from their sin. Don't be afraid, Joseph."

This is what Isaiah was talking about when he said—a young woman will have a baby who will be named Immanuel, which means God is here with us.

When Joseph woke up from that dream, he decided to do just what the messenger from God told him to do. He married Mary, and when her baby was born, he named him Jesus.

The Gospel of the Lord.

The Nativity of Our Lord Jesus Christ: Christmas Day

A Reading from the Book of Isaiah [9:2–7]

The people who have been walking in the dark for so long have finally seen a great light. You have pumped them up and expanded their joy. They are as happy as people who have harvested a fabulous crop and won't go hungry this year, as happy as people are opening birthday presents, or dividing up found money. They no longer feel like they're pulling someone else's wagon. It's time to throw the boots of the soldiers and their bloody clothes in the fire.

A baby boy has been born for us. He will be someone whom we respect and look up to. And his name is Mighty God, Prince of Peace. His influence will keep growing until there is no end of peace for the family of King David and all who followed him. This baby boy will develop a nation held together with justice and goodness now and always.

The Word of the Lord.

Psalm 96

I've got a brand new song to sing to God.
Everyone, join me in singing it.
I'll sing my new song to God and tell everyone God's news
 is the best news ever.
I'll tell people I meet about God's goodness and the wonderful
 things he does.
There really isn't anyone or anything like God.
Which is one reason I love God.

I've got a brand new song to sing to God.
Everyone, join me in singing it.

Other people might think money or family or their job is more important, but it's God who made everything they have and everything there is.
So give your attention to God because God deserves it.
Worship God when you see how beautiful the clouds are, or a rainbow in the sky, or a perfect little snowflake.

I've got a brand new song to sing to God.
Everyone, join me in singing it.

Tell everyone you know about God's goodness and power that he uses to help people.
Even the sky and the stars praise God.
The sea roars and the fields and even the trees shout for joy when they see God coming.
God is good, and God wants us to be the good the world can see.

I've got a brand new song to sing to God.
Everyone, join me in singing it.

A Reading from the Letter of Paul to Titus [2:11–14]

For the grace of God has appeared, saving all of us from ourselves, training us to want goodness, and to live lives that are self-controlled, decent, and kind, while we wait for the hope and glory of our great God and Savior, Jesus Christ. Jesus gave himself for us so that we might be passionate for integrity and justice.

The Word of the Lord.

✠ *The Holy Gospel of Our Lord Jesus Christ According to Luke* [2:1–20]

In order to count how many people there were so that he could tax them, the emperor told everyone to go to their hometowns to be counted. So Joseph went with Mary, his fiancée, who was expecting a baby at any time, from Nazareth to Bethlehem. His family was descended from King David, and King David had lived in Bethlehem. While they were there, Mary delivered a baby boy, wrapped him up tight, and laid him in a feed trough in the barn where they were staying because the inns were all full.

Meanwhile, in the fields, shepherds were watching their sheep during the night. All of a sudden an angel stood right in front of them, and God's glory was shining all around and they were scared to death. The angel told them not to be afraid because there was only good news. "This news is so good," the angel said, "that everyone will be happy. Today in the city of David, the Savior whom everyone's been waiting for was born. I want you to go find him. Here's how you'll know he's the right baby: He'll be lying in a feed trough all wrapped up in strips of cloth."

When the angel said that, the skies burst into song, and angels filled up the entire sky, praising God and saying, "Glory to God in the highest heaven, and peace to those on earth whom God loves."

When the angels had gone back to heaven, the shepherds said to each another, "Let's go to Bethlehem and find this baby boy they were talking about." So they ran and found Mary and Joseph, and the baby lying in the feed trough, just as the angel had told them. They told Mary and Joseph what the angel had said, about who this child was and would become. Everyone was amazed at their story. But Mary kept this entire story in her heart. The shepherds praised God for all that had happened that night, and went back to their sheep who had been wondering where their shepherds had gone.

The Gospel of the Lord.

The First Sunday after Christmas Day

A Reading from the Book of Isaiah [61:10—62:3]

I'm just about to burst with joy. God has bought me a whole new wardrobe! He has dressed me up in salvation and covered my shoulders with a fancy robe of goodness. I look like I'm ready to go to a wedding! Just like the earth pushes little green shoots into the sunshine, and new plants eagerly spring up through the dirt; that's how God is making righteousness and goodness grow all over the world.

I am not going to keep quiet about this. I'm not going to sleep until I know that God's people in Zion and Jerusalem know about God's glory. God will give God's people a new name and a new look about them, so that everyone will be bowled over by their beauty. Then Jerusalem will be like a crown of jewels held in God's hands, ready to place on God's head.

The Word of the Lord.

Psalm 147

Hallelujah! It feels so good to sing God's praises.
    It just feels right to honor God with our songs.
God is building things up again that have been torn down.
Gathering the people who got scattered, healing broken hearts
    and taking care of people's wounds.
God counts the stars in the skies one by one and calls them each
    by name.

The Word actually became one of us, and lived among us.

Our God is so incredibly great.
There is no limit to God's wisdom.

Our God picks up people whose spirits are low and throws the bad ones to the ground.
Sing a song of thanksgiving to God. Make beautiful music on your harp.

The Word actually became one of us, and lived among us.

God is the one who covers the heavens with clouds and gets the rain ready to fall to the earth.
God makes grass grow on the mountaintops and all the green things that are good for us to eat.
God makes sure that there is food in the pasture for our flocks of sheep and herds of goats, and provides food for crying baby birds when they're hungry.

The Word actually became one of us, and lived among us.

There's no point in showing off your biggest, strongest horse or your strongest bodybuilder—God's not impressed.
God is impressed with people who wait patiently with faith and trust.
Jerusalem, worship the Lord. Zion, praise your God.
Because God has strengthened your fortresses to keep you safe and has already blessed the children who live within your borders.
God has established peace around you.
And provides the best wheat for you to eat.

The Word actually became one of us, and lived among us.

God's words ring out all over the world and the earth pays attention.
God sends out the snow and the frost.
Hail falls from the heavens like God was throwing breadcrumbs for the birds.
And when he makes it cold outside, who can stand it?

God's words melt the ice. The winds rage and the waters flow
when God gives breath to the wind.
God speaks to the people in Israel. Hallelujah!

The Word actually became one of us, and lived among us.

A Reading from the Letter of Paul to the Galatians [3:23–25; 4:4–7]

Before we had faith in our hearts, it was like we were in a prison made of laws and faith was not allowed in to visit us. The law was our jailer who kept us in line, until Christ came along, and now faith is what makes us right with God. Now that faith is in our hearts, we don't need a jail or a jailer any more. When God thought we were ready, God sent his Son Jesus, born as a little baby, into a world full of laws, so that he could bring back to himself the people who were living in prisons made of laws. And now, we can all become adopted children of God!

Because we are God's children, God has placed the Spirit of his Son Jesus in our hearts, which makes us cry for God just like he's our father. We don't work in God's house like slaves; we are the kids of the owner! And the owner is God. We are children who will inherit all the goodness God has to offer.

The Word of the Lord.

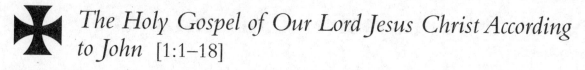

✠ *The Holy Gospel of Our Lord Jesus Christ According to John* [1:1–18]

Before there was anything, there was the *Word*, with God and in God. The *Word* was God! Everything there ever was in the whole universe came to life through the *Word*. In fact, there's nothing that the *Word* didn't make.

Life came into being through him. That life lights up for all people to see. It shines in the darkness, and as you know, darkness cannot put out light.

John the Baptist was a man of God. He understood that Jesus was light, and that Jesus was coming to be our savior. Some people didn't recognize that, but those who did, who let him shine his light into their hearts, had the power to become God's children.

And the *Word* actually became one of us, and lived here on earth with us. You and I have seen his glory, and he is filled with grace and truth.

John cried out in the desert, pointing to Jesus and saying, "He's the One. He's the One I've been talking about!"

Because Jesus is filled with grace, all of us have more than our share of grace. In fact, we have been given grace upon grace upon grace. And even more grace than that.

The law given to Moses served its purpose; now grace and truth is serving its purpose through Jesus Christ. No one knows what God the Father looks like. Jesus, God's only Son, who is close to the Father's heart, is the one who makes God the Father known to us.

The Gospel of the Lord.

The Second Sunday after Christmas Day

A Reading from the Book of Jeremiah [31:7–14]

This is what God says: Go ahead and shout for joy and sing happy songs, people. I am going to round everyone up from the farthest parts of the earth—everybody. The ones who can't see and the ones who can't walk, those who are pregnant and those who are right in the middle of having their babies. This is going to be HUGE! I'll bring them all back home where they belong. They will be weeping for joy as they come. I will let them walk by the beautiful babbling brooks of water, and clear a path for them so they won't stumble and fall. I love you all like a father loves his very first child.

Make sure everyone knows what I'm doing. Tell them about my goodness, about the grain and the wine and the oil and the little lambs. Tell them that my people will be like a beautiful watered garden that always produces beautiful things to eat. Tell them to dance because, instead of crying, they will be laughing. There will be plenty of dancing and laughter and good food to go around.

The Word of the Lord.

Psalm 84

I'm always so happy when I'm at your house, God. I really want to be with you. My heart is full of joy knowing that you are my God, who is alive and close to me.

Little birds are happy at your house where they are safe and can raise their little ones.

My happy place is by your altar, O God.

Because that's where I sing your praises along with all your people.
People who walk in the right direction, on the right path, find their strength in you.
Even people who are going through tough times find your house to be a place where they can fill up their empty places and find the courage to keep on walking.

My happy place is by your altar, O God.

One day with you in your house, God, is better than a thousand days sitting in my own room, or hanging out with people who are up to no good.
You are both my sunshine and my shade, and you have plenty of grace and glory to go around. Those of us who choose to walk your path know we will never run out of grace and glory.

My happy place is by your altar, O God.

A Reading from the Letter of Paul to the Ephesians [1:3–6, 15–19a]

I want to sing God's praises because God has blessed us by sending us Christ Jesus. And because of that, we have every spiritual blessing we could possibly want. God chose us to belong to God, and created us to be adopted as God's children through Jesus Christ. I have heard of the faith you have in Jesus and the love you show all the saints. I always thank God for you and pray for you whenever I think of you. Here is what I pray: that God will give you a spirit of wisdom so that you can know God better. Once God has enlightened the eyes of your heart, you will also know God's hope for you—to have the riches of God's grace, and share in great power that is even bigger and deeper than anyone can measure. That's what I pray for you.

The Word of the Lord.

✠ *The Holy Gospel of Our Lord Jesus Christ According to Matthew* [2:13–15, 19–23]

Once the wise men were gone, an angel from God came to Joseph in another dream. The angel said, "The king is trying to find Jesus to kill him because he heard Jesus was a new king." That woke Joseph right up, and in the middle of the night, they ran away to Egypt. They stayed there until Herod had died and couldn't hurt them anymore. When Herod died, the angel came back and said it was safe to go back to Israel, where they were from. Joseph found out Archelaus was the new ruler, but Joseph didn't trust him either. So, after another dream, he went instead to Nazareth in Galilee. The prophets had said that the Messiah would be called a Nazorean, someone who lived in Nazareth.

The Gospel of the Lord.

or

✠ *The Holy Gospel of Our Lord Jesus Christ According to Luke* [2:41–52]

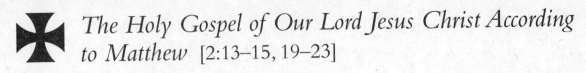

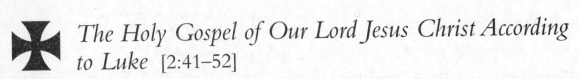

Each year Jesus and his parents walked to Jerusalem to celebrate Passover. When Jesus was twelve, and they were in Jerusalem, they started to go home after the festivities. They walked for a whole day before they realized Jesus wasn't with them, and wasn't with the friends they were walking with either. They looked for him for three days but couldn't find him anywhere. So they went back to Jerusalem. They found him in the temple, listening to the teachers there and asking them questions. Apparently everyone who heard him talk was amazed at how bright he was. His parents weren't happy with him though. His mother said, "I can't believe you, Jesus! What were you thinking? Your father and I have been worried sick about you because we had no idea where you were." Jesus said, "You could have figured I'd be at my Father's house." Mary and Joseph didn't quite get what he meant by that. They all left then, and returned to Nazareth where Jesus was a very good son. His mother loved him very much and kept all these little stories about him in her heart, like any mother does. As Jesus grew older, he grew wiser too, and became more and more the person God and his parents wanted him to be.

The Gospel of the Lord.

or

✠ *The Holy Gospel of Our Lord Jesus Christ According to Matthew* [2:1–12]

When Jesus was born in Bethlehem, wise men from the East came to Jerusalem to ask, "What's this about a child born king of the Jews? We saw a star in the sky that led us here, and we've come to honor him."

King Herod, who was very insecure and a little crazy, said, "King? What king?" Herod was scared that another king was out there. So he called all the priests and smart people together and asked them where this king of the Jews was supposed to be born according to the books.

They looked and found out that he was supposed to be born in Bethlehem. So he told the wise men to go to Bethlehem and made up a story about how he wanted to go and honor this newborn king as well. He actually wanted to destroy him.

The wise men set out for Bethlehem. The star in the sky stopped over the spot where Jesus lived. The wise men were thrilled! When they went inside, they found Jesus and Mary and they got down on their knees to worship him. They opened their packages full of treasures and gave him gifts of incense and gold. They had a dream that told them not to go back to Herod, so instead of going back through Jerusalem, they found another road and went home.

The Gospel of the Lord.

The First Sunday after the Epiphany: The Baptism of the Lord

A Reading from the Book of Isaiah [42:1–9]

This is my servant, and I support him all the way. He's the one I chose and I am thrilled with him. I have given him my spirit, says God.

He will bring justice to everyone, but not by fighting. He is gentle but strong. He will not stop until everyone is treated fairly.

God created the heavens and stretched them out, laid out the earth and everything on it, and gives breath to the people on the earth. Here's what God says:

"I am the LORD, I have called you from the goodness
of my heart.
I have taken you by the hand and I'm holding you close
to me.
I have given you as a gift to everyone, everywhere, a light
to the nations, to open the eyes that are blind and those
who live in darkness, to bring out the prisoners from the
pit they've been in,
I am the LORD, that is my name."

Everything that was supposed to happen has happened. Listen to me, because I'm telling you that from now on, we're doing something new.

The Word of the Lord.

Psalm 29

All glory and strength belongs to God. Worship God in beautiful holiness.
The voice of God is on the waters. The glory of God is in the thunder.
God is on the mighty waters.

At God's house, everybody is shouting, "Glory!"

God's voice is a powerful voice and is full of splendor.
The voice of God is so powerful, it breaks the mighty cedar trees of Lebanon.

At God's house, everybody is shouting, "Glory!"

God makes the whole country of Lebanon skip around like a calf in spring.
And makes Mount Hermon frolic like a young wild ox.

At God's house, everybody is shouting, "Glory!"

God's voice splits the flames of fire and shakes the wilderness.
The voice of God makes the oak trees squirm and strips the trees in the forest bare.

At God's house, everybody is shouting, "Glory!"

Everyone in God's temple is shouting, "Glory!"
God sits high above the floodwaters on a throne like a king for ever.
God will give strength to the people and give them a blessing of peace.

At God's house, everybody is shouting, "Glory!"

A Reading from the Acts of the Apostles [10:34–43]

Peter began to talk to Cornelius and the others: "I understand now that God doesn't see differences between people like we do. Everyone who believes in God and does what is right, no matter who they are or where they are from, is acceptable to God. The message sent to the people of Israel—that Jesus is Lord of all—has now spread throughout the world. The message began with God anointing Jesus with the Holy Spirit. Then Jesus went about doing good and healing people because God was with him. We all witnessed him doing that wherever he went. They killed him, but God raised him up on the third day. And after that we saw him alive, and even ate and drank with him. The risen Jesus told us it was our job to tell people what we'd seen and heard, and to let people know that he was God's appointed one. Everyone who believes in him will be forgiven in his name."

The Word of the Lord.

✠ *The Holy Gospel of Our Lord Jesus Christ, According to Matthew* [3:13–17]

Jesus came to John at the Jordan River to be baptized by him. John thought this was a ridiculous idea. He said, "But Jesus, I should be baptized by you, not the other way around!" Jesus said, "Let's do this because that's what I should do to follow God's law."

"Well, okay then," said John.

After Jesus was baptized, when he was coming up out of the water, suddenly the sky opened and he saw God's Spirit fly out of the clouds like a dove and rest on him. Then a voice from heaven said, "This is my own son whom I love very much, and who pleases me to no end."

The Gospel of the Lord.

The Second Sunday after the Epiphany

A Reading from the Book of Isaiah [49:1–7]

Listen to me, people on the coasts. Pay attention to what I'm saying, those of you who live far away! God chose me before I was even born; while I was still in my mother's belly he gave me my name. He made my mouth like a sharp sword, and kept me safe with the shadow of his hand. He made me into a polished arrow and hid me with all his other arrows. He said to me, "You will work for me, Israel, and you will make me proud." But I said, "This work is too hard. I have tried so hard and yet have gotten nowhere. It's been a big waste of my time. Still, I know that I want to work for you, and you will be good to me, God." Now God who made me says, "Keep working so that the people will be together in my name. I have confidence in you. You don't need to be strong—I will be your strength. You will be a light in this dark world, that my salvation may reach to the edges of the earth." This is what God says to his people, whom other people hate, "The kings will pay attention to you, the princes of the other countries will bow down to you, because you are mine and I have chosen you."

The Word of the Lord.

Psalm 40:1–12

I've been waiting for God for a long time.
Finally God bent down and listened to me.
I was in the pit. I was so depressed that I felt like I was stuck in mud.
God pulled me out of it, and put me on higher ground and made
sure I was safe.

You are God. Don't ever stop loving me and caring for me.

He put a new song in my mouth, a song of praise to God himself.
And many people will see and stand in awe of God. They will put their trust in God.
If you trust in God, you are a happy person.
You don't have to turn to bad people or believe in anything but God himself.
God, you have done such great things. The works of your hand, and the plans you've got in store for us, blow me away. There is absolutely no one like you.

You are God. Don't ever stop loving me and caring for me.

I wish other people could see how great you are. I can't even count the great things you've done for me.
You are not really impressed by all the good things we try to do for you.
I can't believe you even listen to me, but you do.
You don't require offerings, and we don't need to bring you gifts to make sure you'll love us. So I say, let's go be with God. Let's be on God's side.

You are God. Don't ever stop loving me and caring for me.

If someone writes a book about me, it will say this, "I loved belonging to God and doing what God wants. I carry God's Word in my heart."
I stand up in front of everyone and tell them about your goodness, God. In fact, I never stop talking about you. But you already know that, God.
I haven't kept your goodness hidden inside of me. I speak up and talk about how faithful you've been and how you take good care of me. I don't hold back your good news.

You are God. Don't ever stop loving me and caring for me. I hope your love will keep me safe forever.

A Reading from the First Letter of Paul to the Corinthians [1:1–9]

Here's another letter from Paul to us here in Corinth:

I write this to the people of the church in Corinth. You are people God chose to be made holy in Jesus. You are truly saints, along with all those other saints who believe in Jesus. I send you grace and peace from God himself. You know I always thank God for you, and for all the ways God has made your life better. God has given you special gifts—spiritual gifts. Like kindness, and understanding, and being able to talk about God. We all wait for Jesus to be with us in person again. God also will make you strong as you wait, so that at the end, Jesus will be happy to call you his own. God really is faithful, isn't he? It is wonderful that God called you into this relationship with his son, Jesus.

The Word of the Lord.

✠ *The Holy Gospel of Our Lord Jesus Christ According to John* [1:29–42]

John, who was Jesus' cousin who lived in the desert, saw Jesus walking toward him one day and he shouted, "Look, here comes Jesus, the Lamb of God who has come to break down the barriers we put between ourselves and God. He's the one I've been talking about; there is a man who will come after me who is far better than me because he was God's before I was. I didn't always know him. But I've been out here in the desert baptizing people so that Jesus would be shown to be from God."

John said, "When I baptized him, I tell you, I saw the Holy Spirit like a dove, coming down from heaven and land right on Jesus! I wasn't sure what was going on but then God, who sent me to baptize, whispered in my ear: "When you baptize someone and see the Holy Spirit come down from heaven on that person and stay with him, that is the one who will baptize, not with water, but with the Holy Spirit.'

"And sure enough, that's what I saw when I baptized Jesus. That's how I know Jesus is the Son of God."

The next day John was standing around with a couple of his disciples. As he saw Jesus walk by, he shouted out, "Look! There he goes. He's the Lamb of God!" Those disciples believed what he said, and they turned around and followed Jesus from then on.

When Jesus saw them following him, he turned around and said, "What are you looking for?" They said, "Teacher, show us where you're staying." Jesus said, "Come and see. I'll show you." They went with him, saw where he was staying, and stayed with him.

One of those men was named Andrew. He found his brother Simon Peter and said to him, "Guess what? We've found the Messiah, the one we've been looking for!" He brought his brother to Jesus, who took a look at him and said, "I know you. You're Simon, son of John. But I'm going to call you Cephas, which is another word for Rock."

The Gospel of the Lord.

The Third Sunday after the Epiphany

A Reading from the Book of Isaiah [9:1–4]

There used to be a cloud over your heads. But no more. You are now living in a place of sunshine. You used to be walking in the dark, not knowing where you were going. But now there is a light in the darkness. God has given us much more joy than we ever expected. No longer do we feel like oxen pulling someone else's wagon.

The Word of the Lord.

Psalm 27:1, 5–13

God's light shines in my life and makes it worth living. I don't need to be afraid of anything.
I rely on God. No one scares me.

I have only one thing to ask of you, God: Can I live with you forever?

To see God's beautiful face and to live with God would be awesome. God always keeps me safe when I know I'm in trouble. He takes me to a safe place that no one knows about; when the flood waters come, God picks me up and puts me high upon a rock.
When my face is drooping, he lifts up my head in front of those who make fun of me.

I have only one thing to ask of you, God: Can I live with you forever?

Because God does these things for me, I couldn't be any happier. I can't stop singing and making music, which praises God.
Listen to me, God. And then answer me.

I heard you whisper to my heart, "Come find me." And that's
what I'm doing, looking for you.

I have only one thing to ask of you, God: Can I live with you forever?

So don't hide from me, God. Don't turn the other way when
I come.
You have always helped me. So don't leave me now, because I am
counting on you.

I have only one thing to ask of you, God: Can I live with you forever?

A Reading from the First Letter of Paul to the Corinthians [1:10–18]

This is Paul speaking: I want you to do something for me, brothers and sisters, in the name of Jesus—get along with each other! Pay attention to things that really matter, not little things that you disagree about. You should be moving in the same direction as each other. Some of Chloe's people told me you've been arguing with each other, just like brothers and sisters do. Stop it.

Some of you say, "I'm with Paul," or others say, "Well, Apollos is better than Paul, so I'm going with him. Or Cephas or Jesus." Have we divided Jesus up? Did Paul die on a cross for you? Were you baptized in the name of Paul? Now I'm glad I didn't baptize any of you (except Crispus and Gaius), so that none of you can say, "Ha-ha, I was baptized by Paul and you weren't."

Oh yeah, I also baptized Stephanas's household. But I don't think I baptized anyone else.

Jesus didn't send me out to do baptisms but to tell people the Good News. Not so they could be blown away by my fancy words, or thinking, and take power away from what God has done in Jesus. God's message about the cross and Jesus just sounds stupid to those who don't get it, but to those of us who hold on to the cross and Jesus, it is God's awesome power.

The Word of the Lord.

✠ *The Holy Gospel of Our Lord Jesus Christ According to Matthew* [4:12–23]

Jesus heard that his cousin John had been arrested. He left his hometown Nazareth and moved to Capernaum by the sea, just like the prophet Isaiah said the Messiah would. Jesus used to go around sometimes and say, "You'd better change your ways, because God's kingdom is closer to you than you know." He was walking on the seashore one day and he saw two fishermen throwing their nets into the sea. They were brothers, named Peter and Andrew. Jesus said to them, "If you come follow me, I'll show you how to gather people instead of fish." And they did! They dropped their fishing nets right then and there and followed Jesus. Then they saw two fishermen who were mending their nets (because they get torn all the time). These brothers were named James and John, and their father was named Zebedee. Jesus issued the same challenge to them, and they dropped their nets, left their father, and followed Jesus, too.

Jesus walked all around Galilee, teaching in their synagogues and telling about God's goodness and how to live God's way, and curing people of all kinds of sickness.

The Gospel of the Lord.

The Fourth Sunday after the Epiphany

A Reading from the Book of Micah [6:1–8]

God says, "If you've got a problem with me, and what I'm doing, don't just grumble to yourself about it; speak up! We can talk. Let the mountains and the hills hear that you're upset. In fact, let's talk about it right now.

"So, tell me people, what are you upset about? Did I do something you didn't like? Are you tired of me? Answer me, because I want to know. Did it bother you that I rescued you from slavery in Egypt, and gave you Moses to lead you through the desert? Don't you remember all the times I've stood before you and defended you and claimed you as my own?"

The people understood that they made God feel bad. They said, "God, how can we make this up to you? Do you want us to bring special offerings? Shall we bring you a thousand rams, and ten thousand rivers of that oil you like? Do you want our first-born children? Will that make things better between us?"

Then God said, "O people. No. I don't want any of that. Here is what I want from you: I want you to treat everyone equally, I want you to be kind and I want you to remember me with every step you take."

The Word of the Lord.

Psalm 15

Lord, who do you invite into your house?
Who gets to live where you live?
Those who do what is right and speak the truth are already
living with God in their hearts.

Let's go up the hill and live with God.

God's people don't try to trick others, or make fun of their neighbors.
God doesn't even want to look at people who hurt each other.
But God smiles on those who pay attention to God's ways.

Let's go up the hill and live with God.

God's ways are these: Don't hurt other people. Don't go back on your word.
Don't use other people to make money, or use money to make things go your own way.
You'll be sorry in the end if you do those things.

Let's go up the hill and live with God.

A Reading from the First Letter of Paul to the Corinthians [1:18–31]

People make fun of us for believing in Jesus, who died on the cross. But we know that Jesus and all he taught us is the power of God himself. And the cross reminds us of that.

You know, they say that the people who think they know everything, and know better than God, will get theirs in the end.

Where are they now, the people who know better than God? God makes them look silly. It's not through your head that God comes into your life, but through your heart. Some people want signs to know where God is. Some people want proof. Some people want to "know." But God has spoken to our hearts and opened our eyes and we believe, even when others mock us.

Because we'd rather be with God, who looks silly, than with people who think they know what they're talking about but don't. On God's worst days, God is better and stronger and kinder than any human being.

Look at yourselves, people. Not many of you are all that special. You don't have money. You're not the most popular or famous. You'd never make the cover of a magazine. But God chose you! And in God's choice, the rest of them look like fools. God can take the smallest, least likely person to make the point that it is Jesus we should focus on, not ourselves.

Jesus is our hero. He became everything we should want to be.

If we have something to be proud of, we can be proud of Jesus.

The Word of the Lord.

✠ *The Holy Gospel of Our Lord Jesus Christ According to Matthew* [5:1–12]

Jesus looked around and saw lots of people around him. He went up the mountain to talk to them, so they could hear him better. This is what he wanted to teach them:

When you are feeling down and think you're worthless, know that you are blessed. For God's kingdom is yours.

When you are sad because someone has died, know that you are blessed and you will be comforted.

When you feel like you have nothing to offer, know that you are blessed, because you will be given everything.

When you are hungry and thirsty for God, know that you are blessed and that God will fill you up.

When you are kind, even when you don't have to be kind, know that you are blessed. Because God notices and will be kind to you.

When your eyes and hearts are open to God, know that you are blessed, because you will see and feel God.

When you try to bring people together in peace, know that you are blessed, because that's what God's children are supposed to do.

When people make fun of you because you love me, says Jesus, you can be happy about it, because that's exactly what they have done to all of God's people before you.

The Gospel of the Lord.

The Fifth Sunday after the Epiphany

A Reading from the Book of Isaiah [58:1–9a]

God said this to Isaiah: Don't be shy—speak up! In fact, pretend you're a trumpet and blast this out: Tell people what they need to hear. They say they want to be close to me, yet they turn the other way when they see me coming.

Then I can hear them complaining, "So, why are we doing all this to get your attention, God—we fast, and humble ourselves, but you don't see us and you don't even care."

And here's what I say to that: You are fasting for yourselves, not for me. You don't treat your workers like they were real people. Fasting doesn't make you holier, it just makes you hungry and angry and ready to fight. That kind of behavior is NOT going to get my attention. When you act like that, I won't even listen to you.

Instead of fasting (which means not eating) why don't you NOT do something instead? Why don't you NOT let people remain in awful working situations? Why don't you NOT turn away from people who are hurting? Why don't you NOT pretend there aren't people who are hungry? Why don't you NOT walk right past homeless people and instead bring them into your house?

Instead of fasting, if you do these things, you will be like a really bright light, like the sun coming over the mountains, and your life will get so much better. And my glory will follow you all day long and keep you safe.

Instead of fasting, if you do these things, when you call out for me, I will be right there to listen to you and answer you.

The Word of the Lord.

Psalm 112:1–9

Hallelujah. Those who give to the poor are happy.
Those who are in awe of God and love to listen to God are happy, too.
Not only will they be happy, their children will be good, strong, happy people, too.
They will have everything they need and their love of God will go on forever.

Know your heart is right and you are right with God.

If you love God, it's like having a light in a dark tunnel. Being kind when you have no reason to be, and to be gentle with those who are hurting; that's the kind of light God wants in the world.
It's good to be generous with all you have, and to treat everyone equally.
You'll have a good foundation if you do those things; people will remember that you were good to them.

Know your heart is right and you are right with God.

You won't need to worry about people talking trash about you, when you know your heart is right and you are right with God.
You can stand strong, and watch the people who make fun of you become weaker and weaker.
You can hold your head up high when you are able to share what you have with poor people.

Know your heart is right and you are right with God.

A Reading from the First Letter of Paul to the Corinthians [2:1–12]

Paul says this in his letter:

When I came to visit you, my brothers and sisters, I didn't use fancy words or a preachy voice to talk about the mystery of God. That would only bring attention to my awesome speaking ability. No, I decided to focus only on Jesus and the way he died. I was a little nervous when I came to see you. I didn't know if you'd think I knew what I was talking about. But I relied on God's Spirit and God's power, so that it wouldn't matter how I well I spoke or how smart you thought I was. Only the power of God would matter.

God's Spirit has given us the ideas and the words we need. We don't even understand ourselves. How can we understand God? Thank goodness that God's Spirit helps us to understand the gifts God has given us.

The Word of the Lord.

✠ *The Holy Gospel of Our Lord Jesus Christ According to Matthew* [5:13–20]

Jesus said these things:

You are like salt, which is only good when it's salty. You, like salt, can make a big difference.

You are like light that everyone in the world can see.

You are like a city on the top of the world that no one can hide.

You don't light a lamp and then put a bucket over it. You put it on a table in the middle of the house and then it can light up the whole house.

You should let people see your light because when they see the good you do in God's name, they will turn to God and thank him.

My job isn't to wipe out everything everyone before me has said or done. In fact, my job is to do the right things, according to the law. The point of the law is to have it followed. So don't tell people to break the law or the commandments; that certainly won't make you right with God. But know what the law and the commandments really mean for people, and teach them that. You've got to be better than just following the law, thinking that will get you right with God.

The Gospel of the Lord.

The Sixth Sunday after the Epiphany

A Reading from the Book of Deuteronomy [30:15–20]

Moses said to the people:

Here's the deal, you can choose life and riches, or death and trouble. It's up to you. If you love God and behave like you love God, then life is good and it will get better for you and your children. God will bless us wherever we go next. But if your hearts turn away from God and you would rather bow down to other gods and follow them, there will be nothing but trouble ahead. When we go into our own land, life will not be the good life God wants for us.

I want everyone in earth and heaven to hear me when I say, "It's up to you; choose life or death, blessings or troubles. Choose life, people! So that you and your children may have good lives, and love God and hold onto him as he's holding you close." That's the best way to live. And we can move to our own land, which God has promised us, and be happy.

The Word of the Lord.

Psalm 119:1–8

I will be happy and have nothing to worry about when I follow
God and God's ways.
I will be happy when I pay attention to God's words and offer
my heart to God, turning away from bad choices and walk
on the path God has before me.
God laid out a path for me to keep. Oh, I really hope I can walk
that path God wants me to walk.

I will be happy when I follow God's ways.

Then I won't be ashamed of myself.
Then I will thank God with my whole, happy heart; don't let me down, God, I will try my best to follow you.

I will be happy when I follow God's ways.

A Reading from the First Letter of Paul to the Corinthians [3:1–9]

Paul says in his letter to us:

You know, people, that in your new life in Christ, you're like babies all over again. It's like you've gotten a whole new life when you follow Jesus. So, I have to feed you a little at a time, and give you milk rather than solid food. You'll grow up in the faith, but you're not there yet. You know how I can tell you're not grown up yet? Because you bicker with each other and you are jealous of each other. Some of you think if you follow me you're better than people that are following Apollos. But, what difference does that make anyway? Good grief! Apollos and I were just the people who brought you to God. We're not God! It's like you're seeds that I planted. And then Apollos came along and watered you. But only God can make you grow. We work together in the garden of faith but the garden belongs to God.

The Word of the Lord.

✠ *The Holy Gospel of Our Lord Jesus Christ According to Matthew* [5:21–37]

Jesus said this:

You know you're not supposed to murder anybody, don't you? Well, I say that if you are angry with each other, and call each other names, it's just as bad. On your way to church, if you remember that there is something that keeps you from loving a sister or a brother, just turn around and go talk to them. Tell them you're sorry; tell them that you want to make things right between you. And then come to church to worship. Make the extra effort to work things out in your relationships.

You know when you're married you're supposed to be faithful to each other, don't you? I say that if you look at somebody else and wish you could sleep with them rather than your husband or wife, you're being just as unfaithful as if you actually made that wish come true.

Don't listen to that part of you that wants to make bad choices. It's just not worth it.

And don't think you can just throw away your marriage because it's just too much work. Keep working at it.

You know you're not supposed to swear and then break your oath, don't you? I tell you, don't swear at all. Just say what you mean and mean what you say. Keep your word. Anything other than the truth is just wrong.

The Gospel of the Lord.

The Seventh Sunday after the Epiphany

A Reading from the Book of Leviticus [19:1–2, 9–18]

The Lord said this to Moses:

Tell all my people this, Moses. You need to be holy, because I am your God and I am holy. Here are some ideas about how you can live holy lives:

> When you harvest the crops in your field, leave some grain unharvested around the edges. And don't pick every grape off your vines, or pick up every grape that falls. Leave those for the poor people and the immigrants.
>
> Remember I am God.
>
> Don't steal. Don't trick people. Don't lie to one another. Don't use my name when you don't mean it.
>
> Remember I am God.
>
> Don't cheat your neighbor. Don't steal. Don't hold back the money someone has earned. Don't make life any harder for people who can't hear or see. Don't talk about a deaf person just because he can't hear you. And don't put something in the path of a blind man so he'll trip over it and you can laugh.
>
> Remember I am God.
>
> If you make a decision, be fair. Be fair to poor people and rich people alike. Don't talk trash about other people. And don't be happy when your neighbor fails.
>
> Remember I am God.
>
> Don't hate anyone in your family. If you see that you can help your neighbor with something that is troubling him, do it. Don't try to get back at people for what they've done to

you. Don't hold a grudge in your heart. Instead, I tell you, love your neighbor as yourself.
And remember I am God.

The Word of the Lord.

Psalm 119:33–40

I want to learn how you want me to live, God. Teach me, and I will always keep it in my heart.
Help me to understand how I can live the way you want me to live.

God's way gives life. That's the life I want to live.

Show me the path I can walk that will please you. That is what I really want to do.
Make my heart lean toward you, and not toward money and greed and selfishness.
Turn my eyes away from hurtful scenes. Give me life, your life.

God's way gives life. That's the life I want to live.

Make good on your promise to me.
Don't punish me when I know I'm wrong. And you have every right to punish.
You know I yearn to do the right thing and to be without blame as I come before you.

God's way gives life. That's the life I want to live.

A Reading from the First Letter of Paul to the Corinthians
[3:10–11, 16–23]

God has given me grace to lay a foundation as if I was in construction. Someone else is building on that foundation. Each builder works a little differently. But each of us builds on the foundation that is Jesus Christ.

I hope you know that you are God's temple and that God's Spirit lives inside of you. No one dares destroy God's temple because it's holy. Don't trick yourselves into thinking that you know everything. Knowing everything is *not* the way to God. God is the only one who knows everything.

Human leaders may think they're special. But they have nothing on you. You already know what you need to know. You belong to Christ. Christ belongs to God.

The Word of the Lord.

✠ *The Holy Gospel of Our Lord Jesus Christ According to Matthew* [5:38–48]

Jesus said this:

They say, "An eye for an eye, a tooth for a tooth." In other words, you poke out my eye, I can poke out yours. But I'm telling you, don't put up a fight with someone doing wrong. If someone smacks your right cheek, turn your left cheek to him. If someone takes you to court and wants to take your precious things, let them. If someone wants you to go this far, go even farther than that. Give to everyone who begs from you. If someone wants to borrow something from you, give it to him. They say, "Love your neighbor, but hate your enemy." I am telling you, love your enemies. Pray for those who want to hurt you. That's what your Father in heaven does. He makes the sun shine on everybody, doesn't he? On the good people and the bad alike.

If you only love the people who love you, does that make you special? Everybody does that! Live the way God would have you live. Watch how God treats people. Then treat them that way.

The Gospel of the Lord.

The Eighth Sunday after the Epiphany

A Reading from the Book of Isaiah [49:8–16a]

This is what God said:

I helped you when you called me; I saved you when you needed saving. I protected you and gave you as a promise to the people, to establish a home. I have said to the prisoners, "Come out of your prison." And to those who are hiding in the darkness, I said, "Let me see you." You're like sheep that I lead. You can stop and feed along the way. You won't be hungry or thirsty any more. And I'll keep you from the sun and find you springs of water. The mountains will become roads. The heavens will sing for joy because God comforted his people and his heart has softened toward those who are suffering.

You may think I've forgotten you. How could I? Can a woman forget a child she's feeding? Can a woman not care about the baby inside of her? Even if mothers could forget their children, I could never forget you. Look, I have drawn your face on the palms of my hands.

The Word of the Lord.

Psalm 131

Lord, I know exactly who I am, and what I can accomplish. So I don't force myself into things that I don't understand or are beyond me.

I calm myself down, like I was child on my mother's lap. I find a quiet place inside of me.

People of God, wait patiently for God. Quiet yourselves, and always wait patiently for God.

A Reading from the First Letter of Paul to the Corinthians [4:1–5]

Think about this: We work in Christ's household. He has asked us to take care of God's mysteries. People who take care of things that belong to other people are called stewards. And they have to be trustworthy.

I don't need you to decide whether or not I am trustworthy. God has already done that. So, hold back your judgment. God will bring to light those things that seem to hide in the darkness, those things you can't understand. God will reveal the purposes in our hearts, and then God will be glad.

The Word of the Lord.

✠ *The Holy Gospel of Our Lord Jesus Christ According to Matthew* [6:24–34]

Jesus said this:

You just can't be totally loyal to two masters. You'll either love one or the other. That's how it is with God and lots of money. Don't worry so much about what you'll eat or drink, or about the clothes you'll wear. Isn't your life more important than any of those things? Take a look at the birds in the air. They don't plan a future for themselves, and yet your Father in heaven feeds them. Aren't you more valuable to him than a bird?

Think about it. Can you add a single hour to your life by worrying about anything?

Why worry about clothes? Think about the flowers. They grow without even trying or working at it. The richest person in the whole world doesn't wear clothes any more beautiful than a flower.

If God provides for the grass that grows in the field, which lasts such a short time before it gets cut down, do you think he won't provide for you?

Sometimes you have such little faith in God's goodness.

Don't worry. God knows what you need. First, work for the kingdom of God, and what God wants for you and all those who belong to God. And all these things that you need will be given to you.

Again I tell you not to worry about tomorrow. Tomorrow will have enough trouble without you worrying about it. Today's trouble is enough for today.

The Gospel of the Lord.

The Last Sunday after the Epiphany

A Reading from the Book of Exodus [24:12–18]

God said to Moses, "Meet me on the mountain and I will give you some instructions for people on how I want them to live. They'll be written on tablets of stone." So Moses and his assistant Joshua hiked up the mountain. Moses's brother Aaron and his friend Hur were in charge until they returned. When Moses got to the top of the mountain, a cloud covered it. The glory of God was in that cloud and it settled on Mount Sinai for six days. On the seventh day, God called out to Moses from the cloud. From the valley below, the people looked up to see if they could see God on the mountaintop. What they saw was a raging fire that held God's glory. Moses walked straight into the cloud to talk to God. He was there for forty days and forty nights.

The Word of the Lord.

Psalm 2

I can't believe all of the plotting and conspiring going on
  between people and nations. Do they think they will
  overthrow God by joining forces?
God in heaven laughs when he watches them scheme. And then
  when he talks to them, they're terrified to hear him say,
"I have anointed my king
And he sits on the holy mountain."

Let God shelter you from any storm.
Find your protection in God.

God said to me,
"You know, you are my son and I am your Father.

If you ask me, I will give you the whole earth.
You will be stronger than any of the nations around you.
They will break like pottery if you drop them on the ground."

Let God shelter you from any storm.
Find your protection in God.

So, the rest of you kings in charge of countries would be wise to serve my God.
And be a little frightened of what God can do.
Don't do anything that might make him angry.
In fact, let God shelter you from any storm. Find your protection in him.

Let God shelter you from any storm.
Find your protection in God.

A Reading from the Second Letter of Peter [1:16–21]

We weren't making up stories when we told you about the power of Jesus Christ our Lord. We were eyewitnesses to his majesty! We watched as honor and glory flowed into him from God the Father on the mountaintop, and we heard the Father's voice say out loud, "This is my Son whom I love very much; I am so proud of him." I'm telling you, that's what we heard on top of that holy hill!

That really cemented our faith and our message. You'd be smart to listen to us. Our message is like a lamp that helps you see in the dark, until the sun comes up and you can see the morning star in the sky and hold it in your heart. Remember, none of this is a matter of your own interpretation or ours. When God speaks through us, the Holy Spirit moves us to speak God's Word.

The Word of the Lord.

✠ *The Holy Gospel of Our Lord Jesus Christ According to Matthew* [17:1–9]

It had been six days since Peter figured out that Jesus was the Messiah. Jesus was going on a hike and took Peter and James and John with him. When they got to the top of the mountain Jesus started to glow from the inside! His face was shining like the sun. Even his clothes were dazzling white. And then, Moses and Elijah were there with them and they started talking with Jesus.

Peter was so excited and said to Jesus, "This is so awesome! I think we should make three houses here and stay here forever. A house for Jesus, a house for Moses, and a house for Elijah." Then, all of a sudden, a bright cloud came over them and a voice from inside the cloud said, "This is my very own Son whom I love very much. I am so proud of him. I want you to listen to what he has to say."

When Peter, James, and John heard this, they fell to the ground and were scared to death. But Jesus came and touched them, saying, "Get up and don't be afraid." And when they looked up, Moses and Elijah were gone. Only Jesus was there with them.

As they were coming down the mountain, Jesus ordered them, "Don't tell anyone about what you just saw until after I've been raised from the dead. The time isn't right."

The Gospel of the Lord.

Ash Wednesday

A Reading from the Book of Isaiah [58:1–12]

Here's what the Holy One who takes up all of eternity has to say to us:

Do NOT be quiet, people. Use your voice like a really loud trumpet. Tell my people that they are doing it all wrong. They act like they listen to what I say and like they care about me, but they don't. They act like they haven't forgotten how to behave like faithful people, but they have. They sidle up to me, pretending, and say to me, "Why do we bother fasting, if you're not going to pay attention to us? Why should we bother if you don't even notice?"

Look, people. Here's how God sees it. When you are fasting, you have your own interests in mind. You fast at the same time you make life miserable for the people who work for you. And while you're fasting you're picking fights. God won't even listen to you when you fast like that.

Here's the kind of fast that God wants. God wants you to humble yourselves and help people be free of everything that keeps them oppressed. God wants you to share the food you have with hungry people, and open your house to people who are homeless. God wants you to offer clothing to people who have none.

When you do THAT, then your light will shine all over the world, like the sun coming up. And you yourselves will be healed. God will go in front of you to guide you and God's glory will have your back. Then, when you call on God's name, God will answer. When you cry out for him, he will be quick to say, "I am right here."

If you help people find their freedom, if you stop pointing fingers and talking trash, if you offer hungry people food and think about others before thinking about yourselves, then you will be a light in this dark world.

God will always be there to guide you, and give you what you need and make you strong. You will be like a garden that has plenty of water, and like a spring that never, ever dries out. All your past dreams will be rebuilt. And your future will rest on them. You will be called the one who fixed the broken bridge, the one who made life make sense again.

The Word of the Lord.

Psalm 103:8–14

God is full of compassion for us.
It takes a lot to get God angry.
God is incredibly kind.
Even though he could,
He doesn't always point to what we've done wrong.
And God's anger? It doesn't last long.
He chooses to pay attention to who we are, and not our sins.
Thank God we don't always get what we deserve!

God is full of compassion for us.

You know how high the heavens are above the earth?
That's how much mercy he has for those who love him.
He removes our sins and takes them as far away,
as the east is from the west.

God is full of compassion for us.

God cares for us like fathers care for their children.
God knows us inside and out.

God knows what we are made of.
God remembers that we are made of dust.

God is full of compassion for us.

We will only last a little while, like the grass.
We are like wildflowers growing in the field.
Wildflowers grow strong and beautiful
but when the wind blows they are gone
and no one knows they were ever there.

God is full of compassion for us.

A Reading from the Second Letter of Paul to the Corinthians
[5:20b–6:10]

Please, please, *please!* Let God do his work in you so that you can have a good relationship with him. Jesus shared our sinful world so that we might be made right with God. So work with him and take what God offers you. God said, "When the right time came, I was there for you." Don't you see, NOW is the right time; see, God is there for you *now!* We don't want to be in anyone's way, and we hope that no one puts down our ministry because of this, but looks at us as good examples. We've put up with a lot because we have been working on God's side. We've been beaten up, thrown in jail, gone without sleep and food; but God has given us the tools we need to do God's work—patience, kindness, goodness in our hearts, and truth on our lips and especially God's very own power. People treat us as fakes, yet we're really true believers. Some think we're losing our faith, but it's still alive; we may be brought to our knees, but we get up again. You might think all this makes us want to give up, and yet we can't stop singing God's praises. We might be poor, yet we have so much to give to others. You might think we have nothing, but we have everything we could possibly need in God.

The Word of the Lord.

✠ *The Holy Gospel of Our Lord Jesus Christ According to Matthew* [6:1–6, 16–21]

Jesus said, "Make sure you don't show off how good you are so people will think you're really holy. God does NOT like that at all. If you give money to help the poor, that's a really good thing. But don't make a big deal out of it so everyone knows. In fact, give that money with your right hand so quietly that your left hand doesn't even know about it! God knows when you give and that's what counts.

"When you're praying, you don't need to do it loudly or even in public so that everyone knows. You can always pray to God inside your heart, wherever you are, without letting everyone else hear just so they're impressed.

"If you're going to go without food so you can get closer to God, don't tell everyone and whine about how hungry you are so they know you're fasting. Put a smile on your face instead and look your best. God knows what you're doing and it's God who counts.

"Don't keep buying more and more things that you want but don't need. All those things could be destroyed in a minute or stolen by burglars. Instead, invest in your relationship with God because nothing and nobody can take that away from you. Remember, wherever you invest your time and money, that's where your heart will be."

The Gospel of the Lord.

The First Sunday in Lent

A Reading from the Book of Genesis [2:15–17; 3:1–7]

God took the man he made and put him in the Garden of Eden to take care of it. God told him, "Go ahead and eat anything you want from the garden, but don't eat from the tree of the knowledge of good and evil, because you'll die if you eat that."

The serpent was the wisest and sneakiest wild animal that God made. He asked the woman, "Did God really say you can't eat fruit from any tree in the garden?" "No, that's not what God said," said the woman. "God said we can eat from any tree except the one in the middle, and we shouldn't even touch it or we'll die." The serpent said, "You won't die if you eat it. God knows that if you eat fruit from that tree, all of a sudden you will be like God, and know right from wrong, good from evil."

The woman looked at that tree, and thought the fruit on it looked pretty good to eat. Then she really wanted it, especially if it was going to make her wise like God. So she took a piece and ate. Then she gave some of it to her husband as well. And he ate it. Sure enough, it was like their eyes were opened and they saw things they'd never seen before. They hadn't realized it earlier, but now they saw that they didn't have any clothes on. So they took some fig leaves and sewed them together to make some clothes for themselves.

The Word of the Lord.

Psalm 32

People whose sins are forgiven are happy people.
When the Lord says, "You're not guilty of anything," you're a
 happy person, too. You can be happy there's nothing in you
 that wants to cause any trouble.

For a while I was quiet about my sin, and I felt like I was wasting away, and I groaned all day long.

God, you are the place I can hide.
You keep me safe from trouble.

I felt like God's heavy hand was on me day and night. My mouth was all dried up like it was the middle of summer. I was so thirsty.

But then, I told God about my sin, and didn't hide anything from him.

God, you are the place I can hide.
You keep me safe from trouble.

I said, "I'm going to come clean to God about what bad things I've done." And God forgave me and my guilty feelings went away.

People who love God should tell God when they've caused trouble for themselves, then when the times get worse, they won't feel like the floodwaters will cover them up.

God, you are the place I can hide.
You keep me safe from trouble.

And I can hear you calling for me to find me and help me out of tough spots.

God says, "I will teach you how you should act, and show you the way. I've got a really good eye, and I will use it to guide you."

So, don't be like a horse or a mule—they don't know what's going on. They have to be fitted with a bridle or else they'll just wander away.

God, you are the place I can hide.
You keep me safe from trouble.

People who don't want to go God's way will always find themselves in trouble.

But if you love God and trust in God, God will hug you in his loving arms.
You've got lots to be happy about, and you can be happy about God.
Shout for joy, those of you who have given your hearts to God.

God, you are the place I can hide.
You keep me safe from trouble.

A Reading from the Letter of Paul to the Romans [5:12–19]

From the very first person on earth, we all have been separated from God. Not because of what God did, but because humans, *all* humans, constantly put up a barrier between themselves and God. Our sin keeps that barrier up. And then we die. But just as everyone is sinful, everyone has been given God's grace through Jesus Christ! Everyone! We can either focus on how we're all sinful, or how through Jesus we all have God's forgiveness and salvation.

The Word of the Lord.

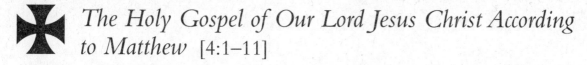

✠ *The Holy Gospel of Our Lord Jesus Christ According to Matthew* [4:1–11]

After Jesus was baptized, the Holy Spirit took him into the desert where he faced a lot of temptations. He stopped eating for a really long time to get a clearer picture of what God wanted him to do with his life. Afterwards, he was really, really hungry. The one who tempts us came to Jesus and said, "So, if you're really the Son of God, why don't you just turn these rocks into bread? What are you waiting for?"

Jesus answered him, "That's not what God's power is all about. Don't you know that the Bible says, 'Bread isn't everything; God's Word is everything'"?

Then the devil took him to the holy city and flew him up to the very tip of the temple. He said, "So, if you are the son of God, jump off, because the Bible said, 'God will make sure his angels take care of you. They'll lift you up so you won't even hurt one foot on a stone below.'"

Jesus said to him, "But the Bible also says, 'Don't test God.'"

Then the devil tried a third time. He took him to the peak of the high mountain where he could see the whole beautiful world and everyone in it. The devil said, "You can have all this, if you will just fall on your knees and worship me instead of God."

Jesus told him to just go away. Because Jesus knew the Bible said, "You're only supposed to worship God and only follow him."

With that, the devil gave up and went away. And then Jesus was surrounded by messengers straight from God who came and took care of everything he needed.

The Gospel of the Lord.

The Second Sunday in Lent

A Reading from the Book of Genesis [12:1–4a]

God was talking to Abram and said, "Leave everything you know behind—your country, your cousins, the home you grew up in, and go to the place I will show you. You are going to be something special. . . . I will bless you so that you can bless others. I will be on your side—those who are good to you, I will be good to them. But those who cause you trouble will find themselves in more trouble than they can imagine." So Abram packed up his things and left, just as God told him to do.

The Word of the Lord.

Psalm 121

When I am down, I look up.
I look up to the mountains for help.

My help comes from God, who made heaven and earth.

God's got my back.
And God never sleeps, but is always watching over me.
God is always watching over Israel too.

My help comes from God, who made heaven and earth.

God's watching over us.
God is our shade, so we're not blinded by the sun
or even the brightness of the moon.
God will keep me safe every time I come in the door and every
time I go out,
today and always.

My help comes from God, who made heaven and earth.

A Reading from the Letter of Paul to the Romans [4:1–5, 13–17]

We all brag because we are children of Abraham. But so what? If Abraham got us closer to God, that would be something to brag about, but he didn't. Nothing Abraham himself did made any difference to God. But Abraham *believed God*. That's what mattered to God.

If you work to earn money, that money isn't a gift. You yourself can't get right with God, but God makes it right between you. That is God's gift to you. You can't do anything to make God love you. He offers his love to you because of grace, not because you've earned it. Those of you who have faith are children of Abraham. God made him the father of us all. God does what only God can do, give life to the dead and create things with a single word from his mouth.

The Word of the Lord.

✠ *The Holy Gospel of Our Lord Jesus Christ According to John* [3:1–17]

One of the Jewish leaders named Nicodemus came to Jesus after dark. Nicodemus said, "Jesus, we know you are a teacher from God, because of the amazing things we've seen you do—no one could do those things unless they'd been in God's presence."

Jesus said, "I'm telling you that being in God's presence isn't even possible without being born from above."

Nicodemus asked Jesus, "How is somebody going to do that? What, am I supposed to crawl back into my mother and be born again?"

Jesus replied, "No, I'm talking about being born with water and the Spirit. What do you think about that? The wind is free, and goes wherever it wants to go. Just like the Spirit."

Nicodemus said, "I still don't get it."

"How can you be a leader of your people and still not get it?" Jesus said, "These are heavenly things I'm talking about. Here's the most important thing you need to know—God loved everything and everyone in the world so much that he gave up his Son for them, and everyone who believes in God's Son will live with God in their hearts forever. God didn't send his Son to make us all look ridiculous. God didn't send his Son to tell us we were going to hell, but to save us from ourselves for God."

The Gospel of the Lord.

The Third Sunday in Lent

A Reading from the Book of Exodus [17:1–7]

God's people were on the move, just as God commanded. They made camp at Rephadim, but there was no water for anyone to drink. The people were mad at Moses and yelled, "GIVE US WATER!" Moses said, "Why are you yelling at me? You people are a pain." And the people whined, saying, "Why did you bother to take us out of Egypt, only to let us and our kids and our animals die of thirst?"

Moses wasn't happy with God. "What am I supposed to do with these people?" Moses said, "They're so angry and thirsty they are ready to kill me."

God said, "Get some of your best men together. Take the staff with which you turned the Nile into blood, and go on a hike. Walk as far as Horeb, and I will be there standing on a rock. Hit that rock with your staff and you will have water for everyone to drink. Water will gush from that rock."

Moses did as God told him to do. And water came from the rock, just as God said it would. God's people had whined and pushed God to the edge, but now they had water to drink.

The Word of the Lord.

Psalm 95

Come on, let's sing to God. Let's make lots of noise for our
Rock, our salvation.
Let's surround God with thanks.

For God is the best, the best there could ever be.

He holds in his hands the lowest caves and the highest mountains.
The oceans belong to him because he made them and with his own hands he molded the earth like clay.

For God is the best, the best there could ever be.

So let us bow our heads, and bend our knees and kneel before God who made us.
He is our God, and we are his people. We are the sheep who eat in his pastures.
Let's pay attention to God when he calls us to follow.

For God is the best, the best there could ever be.

A Reading from the Letter of Paul to the Romans [5:1–11]

We have faith and are good with God, so we have peace in our hearts. It is because of Jesus that we can hope to share God's glory. We also share in God's suffering. But suffering helps to make us patient, and patience helps to make us better people. God's love has been poured into us because we've been given the Holy Spirit.

It's awesome to think that Jesus died for us. If that's not proof of God's love I don't know what is, because we're a bunch of sinners. Why would Jesus do that? Because God loves us. Even more than that, we can tell God loves us by the way Jesus lived his life. Living the way Jesus lived his life will bring us closer to God's Way. We'll be going in the same direction with God, not in opposite directions from God anymore.

The Word of the Lord.

✠ *The Holy Gospel of Our Lord Jesus Christ According to John* [4:5–42]

Jesus came to Jacob's well and sat down because he was tired. His disciples had gone into town to buy food. It was the middle of the day. A Samaritan woman came to get water from the well and Jesus asked her if she'd give him a drink of water.

The woman was shocked because Jews don't usually talk to Samaritans, much less share their water. "You're asking ME for water?" the woman said. Jesus answered her, "If only you knew who I was, and what I could give you, you would have asked ME for LIVING water."

The woman said, "Living water? This is one deep well and you don't even have a bucket. How do expect to give me living water? You think you're more special than our ancestor Jacob, who gave us this well?"

Jesus said, "You drink from this well, and you'll just be thirsty again. But if you drink the 'water' I give you, you will never be thirsty again. The water I have for you will gush up from a spring of eternal life."

The woman said, "Oh please sir, I'd like some of that water, so I'll never be thirsty and I won't have to work so hard to get water here at this well."

Jesus said, "Why don't you go get your husband and tell him?"

"But I don't have a husband," she said.

Jesus said, "You're right about that. You've gone through five husbands, and the man you're living with now isn't your husband."

"Whoa! How did you know that? You must be a prophet. My people worship here, but you Jews say the only place to worship is in Jerusalem. What do you say about that?"

Jesus said, "You know, someday it won't matter where we worship, because the only place to worship God is in your heart. God doesn't 'belong' anywhere; God is spirit and we must worship him with our spirit."

The woman agreed with him. "And I agree that the Messiah is coming soon, and when he gets here, he will tell us all what's going on."

Jesus said, "You're talking to him, the Messiah."

Just then his disciples came back with food. They were shocked that he was talking on and on with this woman. They saw her leave her water jar at the well. When she was in the city, she told everyone she knew about this remarkable man who seemed to know everything about her. "I think he's the Messiah," she said.

Meanwhile the disciples tried to get Jesus to eat something. "Oh, I have food alright," Jesus said. "Food you don't know about."

"What?" the disciples said. "We walked all the way into town to get some food for you, and now you say you already had some?"

But Jesus was talking about food in a different way, just as he talked with the woman about living water.

"The food that keeps me going is doing what God wants me to do," said Jesus.

The Samaritan woman brought her friends from town to meet Jesus. They all believed in Jesus because of what she told them. They invited Jesus to stay with them, so he did. Even more people believed in him then and knew that he was the Savior of the world because of all he told them.

The Gospel of the Lord.

The Fourth Sunday in Lent

A Reading from the First Book of Samuel [16:1–13]

God said to Samuel, "I know you're upset that Saul won't be king of Israel, but how long are you going to cry about it? Fill your horn with oil and hit the road. I will send you to Jesse, because one of his sons will be the next king."

Samuel said, "I can't do that. If Saul hears about it, he'll kill me."

God said, "Here's what you do. Take a heifer with you and say, 'I've come to sacrifice this to the Lord.' Invite Jesse to the sacrifice. Then I'll show you what you should do next, and which of his sons you shall anoint."

That's what Samuel did. When he got to Bethlehem, the leaders of the city were scared, and asked if he'd come in peace.

Samuel replied, "Yes. I've come to make a sacrifice to the Lord, and want you to join me."

Jesse and his sons went with Samuel. Samuel saw Eliab, a son of Jesse. Everyone thought for sure he's come to make Eliab the next king.

But God whispered to Samuel, "Nope. He looks like a king, all tall and handsome, but he's not the one. I'm looking for someone with a special heart, not someone with special looks. Keep looking."

Jesse called another son to meet Samuel. But he wasn't the one either.

Then another son. And another son. Seven sons in all came by Samuel to see if they'd been chosen king.

Samuel finally said, "Is that the last of your sons, Jesse?"

Jesse said, "Well, the youngest is out in the field keeping his sheep."

Samuel said, "God told me the next king would be one of your sons. So I'm not leaving until I meet the last one."

They went and called David in from the fields. He was rugged and handsome and had beautiful eyes. Then God whispered in Samuel's ear, "Anoint this one. He's the next king."

So Samuel emptied his horn of oil on David's head, surrounded by his brothers. And God's spirit came upon David that day, and stayed with him.

Then Samuel left and went on to Ramah.

The Word of the Lord.

Psalm 23

The Lord is my shepherd and I am the sheep.
I have everything I need.
He takes me to places where I can rest in peaceful, green pastures,
and lie down beside deep, still, soothing waters.
He puts new life back into me, and shows me the right ways to go.

The Lord is my shepherd and I am the sheep.
I have everything I need.

Even though I walk through the valley of the shadow of death,
I'm not scared because the Lord is with me. He carries a big stick, and a crook to grab me if I fall down a ravine. That makes me feel a lot better.

The Lord is my shepherd and I am the sheep.
I have everything I need.

When those who make fun of me are watching, he spreads out a feast in front of them. A feast just for me. And he anoints me just as a king would be anointed. My cup is running over. My happiness is complete.

The Lord is my shepherd and I am the sheep.
I have everything I need.

There is nowhere I can go that the Lord's goodness and mercy isn't already there. It's like living in the Lord's house for ever and ever.

The Lord is my shepherd and I am the sheep.
What more could I need or want?

A Reading from the Letter of Paul to the Ephesians [5:8–14]

Once upon a time you were full of darkness but now, because of God, you are filled with light! So live like you are children of the light, and do things that are good and right and true. Figure out for yourselves what pleases God. Don't take part in the darkness anymore. Instead, shine the light into the dark so everyone can see what's going on.

Like the scriptures say, "Wake up! Rise from the dead, and Christ, your light, will shine on you."

The Word of the Lord.

✠ *The Holy Gospel of Our Lord Jesus Christ According to John* [9:1–41]

As Jesus was walking along on a Sabbath day, the day when you weren't supposed to do any work, he saw a man who had been born blind. His disciples asked him, "Teacher, whose sin caused this man to be born blind?" Jesus said, "Nobody's sin caused his blindness. But now God's goodness can be revealed in him. You know, I am the light of the world."

Just as Jesus said that, he spit on the ground, and made mud with his saliva, and spread it on the man's eyes. Then he sent the man to wash his eyes in the pool of water. When the man came back to Jesus, he could see.

"Whoa!" said his neighbors. "Isn't this the blind man who used to beg? It can't be. It looks like him. But this man can see. What is going on? "

The man laughed and said, "Yup. It's me. I can see alright."

"Who opened your eyes for you?" they asked him.

"Jesus did," the man said. "He put mud on my eyes, and when I washed it off, I could see for the first time in my life."

"Where is Jesus? We want to talk to him."

"I have no idea where he went," said the man.

The neighbors took the man to the leaders of the church. They asked him a bunch of questions about how he'd been made to see again. So the man told them his story.

"Hmpf," said the leaders. "Well, this can't be God's doing, because it's the Sabbath. And nobody who believes in God works on the Sabbath."

The other leaders said, "But how can anyone except God do such a miracle?

So they asked the man formerly known as the blind man, "What do you think about this Jesus? It was your eyes that he opened."

"Well, I think he's a prophet," said the man.

Some people refused to believe he'd ever been blind at all. So they called the man's parents and asked them. "Is this your son and was he born blind? How is it that he can see again?"

The parents said, "Yes, this is our son who was born blind. We have no idea how he can see now or who opened his eyes. Ask him. He's an adult. He'll tell you."

His parents were afraid of those people, because they had said they were going to kick anyone who believed Jesus was the Messiah out of the synagogue.

The church leaders found the man again. The man said, "You know what? All I know is that I have always been blind, and now I can see."

"But how did he do it?"

The man said, "I already told you my story and you didn't listen to me. Why do you need to hear it again? Is it because you want to be a follower of Jesus?"

"Ha! Not us. You may be a follower of Jesus, but we are followers of Moses. We know God spoke to Moses, but we have no idea where this Jesus comes from."

"Here's the thing," the man said. "We may not know where he comes from, but he opened my eyes. God may not listen to people we think are sinners, but he listens to those who listen to him. I've never heard of anyone born blind being able to see. If Jesus weren't from God, he wouldn't have been able to do that."

Then the church leaders ran him out of there. Jesus heard they'd chased him away, and found him. Jesus asked him, "Do you believe in the Son of Man?"

"Who would that be? Tell me who he is and I will believe in him," said the man.

Jesus said to him,"You have seen him with your very own eyes. He's the one who is speaking to you right now."

The man, said, "Lord, I believe." And he worshiped Jesus.

Jesus said, "I came into this world so that people who had been blind could see. Those who are able to see might become blind though."

Some of the leaders heard Jesus say this. And they said, "We're not blind, are we?"

Jesus said, "If you were blind, and you knew it, there wouldn't be a barrier between you and God. It's because you think you can see everything, that a barrier between you and God exists."

The Gospel of the Lord.

The Fifth Sunday in Lent

A Reading from the Book of Ezekiel [37:1–14]

God plucked me with his fingers and lifted me up. He set me down in the middle of a valley full of all kinds of bones, which were very dry. God said to me, "Do you think these bones can come back to life?"

I said, "I don't know, God. You tell me."

"Tell these bones to listen. Tell them that I will cause breath to enter them so that they might live again. I will put cartilage on them and muscles and skin. And they will live and they will know that I am God."

So I told them that. And suddenly, I heard rattling as the bones came together into skeletons. And then cartilage formed and muscles and skin covered them. But there was still no breath.

God said to me, "Say this to the breath, 'Come from the four winds, O breath, and breathe into these bones that they might come alive.'"

And they lived and stood up on their feet. There were a lot of people all of a sudden standing before me.

God said, "These bones belong to the whole house of Israel. They think they're all dried up, and they have no hope of living again. But say this to them for me, 'I will open your graves, and bring your people back to life and to the land of Israel. I will breathe my Spirit into you and you will live again as my people in Israel. And you will know that I am the Lord and that I have acted.'"

The Word of the Lord.

Psalm 130

From the depths of my soul I have cried to you, God. Please hear my voice. Let your ears hear me and listen to what I have to say.

With you, God, there is plenty of mercy and goodness to go around.

If you were to count up everything anyone has ever done wrong, God, who would be left standing?
But you are a forgiving God. And I am astounded by the forgiveness you offer.

With you, God, there is plenty of mercy and goodness to go around.

I wait for you patiently. My soul waits for you. As I take your word into my heart I can feel the hope.
My soul waits for you more anxiously than people who wait for a long, dark night to come to an end.

With you, God, there is plenty of mercy and goodness to go around.

People of God, people of Israel, wait with me for God, because I know God has mercy.
With God, there is plenty of mercy and goodness and God will bring all of you back into relationship with him.

With you, God, there is plenty of mercy and goodness to go around.

A Reading from the Letter of Paul to the Romans [8:6–11]

It's no good to be thinking only of yourself and your body and your own needs. That's no way to live. But if you set your mind on God's Spirit instead, you will have life and peace. You may be made of flesh, but you are not made of flesh alone. You have the Spirit of God breathing in and out of you. And the Spirit of God, who raised Jesus from the dead, makes Jesus a living, breathing part of you.

The Word of the Lord.

✠ *The Holy Gospel of Our Lord Jesus Christ According to John* [11:1–45]

Lazarus lived with his sisters Martha and Mary. They were all good friends of Jesus. Lazarus got very sick and his sisters sent word to Jesus that he was sick. When Jesus heard this, he said, "I think this sickness will allow God's glory to show through, even if Lazarus dies." So Jesus stayed put where he was rather than going to see Lazarus right away.

A couple of days later, Jesus said to his disciples, "Let's go to Judea." His disciples said, "But the last time we were there, they tried to stone you. And you want to go back?"

Jesus replied, " We've only got so much time on this earth to do good. Lazarus is sleeping and I want to go wake him up."

The disciples said, "Well, if he's sleeping, there's really no reason to go. He'll be fine."

Jesus said, "No, I meant that Lazarus has died. I'm glad I wasn't there when he died, because now I've got something I want to show you so you can believe. Let's go."

Thomas the Twin said to his fellow followers, "Oh well, here we go. Might as well go with him and die with him."

When they got there, Lazarus had been in his grave for four days. Many people had come to comfort his sisters. Martha heard Jesus had come and ran out to meet him, while Mary stayed at the house. Martha said, "Jesus, if you'd been here, my brother wouldn't have died. I know even now that God will do whatever you ask of him."

Jesus said, " Martha, you know your brother will rise again."

"Of course, I believe in the resurrection on the last day," Martha said.

Jesus looked at her and said, "Martha, I am the resurrection and the life. Whoever believes in me will be alive, whether they live or they die. Do you believe this?"

Martha said, "Yes, Lord. I believe that you are the one God has sent into the world, the Messiah."

She went back and told Mary that Jesus was asking for her. Mary knelt at Jesus' feet, saying, "Lord, if only you'd been here, my brother wouldn't have died."

When Jesus saw her crying, and saw that all the people at the house were crying, he felt the deep pain of losing Lazarus to death. The pain shook him to his core.

"Where is his grave? Show me." Jesus said.

"Come and see, Lord." And Jesus started to cry.

Some people could see how much Jesus had loved his friend Lazarus. Others wondered why, if he could open the eyes of a blind man, he couldn't have kept Lazarus from dying.

Jesus came to the grave, which was in the side of a cave with a big stone rolled against the opening. He told them to roll away the stone. Martha said, "Don't do that. He's been in there four days and the smell will be awful."

Jesus said, "Haven't I told you that if you believed, you would see God's glory?"

So they took the stone away.

Jesus looked up to heaven and said, "Father, thank you for hearing me." And he yelled really loud, "Lazarus, come out of there!"

And the dead man came out, his hands and feet still bound with strips of cloth and his face wrapped up.

Jesus said to the people around, "Set him free from the cloth that is binding him, and let him go."

Many of the people who saw what happened believed in Jesus after that.

The Gospel of the Lord.

The Sunday of the Passion: Palm Sunday

At the Liturgy of the Palms

✠ *The Holy Gospel of Our Lord Jesus Christ According to Matthew* [21:1–13]

When Jesus and his disciples were at the Mount of Olives just outside Jerusalem, Jesus called two of the disciples and said, "Go into town. Right away you will see a donkey tied up, with a colt. Untie them and bring them here. If anyone asks you what you're doing, just say, 'The Lord needs them,' and he will let you take them." (The prophets had said that the king would ride into Jerusalem on a donkey and a colt—so this pointed to Jesus as that king.)

So they went as Jesus asked them to, got the donkey and colt, and Jesus rode into town. There were lots of people around when they heard Jesus was in town. They began to spread their coats on the road in front of them, and cut down branches from the trees, and put them on the road for him to ride on like a carpet. The crowd was shouting "Hosanna to the Son of David! He is so blessed. Hosanna way up in heaven!" When they finally reached Jerusalem, everyone was abuzz. "Who could this possibly be that is causing such excitement?" Of course, the crowds answered, "It's Jesus, the prophet from Nazareth!"

The Gospel of the Lord.

At the Liturgy of the Word

A Reading from the Book of Isaiah [50:4–9]

God has given me the gift of teaching. I know how to catch people's attention with words. God wakes me in the morning with lots to teach me. He has opened my ears, and I let him. I understand that I shouldn't hit those who would hit me, and I have let people spit on me and insult me to my face. God helps me be strong. I have not been humbled even when they try to humiliate me. God helps me be confident that I can take it. If God is on my side, then I say, bring it on, enemies.

The Word of the Lord.

Psalm 31:9–16

I need your help, God, because I'm in big trouble.
I can't stop crying, and I'm so sad my stomach and my throat even hurt.
Everything is just awful. All I can do is sigh.
I feel so old because my bones ache.
I'm just not as strong as I used to be.

I need your help, God, because I'm in big trouble.

People down the street laugh at me. When my old friends see me on the street, they cross to the other side to avoid me. That's how much they don't like me.
No one remembers I'm here. I am as useless as a broken pot.

I need your help, God, because I'm in big trouble.

I hear them whispering behind my back.
All of them talk about me, and what they're planning to do to me.
I remember though, that I trust in you. I've always said, "You are my God."
My life is in your hands. Keep me safe from people who would hurt me.
Smile on me, and let me see your face, God; and please, because you are so kind, save me.

I need your help, God, because I'm in big trouble.

A Reading from the Letter of Paul to the Philippians [2:5–11]

I want you to think the way Jesus thought. He was God and yet he wasn't so full of himself that he needed to take advantage of being God. He emptied himself of the privileges God has, and was born as a servant. He humbled himself and became obedient, as we should be. Jesus let God lead him wherever God wanted him to go. God rewarded him and lifted him on his shoulders. Now Jesus' name is the name that makes us all bow down to him. All of creation knows him and worships him. Everyone should know that Jesus is Lord, and brings glory to the Father.

The Word of the Lord.

✠ *The Holy Gospel of Our Lord Jesus Christ According to Matthew* [27:11–54]

Jesus had been arrested and taken to meet the governor. The governor asked him, "So, are you the King of the Jews?" Jesus replied, "You say so." That's all he would say. He didn't answer any of the accusations anyone made against him. The governor even asked Jesus if he'd heard what people were saying he'd done, because he couldn't believe Jesus just stood there and didn't say a word.

Once a year at festival time the governor would release a prisoner for the crowd. Any prisoner the crowd wanted. The governor was sure they would want Jesus released. The chief priests talked the crowd into asking for Barabbas to be released rather than Jesus. The governor said, "Okay, but what do you want me to do with Jesus then?"

The crowd yelled, "Nail him to a cross!" "Why?" asked the governor. "What has he done to deserve to die?" They shouted even louder, "Nail him to a cross!"

So the governor released Barabbas, and had Jesus whipped and ordered him to be nailed to a cross. The soldiers stripped Jesus, put a purple robe on him to make him look like a fake king, twisted some thorns into a fake crown and smashed it into his head. They put a stick in his hand and knelt in front of him, saying, "Hail, King of the Jews." Then they spit on him and took the stick out of his hand and bashed him over the head with it. When they were done mocking him, they put his own clothes back on him and marched him off to nail him to a cross.

They took him to Golgotha, which means the Place of a Skull, and nailed him to the cross. They wrote a sign to hang over his head that read: This is Jesus, King of the Jews. Then they sat down to watch him die.

People walked by and made fun of Jesus hanging there. "If he's the Son of God, why can't he save himself? We'd believe him if he did." Even the criminals who were hanging on crosses next to him made fun of him.

At noon, the sun went dark. At three o'clock in the afternoon Jesus cried out, "Why have you abandoned me, God?" He cried out again and then took one last breath and died. When Jesus died, the earth shook and rocks were split in two. A Roman soldier, who was watching over Jesus, was terrified at the earthquake the moment of Jesus' death. "This man was the Son of God for sure," he said.

Maundy Thursday

A Reading from the Book of Exodus [12:1–4, 11–14]

This is what God told Moses and Aaron when they were in Egypt:

The month we're in now will be the first month of the year for you from now on. Tell everyone in Israel, that on the tenth day of this month, they should take a lamb for each household, or share one with their neighbors. Cook it, and here's how I want you to eat it: Put your shoes on and have your walking stick and be ready to go. So eat quickly.

This is the Passover of the Lord. On that night I will pass through Egypt and take the life of every firstborn, both animals and humans. If you put the blood from your lamb that you are eating on the top of the doorpost, I will know where you live and nothing will hurt you or your children or animals. Always remember this day, and each year celebrate it as long as you live.

The Word of the Lord.

Psalm 116:1, 10–17

I love God, because he knows my voice and God always listens to me.

Can I ever repay you, God, for all the good things you've done for me?

My cup of salvation is full and I lift it up to offer God a toast.
Everything I vowed to do for God I will do, and everyone will
know that God is good.

Can I ever repay you, God, for all the good things you've done for me?

I know I will always be precious to God, even when I die.
God, I owe you my life. You have cut me loose from the ties that were holding me back.

Can I ever repay you, God, for all the good things you've done for me?

Thank you, God. I can't thank you enough.
I've promised to do good in your name among your people.

Can I ever repay you, God, for all the good things you've done for me? Hallelujah!

A Reading from the First Letter of Paul to the Corinthians
[11:23–26]

Here's what was given to me by the Lord and now I'm passing on to you. On the night when he was betrayed by one of his friends, Jesus took a loaf of bread and gave thanks to God for it. He broke the bread and handed it around the table, saying, "This is my body, which is given for you. Remember me when you do this." Then after supper he took the cup of wine and lifted it up and said, "This is the agreement between you and God. Remember me every time you drink it. Whenever you eat this bread and drink this wine, you proclaim the Lord's death until he comes."

The Word of the Lord.

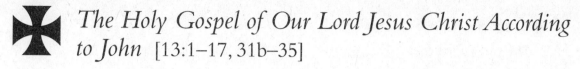

✠ *The Holy Gospel of Our Lord Jesus Christ According to John* [13:1–17, 31b–35]

Jesus knew his time was short, and he loved his disciples now even more, right until the end. Judas was ready to hand Jesus over to the authorities so they could arrest him. During supper Jesus took off his outer robe, and tied a towel around his waist like a servant would. He poured water into a basin and began to wash his disciples' feet and wipe them with the towel he had wrapped around himself. He came to Simon Peter, who was shocked and said to Jesus, "What are you doing? Are you going to wash my feet?"

Jesus answered him, "I know you don't know what I'm doing now, but you will. You'll understand later." Peter said to him, "You will never wash my feet." Jesus answered, "Unless you let me wash you, there is no point in following me." Simon Peter said to him, "Lord, okay. Don't just wash my feet, then. Wash my hands and my head too, please!" Jesus said to him, "You are already clean, Peter. But not all of you in this room are clean." Jesus said that because he knew what was in Judas's heart.

After he had washed their feet, had put on his robe, and had returned to the table, he said to them, "Do you understand what I have just done? You know I'm your teacher. So if I, your teacher, have washed your feet, you also should wash one another's feet. I just gave you an example that you should follow, that you also should do what I just did for you. You will be blessed if you follow my example. If you love each other, everyone will know by looking at you and how your treat each other that you are my disciples."

The Gospel of the Lord.

Good Friday

A Reading from the Book of Isaiah [52:13–53:12]

God says, look at my servant, held high for all of you to see. You will be astonished at his appearance. He no longer looks human. The sight startles the people; the kings who look upon him are stunned into silence. Suddenly they understand what has been revealed.

He grew before their eyes like a young plant growing from the dry ground. There was nothing remarkable about him. He was hated and rejected by those around him. He knew what suffering was. He is the one to carry our diseases and infirmities for us, and yet we turned away from him. His wounds belonged to us. His punishment made us whole and his bruises healed us.

We are like sheep who have wondered off, each going our own way. Our sin was laid on his back. Through all this, he did not open his mouth. He was like a lamb being led to slaughter. Like a sheep who lets his shearers do what they want with him. It's outrageous to think that this could have happened. He was cut off from the living. Laid in his grave with the wicked, although he had done nothing wrong and had never spoken a lie. He was crushed with pain. Through him God's will is done. From deep inside his anguish, he will see light. Through him many will be made right. He poured himself out like a cup, even as he was dying with all the other sinners. He carried sin for many, and prayed for sinners.

The Word of the Lord.

Psalm 22

My God, have you forgotten about me? Why have you left me all alone?
Do you even hear my cry? Can you hear in my voice how distressed I am?
I cry for you in the day, and I hear no answer from you.
During the night I cry out, and I cannot sleep.

My God, have you forgotten about me?
Why have you left me all alone?

I know that you are the Holy One,
the one all Israel praises.
Those who came before me trusted you and you came to help them.
They cried out to you and you heard their voice.
They trusted in you and were not disappointed.

My God, have you forgotten about me?
Why have you left me all alone?

As for me, I am a worm, not even human. Everyone makes fun of me and hates me.
They laugh at me, saying, "Look what she gets for trusting in God. If God loves her, let's see him rescue her."
Yet I know that you are the one who brought me to life
and kept me safe on my mother's breast.
I have been yours ever since I was born.
You were my God even when I was in my mother's body.

My God, have you forgotten about me?
Why have you left me all alone?

Don't be so far away, because trouble is so near
and there is no one else to help me.

It's like bulls are circling around me
    and their jaws are wide open, ready to eat me.
Like roaring, hungry lions they come after me.

My God, have you forgotten about me?
Why have you left me all alone?

I am poured out like water out of a bottle.
    All my bones are out of joint;
    my heart is like wax that is melting.
My mouth is dried out and
    my tongue sticks to the roof of my mouth;
    I feel like you've laid me in my grave.

My God, have you forgotten about me?
Why have you left me all alone?

Packs of dogs close me in, and gangs circle around me;
    they stab my hands and my feet;
    I am skin and bone.
They stare and gloat over me;
    they rip at my clothes and divide them between
    themselves.

My God, have you forgotten about me?
Why have you left me all alone?

Don't be so far away, God,
    you are my strength; hurry to help me.
Save me from the knives that will cut me
    and the dogs who would rip me to shreds.
I will tell people about you;
in the middle of the crowd I will praise you.
I will say to them, "Praise God, people.
Stand in awe of him, Israel."

He doesn't leave people in their poverty or turn and look the other way. When they cry to him, he hears them.

My God, have you forgotten about me?
Why have you left me all alone?

The poor will have enough to eat,
and those who look for God will find him and say,
"May your heart live forever!"
Everyone in the world will turn to you, God.
All the families in every country will bow down before you.
For you are the king over all, even those who have died.

My God, have you forgotten about me?
Why have you left me all alone?

My soul will live for God;
my children and their children will serve God, too;
they will always be known as God's children.
They will make you known to people who haven't even been born yet.

My God, have you forgotten about me?
Why have you left me all alone?

A Reading from the Letter to the Hebrews [10:16–25]

Jesus is the Son of God and acts on our behalf before God, like a priest. He knows our weaknesses, and can understand the troubles we have, because he was one of us and suffered himself. We can march right up to God with confidence that we will find mercy and grace for our lives. Jesus prayed to God just as we do, and God heard him. He learned how to obey God's ways and is the source of eternal life for all who now obey him.

The Word of the Lord.

✠ *The Holy Gospel of Our Lord Jesus Christ According to John* [18:1–19:42]

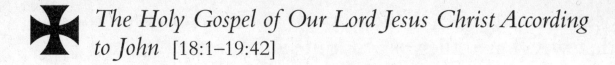

Jesus and his disciples were in a garden where they liked to go and pray. Suddenly soldiers with torches and weapons came into the garden, led by Judas, who was a disciple of Jesus. Jesus knew what was happening and asked them who they were looking for. When they replied, "Jesus from Nazareth," he answered, "That's me." The disciples were shocked. Jesus asked the soldiers if they would please let his disciples go since he was the only one they wanted.

Peter had a sword with him and he swung it around and cut off someone's ear with it. Jesus told him to put the sword away. "I am willing to drink the cup the Father has poured for me."

So the police arrested Jesus and tied his hands. They marched him to the high priest.

Meanwhile, Peter and another disciple followed Jesus. The disciple went inside, but Peter stayed outside the building and waited. A woman guarding the gate said to Peter, "I know you. You're one of Jesus' disciples, aren't you?" Peter said, "No, I'm not. You're thinking of somebody else."

Inside Jesus was being questioned about his teaching. He told them, "Don't ask me. I've always taught where plenty of people could hear me. Ask them what I taught." When he had said this, one of the police standing nearby slapped Jesus on the face, saying, "Is that how you answer the high priest?" Jesus answered, "It's true. Why did you hit me if what I said is true?" They sent him on to another priest.

It was cold outside so the police and slaves and Peter were standing around a fire warming themselves. Someone said to Peter, "You're not one of his disciples, are you?" Peter said, "No, I'm not." One of the slaves of the high priest, a relative of the man whose ear Peter had cut off, asked, "But didn't I see you in the garden with him?" Again Peter denied it, and at that moment a rooster crowed.

Then they took Jesus to Pilate's headquarters. It was early in the morning. Pilate said, "Tell me what this man is being accused of."

They replied, "He's a criminal or we wouldn't have brought him to you." Pilate, who was a Roman, said to them, "Judge him according to your own law. Why bother me?" They replied, "We are not permitted to put anyone to death. We want you to do it for us."

Then Pilate asked Jesus, "Are you the King of the Jews?" Jesus answered, "Do you ask this on your own, or did others tell you about me?" Pilate replied, "I am not a Jew, am I? I am a Roman. Your own people handed you over to me. What have you done?" Jesus answered, "My kingdom is not part of this world." Pilate asked him, "So you are a king?" Jesus answered, "You say that I am a king. Everyone who belongs to the truth listens to my voice." Pilate asked him, "What is truth, anyway?"

Pilate told the people, "I find no case against him. But every year I release someone from prison for you during Passover. Do you want me to release for you the King of the Jews?" They shouted in reply, "Not this man. Release Barabbas instead!"

Now Barabbas was a man who had been stirring up revolution among the people.

Then Pilate took Jesus and had him flogged. The soldiers wove a crown of thorns and put it on his head. They dressed him in a purple robe so that he looked like a king. They made fun of him, saying, "Hail, King of the Jews!" and hitting him in the face. Pilate went out again and said to them, "Look, I told you I am not going to do anything more with him." Jesus came out, wearing the crown of thorns and the purple robe. Pilate said to them, "Here is the man! Look at him."

When the chief priests and the police saw him, they shouted, "String him up on a cross to die!" Pilate said to them, "You do it; I find no case against him." The Jews answered him, "We have a law, and according to that law, he ought to die because he has claimed to be the Son of God."

When Pilate heard this, he was scared of the people. He entered his headquarters again and asked Jesus, "Where did you say you're from?" But Jesus said nothing. Pilate said to him, "Do you refuse to speak to me? Don't you know that I can set you free or execute you?" Jesus answered him, "You don't have any power that God hasn't given you." From then on Pilate tried to set him free, but the people cried out, "If you release this man, you are no friend of the emperor. Everyone who claims to be a king sets himself against the emperor."

When Pilate heard these words, he brought Jesus outside and said, "Here is your King. You want me to execute your King?" The people cried "Do it! Do it! Do it!" The chief priests answered, "We have no king but the emperor." Then he handed him over to them to be crucified.

So they took Jesus and made him carry the cross by himself to what is called The Place of the Skull. There they crucified him, and with him, two others. Pilate had a sign put on the cross that read "Jesus of Nazareth, the King of the Jews."

The chief priests of the Jews said to Pilate, "Don't write, 'The King of the Jews,' but, 'This man *said*, I am King of the Jews.'" Pilate answered, "What I have written I have written." When the soldiers had crucified Jesus, they took his clothes and divided them into four parts, one for each soldier. Meanwhile, standing near the cross of Jesus were his mother, and his mother's sister, Mary, and Mary Magdalene. When Jesus saw his mother and the disciple whom he loved standing beside her, he said to his mother, "Mother, here is your son." Then he said to the disciple,

"Here is your mother. Take care of her for me." After that, the disciple took her into his own home.

When Jesus knew that all was now finished, he said, "I am thirsty." A jar full of sour wine was standing there. So they put a sponge full of it up to his mouth. When Jesus had received the wine, he said, "It is finished." Then he bowed his head and breathed for the last time.

A man named Joseph from Arimathea was a secret admirer of Jesus and asked to let him take Jesus' body to bury it. Nicodemus was there too, and used a mixture of spices to wrap in the linen cloths around Jesus' body, the way they did back then. They laid his body in a brand new tomb.

The Great Vigil of Easter

At the Liturgy of the Word

The Story of Creation [Genesis 1:1–2:2]

In the beginning when God created the heavens and the earth, the earth had no shape at all. There wasn't any light. The water was in total darkness and God's breath moved back and forth over the sea. God said out loud, "Let there be light." And there was! He separated the light and the darkness and called the light "daytime" and called the dark "nighttime." That was the very first day.

"This is good," God said.

Then he worked on separating the water from the sky. That was the second day.

God said, "Let's put all the water on the earth together in one place and call it 'sea' and the places of dry land we'll call 'earth.'" He called them "seas" and "earth." God was very pleased with how things were coming together. Then God said, "Let the earth put forth plants and trees. Let's have plants that grow food! Great!" God said, "This third day was very good."

God said, "Now let's put some order to the light in the skies. We need something to separate day from night, and days from years, and seasons from seasons." And it was so. The big light is the sun, which we see in the day, and the smaller light is the moon. Then God made all the stars in the sky. That was the fourth day.

God said, "I'd like to see some living creatures—like fish in the sea and whales and all kinds of birds in the sky. Let's make some huge sea monsters that live way down deep, and then some little fish who like to flip out of the water. Oh, I've got so many great ideas about animals. Let's make them all." Every kind of animal that crawls or runs or flies was made by God. And God was delighted. He blessed them so that they could multiply, and said, "Please, fill up the oceans with things that swim and fill the skies with birds." That was the fifth day.

God said, "Now, let's see. What kind of animals should live on the dry parts? How about cows, and bugs, and cats? And all kinds of wild animals." And the earth was filled with every kind of animal he could imagine. And God saw that it was really, really good.

Then God said, "Let us make people in our image, who are more like us; and they can take care of the earth and the seas and the animals and the birds in the air and the fish in the sea." So God created man and woman. He blessed them and told them to be productive and have children so there would always be someone to take care of God's creation. God explained that they could use the plants to feed themselves.

God stepped back and looked at everything. Such excellent work! That was the end of the sixth day.

On the seventh day, God took a break, blessed and declared that day a day of rest. That rest felt very, very good.

The Word of the Lord.

Psalm 136:1–9, 23–26

Give thanks to God, for he is the best.

God's mercy goes on forever.

God does great wonders.

God's mercy goes on forever.

God made the heavens above us.

God's mercy goes on forever.

God spread the earth out over the waters.

God's mercy goes on forever.

God created the "great lights" in the sky.

God's mercy goes on forever.

The sun rules the hours of the day.
The moon and stars govern the night sky.

God's mercy goes on forever.

God remembered us and rescued us.

God's mercy goes on forever.

God gives food to every living thing.

God's mercy goes on forever.

Give thanks to the God of heaven.

God's mercy goes on forever.

The Flood [Genesis 7:1–5, 11–18; 8:6–18, 9:8–13]

Noah was a very old man. He and his wife liked to talk with God. They and their children tried very hard to live in God's Way. But it wasn't easy. All the other people where the Noah family lived didn't even think about God. They fought with each other and killed each other. They stole things and told lies. They were mean to each other. That made God very unhappy.

God became so unhappy, God finally decided to start the world all over again with new people. So God said to Noah and his family, "Build a boat. A special kind of boat called an ark. It must be huge so that it can hold two of every kind of animal and bird in the world."

The people who didn't listen to God thought Noah was very silly. "There's no water around here," they said. "It's just stupid to build a boat where there isn't any water!"

Noah and his family knew it looked pretty strange, but God told them to build this boat, so they were going to build it.

Mr. and Mrs. Noah and their kids built the boat together. When it was finally done, God told them to find two dogs, two cats. Two horses. Two tigers. Two snakes. Two wallabies. Two bugs. Two skunks. Two of everything. It was crowded and noisy and smelly when they all got into that boat together. Then Noah, and Mrs. Noah, and their kids got in the boat with them. And they waited for the rain.

Still no water. Noah's kids would ask, "Do we have to sit in this awful boat forever? When it's not even raining?" Noah told them to be patient. The rain would come. But it was hard to be patient.

Then all of a sudden, it started to rain. And it kept raining and raining for forty days and forty nights. And only Noah, his family, and those animals inside were safe.

The ark floated up on the water and drifted around for a long, long time. All they could see when they looked outside was water. Water everywhere. Then, one day, the sun came out. And the wind began to blow. Noah decided to see if there was dry land anywhere, even though he couldn't see any. He wanted to get off that smelly ark more than anyone.

So Noah took one of the birds, a raven, and let it fly away. The raven couldn't find any place to land so he came back to the ark. Then Noah tried sending out a dove, and the same thing happened. He waited another week and tried sending the dove out again. It stayed away a long time, but when it finally came back, it had some olive leaves in its beak. "Look!" yelled Noah. "The dove found some leaves! That means that somewhere out there is land with a tree on it!"

Everyone cheered and danced and partied. They had been on that boat for forty days and couldn't wait to get on dry land again. Noah gathered his family and told them, "The first thing we do, when we get off this stinky boat, is say thank you to God."

When the ark came to dry ground, everybody got off that boat as quickly as they could. The Noah family piled up some rocks to make an altar. They put some wood on the altar to make a fire, and good food on the fire. They hoped God could smell the delicious food and know that they were saying thank you to him!

They let all the animals out of the boat. The animals ran around and jumped up and down, and smelled the grass and the trees. It was like they were saying "Thank you" to God in their own way.

Everyone was happy.

God was happy too.

The Word of the Lord.

Psalm 46

We run to you for protection and strength,
when there is no other place for us to go.

Even when we're in deep trouble, we won't be afraid.

We won't be afraid although the earth changes shape, and the mountains quiver beneath the waves of the sea,
even though the oceans get angry and roar,
and the mountains are frightened by storms.

Even when we're in deep trouble, we won't be afraid.

I like to imagine a beautiful river running through the city where God lives.
That city is grounded in God and has nothing to fear.
When the sun comes up, and the world surrounding that city is at war and nations are about to fall, God speaks and the whole earth melts.
Thank God that the Lord is with us
and the God of Jacob is our protector.

Even when we're in deep trouble, we won't be afraid.

Look around and see what God has done.
God has changed everything.
He makes wars end, destroys weapons.
We hear God say,
"Quiet. Be still. Know this: I am God.
I am the God of all of you."

Even when we're in deep trouble, we won't be afraid.

Abraham's sacrifice of Isaac [Genesis 22:1–14]

God gave Abraham a test. When God said, "Abraham!" Abraham said, "I'm here, God." God told Abraham to take his only son, Isaac, whom he loved a lot, and offer him to God in the mountains. So Abraham got up early in the morning, put a saddle on his donkey, took two men and his son Isaac, and started out for the mountains. He cut the wood for the burnt offering, and traveled to the place God had told him he should go. After three days, Abraham and Isaac left the others to go worship. They carried the wood for the fire. Isaac wondered where they would get the lamb for the offering, like they usually did. Abraham told Isaac that God himself was providing the lamb. They kept walking until they came to the place that God had showed them. Abraham built the altar, laid the wood. Then put his son Isaac on top of the wood. He was ready to take his son's life and offer Isaac to God, when the angel of the Lord yelled, "Abraham! Don't do it! God doesn't want your son, he wants you. God wants all of you." Abraham stopped what he was doing, and saw a ram in the thicket, and knew God had indeed provided him with an offering. Abraham called that place "God provides."

The Word of the Lord.

Psalm 16

Keep me safe, O God. I've come to you for protection.
I always say, "God is the best."
I want to be just like the people who follow God's ways and do good things for other people. The ones who put other things before God will have no end of trouble in their lives. I don't want to do what they do.
You are the one I want, God. I know you have my back.

Everything I see before me is good. You have been so good to me.

I bless you, because you guide me in the right direction. Your words are in my heart when I go to sleep at night. And when I wake up, you're the first thing I think about. You are beside me all day long, so I know I can't go wrong.

Everything I see before me is good. You have been so good to me.

My heart is happy, and my spirit jumps up and down with joy inside me. And when I lay down, I have hope on my mind.
Even when I die, I know you won't abandon me. Even there, you will show me the path of life. When you are with me, I'm full up with joy. Being with you always makes me happy.

Everything I see before me is good. You have been so good to me.

Israel's deliverance at the Red Sea [Exodus 14:10–31; 15:20–21]

The people of Israel had been slaves in Egypt for four hundred years. God asked Moses to lead them back to the place where their ancestors had lived. Pharaoh and the Egyptians didn't want them to leave and followed them into the desert.

The people of Israel turned around and saw that the Egyptians were catching up. They were scared and cried out to God to save them. They yelled at Moses, "Why did you bring us out here, because there weren't any graves in Egypt? It would have been better to stay in Egypt as slaves than to die out here in the middle of nowhere!"

But Moses said to the people, "Get a grip! Don't be afraid. Today God will fight for us, you'll see. And those Egyptians you see chasing us? That's the last we'll ever see of them. Let God do his work."

When Moses told God that the people were complaining, God said, "Why? Tell them to put one foot in front of the other. When you reach the sea, lift up your walking stick, stretch your hand out over the water, and it will divide in two, and they'll be able to walk on dry ground to freedom. The Egyptians will follow you in, but they won't come out the other side. They'll know that I am God."

The angel of God had been leading the people of Israel, but moved to the back. A pillar of cloud that had been leading them moved behind them too, between the people of Israel and the Egyptians to keep them apart during the night.

When they got to the sea, Moses did what God told him; he lifted his walking stick and his hand over the water. And God used the wind to divide the sea and make a dry path right through the water. The people of Israel walked through the sea, with walls of water on either side of them. The Egyptians came in after them. They started to panic and they got stuck in the mud. They tried to turn back, but they couldn't. They said to themselves, "It looks like God is on the side of the people of Israel. Let's get out of here."

God told Moses to stretch out his hand over the water again. Not a single Egyptian or his chariot got out before the sea returned back to normal. That's how God saved the people of Israel. They were amazed at what God had done for them. They believed that God was on their side and believed in his servant Moses.

Moses's sister Miriam and the women danced and sang with tambourines, "Sing to the LORD, for he has triumphed gloriously; horse and rider he has thrown into the sea."

The Word of the Lord.

Canticle 8: The Song of Moses [Exodus 15:1–6, 11–13, 17–18]

I'm singing to God with my loudest voice because God's the best.
My enemies have been hurled into the sea.
God is my protector, my strength, and now God has become
the one who saved me.
This is my God and I will praise this mighty warrior whose
name is Yahweh.
My enemies are nowhere to be found. They are long gone.
Who can compare to you, God? Is there anyone else who is
so holy, so glorious, so awesome?
We watched you stretch out your hand and the seas devoured
our enemies.
You led us to safety with your constant love.
You will bring us to a place of honor with you.
We will honor you wherever you choose to dwell.
You will reign forever.

Salvation offered freely to all [Isaiah 55:1–11]

If you're thirsty, I've got water for you. Even if you don't have any money, come and eat. You don't need to be thirsty and hungry. You can have free wine and milk.

Why spend your money on food that doesn't fill you up? Why spend your time doing things that don't matter? Listen carefully to me. Eat what is good, and delight yourselves in rich food. As much as you want. Lean close to me and listen. I will make you a promise, just as I made a promise with my steadfast, sure love for King David.

I made him someone people could look up to, a leader and commander of the people.

You can be people that everyone looks up to because I, the LORD your God, the Holy One of Israel, have glorified you.

Look for God while he can be found. Talk to God while he is near.

Give up going the wrong way, where people get hurt, and return to God. Come back to God who is ready to forgive you. God's mercy has no limits. God says, "My thoughts are not your thoughts, nor are your ways my ways.

"Just as high as the skies are above the earth, that's how much higher my thoughts are than yours. The rain and the snow come down from heaven, and they don't return until they have watered the earth. They make it ready for things to sprout, giving seed to the sower and bread to the eater. That's how my word is—once I have spoken it, it won't return to me without results. But it will do what I send it to do."

The Word of the Lord.

Canticle 9 [Isaiah 12:2–6]

For sure, you are the one who saves me. I'm not afraid, God,
when I trust in you.
I can count on you. I just hold on tight and you defend me.
There is always water in the well of salvation to drink.

And I'm happy to call out your name and give you thanks
out loud.
Tell everyone what God has done, people. Don't let them forget
God's name.
Sing whenever you can about God.
Ring all the bells in Zion and keep them ringing because the
Holy One is right there with you.

A new heart and a new Spirit [Ezekiel 36:24–28]

God came to me and said, "Here's what I want you to say to the people of Israel.

"I am going to gather you from wherever you are, and bring you into a new land you can call your own. I will sprinkle fresh water on you, and you will be clean. From all those things that keep you from me, I will clean you. I will give you a new heart. And put a brand new spirit inside you. I will cut out your heart of stone, and put in its place a heart of flesh. I will put my own spirit within you as well and you will follow my ways. When you live in your new place, with your new heart, you will be my people and I will be your God."

The Word of the Lord.

Psalm 42:1–7

I am like a deer who longs for flowing streams;
that's how my soul longs for you, O God.

**My soul is thirsty for you;
you are the living God.**

When can I see your face?
I've done nothing but cry heavy tears day and night.

People around me wonder where you are. They ask me, "Where is your god now?"

My soul is thirsty for you;
you are the living God.

In my mind I go over the times when you were with me and my heart aches:
All those times I went with the crowds to your house to praise you.

My soul is thirsty for you;
you are the living God.

I tell myself I shouldn't be so sad. "Soul," I say, "Why do you feel like this?
"Remember your hope in God. Praise God who is your help."

My soul is thirsty for you;
you are the living God.

The Valley of Dry Bones [Ezekiel 37:1–14]
(see the Fifth Sunday in Lent, Year A, p. 74)

Psalm 30

Again, I've got a lot to thank you for, God.
You got me out of a mess again
and kept the bullies from beating me up and laughing.
I yelled for you to help me
and you calmed me down
and settled my heart.

I know that God is good. All the time.
All the time, God is good.

I thought I was a goner, but sure enough,
just like you promised,
there you were to help me put my life together again.
Everyone who loves God has a story like this.
Every one of us should be thankful when God works things out for the good.
Sometimes it seems God might be angry,
but that doesn't last long.

I know that God is good. All the time.
All the time, God is good.

I might cry myself to sleep at night
but in the morning things seem a lot better.
There are times when I feel nothing will ever go wrong,
because I'm just that good at being me.

I know that God is good. All the time.
All the time, God is good.

You have made me the king of the mountain, God.
Way to go! I'm the best.
But when I forget that you are God, and I forget that I am not God,
everything falls apart and I'm scared every time I turn around.
So, once again, I'm knocking on your door, God, begging you to help me.
I'm of no use when I'm like this. You might as well help me out again, God.

I know that God is good. All the time.
All the time, God is good.

I'm glad that you don't laugh at me, God.
I hope you are laughing *with* me instead.

There are sure a lot of ups and downs in my life
and you are there through all of them.

I know that God is good. All the time.
All the time, God is good.

I will sing your praises and do a happy dance today.
Thank you for being with me through it all.
I can't thank you enough.

I know that God is good. All the time.
All the time, God is good.

The Gathering of God's People [Zephaniah 3:12–20]

Sing as loud as you can, O daughter Zion; go ahead and shout, O Israel! Rejoice with all your heart, O daughter Jerusalem! Everything and everybody that could hurt you, God has taken away. God is right beside you and you don't have anything to be afraid of or worry about anymore.

God has won the day
and will rejoice over you with gladness.
    God's love will renew you
and God will sing with you, loudly and for a long time.
God says, "I will take care of the disasters,
    and I will deal with the people who want to put you down.
I will save those who can't keep up with you and gather the
    people on the fringes of your community,
I will change their shame into praise and make their name famous.
I will bring you home, and make you special among all the
    peoples of the earth.
Things will be good again for you. Watch me make it happen."

The Word of the Lord.

Psalm 98

Together we'll sing a brand new song to you, God,
because of all the incredible things you have done.
You are a winner! We'll make sure everyone knows.
You haven't forgotten about us.
Your love for us is faithful through all that we've been through together.
Let's break out in song, everyone all over the world.
Get your harps and trumpets and your voices ready to sing praises to God.
Let the sea roar with delight, and all the creatures that swim in the sea, join in.
Let the floodwaters clap their hands
and the hills sing in harmony because our God is coming.
When you come to us, God, you will make things right and even the score between people.

A Reading from the Letter of Paul to the Romans [6:3–11]

You know, don't you, that all of us who have been baptized, have been baptized into Jesus' death? Our old selves have been buried with him, so that just as Jesus was brought back to life by the glory of the Father, we too might have a brand new life. Our old self died with him, so that sin isn't in charge of us anymore. We know that Christ will never die again. Death has absolutely no power over him. When he died, sin died with him. The life he lives now, he lives for God. You too are dead to sin and alive to God in Christ Jesus. Remember that.

The Word of the Lord.

✠ *The Holy Gospel of Our Lord Jesus Christ According to Matthew* [28:1–10]

As the sun was coming up on Sunday morning, Mary Magdalene and another Mary went to see Jesus' grave. All of a sudden the earth shook. And an angel came down from heaven and rolled the stone away from the grave and sat on the stone. He looked like lightning and his clothes were white as snow. The guards who were at the grave were so scared, they passed out. But the angel said to the women, "Don't be afraid; I know that you're looking for Jesus who was crucified. He isn't here; for he has been brought back to life, just as he said. Come in here, I'll show you the place where he was laid when he was dead. Then go tell his disciples right away, 'He's been raised from the dead, and he's going to meet us in Galilee.'" So they left the tomb and ran to tell the disciples, both as scared and as happy as can be. Suddenly Jesus was right in front of them and said, "Hello!" They fell on their knees, grabbed his feet, and worshiped him. Then Jesus said to them, "Don't be afraid; go and tell my brothers to go to Galilee; I'll meet them there."

The Gospel of the Lord.

Easter Day

A Reading from the Acts of the Apostles [10:34–43]
(see the First Sunday after the Epiphany, Year A, p. 27)

Psalm 118:1–2, 14–24

Thanks, God. You are so good. Your mercy never, ever ends.
Let all God's people say it aloud: God's mercy never, ever ends!
You are my strength and the song I sing, and now you've become my salvation.

Today our God has acted. Let everyone rejoice and be happy.

I hear people singing in their homes, and claiming victory. God has triumphed!
I will shout about the work God has accomplished today.
Sometimes I am punished, but I get back up and try again.
When God opens his doors to me, the doors to good things, I will walk right through them. Thanks for inviting me in, God.

Today our God has acted. Let everyone rejoice and be happy.

The stone that the builders threw out because they didn't like it, is now the cornerstone that the whole building is built upon.
It's all because of the amazing things that God has done for us.

Today our God has acted. Let everyone rejoice and be happy.

A Reading from the Letter of Paul to the Colossians [3:1–4]

Since Jesus rose from the dead, we have been raised from our old life to a brand new life. So we should work for God's purpose now. We can now focus on things that God wants for us, not on things from our old life. That old life is over and a new life has begun with Jesus. When God is done working in us through Christ Jesus, we will be revealed with Christ in God's glory.

The Word of the Lord.

✠ *The Holy Gospel of Our Lord Jesus Christ According to John* [20:1–18]

Early on Sunday morning, before the sun even came up, Mary Magdalene went to the tomb where they had laid Jesus' body. She saw that the stone they'd rolled across the entrance had been removed. She wasn't sure what had happened so she ran to find Simon Peter and the other disciple that Jesus loved and said, "Someone has taken Jesus out of his tomb, and I have no idea where they've taken him."

Peter and the other disciple went running right away to check things out. The other disciple beat Peter to the tomb. He looked in the tomb and saw the cloths they had wrapped Jesus in, but no Jesus. Peter caught up with him and walked right into the tomb. He saw the cloths lying there too, but also saw the cloth that had been on Jesus' head rolled up in the corner by itself. Then the other disciple came in, and when he saw what was in there, he believed. At first they didn't understand what they'd been told in the scripture about Jesus rising from the dead.

They left the tomb and went home, leaving Mary standing there crying. When she looked inside the tomb, she saw two angels sitting where Jesus' body had been. They asked her why she was crying. She told them, "Someone took Jesus away and I have no idea where his body is." Then she turned around and saw Jesus standing right in front of her! But she didn't recognize him. Jesus said to her, "Why are you crying? Who are you looking for?" At first she thought he was the man in charge of the tomb, and she said, "Sir, if you took him somewhere else, let me know where he is and I'll take him away with me." Then Jesus said, "Mary." She recognized his voice and turned around and said "Teacher!" (That's what she used to call him.) "It's really you!" Jesus told her not to grab him to keep him here, that he was going to go to his Father. "Go tell my brothers that I'm going to be with our God, the father of us all," he said. So she ran to find the disciples to tell them that she had actually seen Jesus and talked to him. And she told them what Jesus said.

The Gospel of the Lord.

The Second Sunday of Easter

A Reading from the Acts of the Apostles [2:14a, 22–32]

Peter and the eleven other disciples were together in a crowd of people. Peter started shouting about Jesus:

Jesus from Nazareth was the sign that God was among you. You watched him do those signs. This is the man you handed over to the authorities who killed him. But God freed him from death, because he was even stronger than death itself. King David, who lived a long time ago, even talked about him: "My heart is glad and full of hope because your Holy One was raised from death. You have shown me the good life, full of your presence." Fellow people of Israel, King David wasn't talking about himself. God had promised David that one of his descendants would be the Messiah. It was Jesus that God raised and we are all witnesses of that.

The Word of the Lord.

Psalm 16 (see the Great Vigil of Easter Vigil, Year A, p. 100)

A Reading from the First Letter of Peter [1:3–9]

Blessed be God, the Father of our Savior Jesus Christ. God is so very merciful and has given us a whole new life of hope that will never die, because Jesus didn't stay dead. Our new life is one that will never die, and never get old. Even though right now things are really rough for you, and it feels like you are metal in a fire, you are getting stronger in Jesus Christ. Even though you have never met him personally, you still love him. And you believe in him, and have no end of joy because of your faith in him.

The Word of the Lord.

✠ *The Holy Gospel of Our Lord Jesus Christ According to John* [20:19–31]

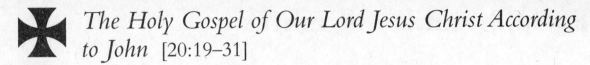

It was Easter Sunday night, and the disciples were all together, in a house with locked doors. They were scared the authorities were going to come get them because they knew Jesus. All of a sudden Jesus was right in the middle of them and said, "Peace, brothers!" He could tell they couldn't believe it was him, so he showed them the holes in his hands and his side. They were so very happy to see him alive. Again he said, "Peace be with you. Just like my Father sent me to you, I'm sending you out as well." He breathed on them and said, "Here . . . receive the Holy Spirit. Now you have the power to forgive."

Thomas hadn't been with them that night. The other disciples told him, "We saw Jesus. He was right here with us." Thomas said, "I won't believe that until I see him for myself and can put my fingers on his wounds."

A week later the disciples were together again in the same house. Thomas was with them this time. Even though the doors were shut, Jesus was able to be in the middle of them again, and again he said, "Peace be with you all." Jesus said, "Thomas, I know it's hard to believe I'm here. Go ahead and put your finger here on my hands. And touch my side. That will help you believe."

Thomas fell to his knees. He didn't need to touch Jesus in order to say, "My Lord and my God! It is you, Jesus!"

Jesus said, "You believe because you can see me. Blessed are those who will never see me in person but believe in me anyway."

I can't tell you all the awesome things Jesus did. I've written what I have written so you can believe that Jesus is the Messiah, and so that you can have the life he offers.

The Gospel of the Lord.

The Third Sunday of Easter

A Reading from the Acts of the Apostles [2:14a, 36–41]

Peter was with the rest of the disciples, still talking. Here's some of what he said. "I want everyone in Israel to know for sure that God made Jesus, the one who was crucified, the Messiah." The people who heard were moved to tears and they asked Peter what they should do now. Peter said, "You can turn your lives around and be baptized in Jesus' name. Your sins will be forgiven and you will receive the Holy Spirit as a gift. God's promise of new life is for you, and your children, and everyone in the whole world."

Peter kept on talking and telling them about how corrupt the world was around them. That day about three thousand of the people, who took into their hearts what Peter said, were baptized and became disciples too.

The Word of the Lord.

Psalm 116:1–3, 10–17 (see Maundy Thursday, Year A, p. 83)

A Reading from the First Letter of Peter [1:17–23]

If you call on God to help you as your father would, just remember that God won't let you get away with things. God paid a price to get you out of the useless life you were living. The price wasn't gold or silver, but the blood of his Son, Jesus. Having you live a holy life through Christ has always been in God's plan. Your faith is set on God now. You know the truth because you know Christ. And through him you have come to trust in God. Now you can love each other deeply from the heart. You have been given a brand new life, not a life that will end, but will go on forever through God's living and endless Word.

The Word of the Lord.

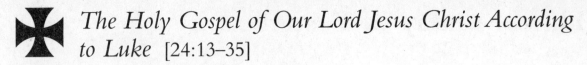

✠ *The Holy Gospel of Our Lord Jesus Christ According to Luke* [24:13–35]

On Easter night, two disciples were walking the seven miles from Jerusalem to Emmaus. They couldn't stop talking about what had happened to Jesus. As they were talking, Jesus himself walked up to them and joined them, but they didn't recognize him (because they thought he was dead!). Jesus asked them what they were talking about. They stopped and looked at him and said, "Are you kidding? You must be the only person in Jerusalem who doesn't know what happened this weekend." Jesus said, "What? What happened?" They told him, "Well, Jesus of Nazareth, who was a prophet from God, got handed over to the Roman authorities, who put him to death. We thought he was the one to save Israel from the Romans! And that's not all. This morning, some women in our group shocked us. They had gone to his grave early this morning but didn't find his body there. Instead there were angels who told them Jesus was alive. Sure enough, others checked it out and it was just like the women said."

Jesus said, "But didn't the prophets say these things would happen?" And he started to explain that the scriptures about the Messiah were all about him. As they got close to Emmaus, Jesus kept on walking. But they begged him to stay with them. "Please," they said. "The sun is setting. Stay here for the night." So he stayed with them.

At the dinner table he took the bread in front of them and blessed it, broke it into pieces, and offered it to them. All of a sudden, it was like their eyes were opened. And they recognized that it was Jesus right in front of them, breaking bread with them! Then he disappeared.

They said to each other, "When he was talking to us about the scripture, wasn't it like our hearts were on fire?"

Immediately they got on the road back to Jerusalem, to find the other disciples to tell them they'd seen Jesus. "Jesus is alive, and Simon saw him too!" the disciples said. They told the disciples the story of what happened on the road and how they finally knew it was Jesus with them in the breaking of the bread.

The Gospel of the Lord.

The Fourth Sunday of Easter

A Reading from the Acts of the Apostles [2:42–47]

The friends of Jesus spent their time in teaching and learning from each other, in enjoying each other's company, in sharing bread and wine and worshipping God. Everyone was amazed at the awesome signs and wonders they did. Together they shared everything they owned, so that no one would go without. They simplified their lives by selling the things they owned, and then distributed the money in ways that helped other people. Each day, they spent time worshipping God, having Eucharist at home with each other, and eating their meals together. Their hearts were glad and generous and full of God's love. And each day, God added more people to their fellowship.

The Word of the Lord.

Psalm 23 (see Fourth Sunday in Lent, Year A, p. 70)

A Reading from the First Letter of Peter [2:19–25]

There's something special about you when you're able to keep your chin up for God's sake as people make fun of you. If you're doing the right thing, it's not always popular, but it's always the right thing to do and you know it. Jesus knew what that was like. He was always being chased and mocked by people for telling them about God and God's ways. When people were abusing him, he didn't return the abuse. He simply let God deal with them. It wasn't easy for him. And it won't be easy for you, either. When he died on the cross, he was hoping that we would be free from the power our sin holds over us and live in an entirely different way. We have been healed by Jesus' wounds. Once, we were going in the wrong direction like sheep who have lost their way. But now, we have returned to the shepherd who watches out for our souls.

The Word of the Lord.

✠ *The Holy Gospel of Our Savior Jesus Christ According to John* [10:1–10]

Jesus talked to them about sheep and shepherds. He said that the sheep know the shepherd's voice and won't follow a stranger whose voice they don't know. The shepherd comes through the gate into the place the sheep are kept, the sheepfold. People who try to get into the sheepfold by hopping over the fence are thieves.

When Jesus said all this, the disciples had no idea what he was talking about. So Jesus explained it to them. He said, "I am the gate for the sheep. Others who have come were thieves and the sheep didn't know their voices so they didn't listen to them. They wanted to steal and destroy the sheep. But whoever comes through me will find good pasture. I have come so that you all may have life, a better life than you could ever imagine."

The Gospel of the Lord.

The Fifth Sunday of Easter

A Reading from the Acts of the Apostles [7:55–60]

Stephen was filled with the Holy Spirit. He looked up into heaven and could actually see God in all God's glory, and Jesus standing there, too. "Everyone, look! I am looking right into heaven itself and can see the Son of Man at the right hand of God!"

Instead of being excited, the people who could hear him covered their ears and yelled really loudly and came at Stephen, all angry. Then they dragged him out of the city and picked up rocks and began throwing them at him to kill him. They laid their coats next to the feet of a young man named Saul.

Even while they were throwing rocks at him, and he knew he was going to die, Stephen prayed, "Lord Jesus, receive my spirit. Let me be with you." While rocks were still hitting him in the head, he got on his knees and cried as loud as he could, "Lord, don't hold this sin against these people who are killing me." And then he died.

The Word of the Lord.

Psalm 31:1–5, 15–16

Whenever I am in trouble, I always run to you, God.
There is no shame in hiding with you. You come to my rescue.
Bring your ear close to me now. And hurry, because I need
rescuing. Again.

Let me see your shining face. Love me, God, and save me.

Be like a strong rock. Be a big castle to keep me safe. I count
on you.
Because you are who you are, show me where I should go.

I'm all tangled up in a net that people secretly set for me.
Come and get me out of this mess. I count on you and your strength.

Let me see your shining face. Love me, God, and save me.

I put myself and my future in your hands.
Because you have kept me for yourself, God of all that is true,
every minute of my life is in your hands now.
You're the only one who can save me from people who hate me and make fun of me.

Let me see your shining face. Love me, God, and save me.

A Reading from the First Letter of Peter [2:2–10]

You're just like little babies who are crying out for milk, for spiritual milk that will help you grow in knowing God in your life. Taste this spiritual milk and see that God is good. Come to God. Even though others would throw you away, you are precious to God. God can use you like a living stone to build a spiritual house. And all you do will be acceptable to God because you know Jesus Christ. You are special to God. And all of you together make up a group of people who are awesome in God's eyes. You are God's own people and God has found you in the darkness and brought you into the marvelous light. Everything has changed for you now. Now you have God and you have mercy.

The Word of the Lord.

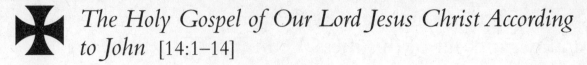

✠ *The Holy Gospel of Our Lord Jesus Christ According to John* [14:1–14]

Jesus told his disciples, "Don't let yourself worry about things. Place your trust in God and me. Do you know that God's house has a place for everyone? I'm going to go to that place and make sure it's ready for you. And then I'll be back to bring you there myself, even though you know the way there."

Thomas said, "What? Why would you think we know the way there? We don't know where you're going much less know how to get there."

Jesus said, "You know the way! I am the way, the truth, and the life. You come to me and you'll have your way to the Father. You know me; you know my Father."

Philip said, "Show the Father to us, Jesus, and we'll stop bugging you about it."

Jesus said, "How long have I been with you guys, and you still don't know who I am? If you've seen me, then you've seen the Father. Don't say show me the Father. I know it's hard to understand but I am in the Father and the Father is in me. And the words I speak, they aren't my own words. They belong to the Father. All the work I do is in the Father's name. Whatever you ask the Father for in my name, I will do it. That's how close the Father and I are."

The Gospel of the Lord.

The Sixth Sunday of Easter

A Reading from the Acts of the Apostles [17:22–31]

Paul stood in front of everyone and said:

As I was walking through your beautiful city of Athens, I noted how extremely religious you all are. I even found an altar with this written on it, "To an unknown god." I have a God I know well. This is what I know about my God: My God made the world and everything that's in it. My God doesn't live in shrines we humans build. My God gives life itself to everything. My God made the first man and woman, and all the people of the earth are related to that one couple. My God made the boundaries of space and time and planted in each of us a space that can only God can fill. We all search for God, even though God's not very far at all from each of us. "In him we live and move and have our being" someone once said. And "we too are his offspring."

God is not something we can hold, like gold or silver or stone, and no one has ever painted a picture of God. God wants us all to turn toward him, and know that we are right with him because of Jesus, whom God has raised from the dead.

The Word of the Lord.

Psalm 66:7–18

Shout it LOUD, people. Bless you, God!
You hold our souls in your hands
and won't let us slip through your fingers.

Come and listen, friends, and I will tell you what God has done for me.

You have tested us, God, just as silver is tested.
We've been in traps and had heavy burdens on our backs.
We've had enemies ride their horses over our heads.

Come and listen, friends, and I will tell you what God has done for me.

We walked through fire and water
and you brought us through all of it, to a beautiful place of refreshment.
I will come to your house with gifts and make good the promises
I made when I was in trouble and you helped me.
I will bring you anything you want.

Come and listen, friends, and I will tell you what God has done for me.

I yelled to God for help and now I yell God's praises.
Bless you, God!
You didn't find evil in my heart when you looked.
You have heard my voice.
Bless you for not throwing me and my prayers out.

Come and listen, friends, and I will tell you what God has done for me.

A Reading from the First Letter of Peter [3:13–22]

If you are anxious to do the right thing, can anyone hurt you? Well, maybe. But even if you get into trouble for doing the right thing, you are blessed. Don't be afraid. Don't let them bully or scare you. In your hearts, you know Christ is Lord. If someone asks you why you have hope, make sure you have an answer for them. But answer them gently and respectfully, not in a way that makes them feel stupid.

Keep your conscience clear so that, when people *do* make fun of you, you will have nothing to be ashamed of. After all, it's better to suffer for doing good than to suffer for doing evil. Christ suffered for all of us, because we are sinful, in order to bring us to God. They killed his body, but he was made alive in spirit. When he was raised, his spirit visited those spirits in prison who were waiting patiently to meet him. Baptism saves you now, not because it removes dirt from your body, but because it connects you with God through Christ's resurrection. Christ makes your appeal to God, and he now sits at God's right hand, with angels and the host of heaven as his servants.

The Word of the Lord.

✠ *The Holy Gospel of Our Savior Jesus Christ According to John* [14:15–21]

Jesus said to his disciples, "If you love me, you will remember what I've said to you and follow my commandments. When I leave I am going to ask the Father to send you the Holy Spirit, the spirit of truth. The Spirit will be inside of you and stay with you. So you see, I'm not going to leave you alone. I will be with you. In a little while, the world won't be able to see me, but you will be able to see me. And because I am alive, you will be more alive, too. You will know that I am one with the Father and you are one with me. And if you love me and keep my commandments, the Father and I love you and know you as well."

The Gospel of the Lord.

The Seventh Sunday of Easter

A Reading from the Acts of the Apostles [1:6–14]

The disciples were together with Jesus and they asked him, "So, Jesus, are you going to rescue Israel from Roman occupation *now*?"

Jesus said, "You know what? You don't need to know everything God is doing. God has a special time line. You will receive special power when the Holy Spirit comes on you. And then, you will speak for me wherever you go."

Just as he said this, they saw him lifted up into a cloud above them, and he was gone. As they stood there with their mouths open, still looking up, two men dressed in white said to them, "Why are you just standing there looking up? Jesus has gone into heaven, and he'll come back the same way."

Then the disciples went back to Jerusalem, to the upstairs room where they were staying. If you want to know the disciples names, here they are: Peter, John, James, Andrew, Philip, Thomas, Bartholomew, Matthew, James, Simon, and Judas son of James. There were some women there, too. Mary, Jesus' mother, was there, as were his brothers. And they spent their time praying constantly.

The Word of the Lord.

Psalm 68:1–10, 33–36

May you rise up, God, and your enemies run away like scared little kids.

May they disappear like smoke in the wind, like wax that melts when it gets too close to the fire.

And then, the faithful people can be happy.

Everyone on earth, no matter who you are, or where you live . . . sing God's praises!

Sing good and loud to God whose name is YAHWEH. Shout it wherever you go!

God is on the side of those who have no parents or spouses to care for them.

God gives those without families a home and sets prisoners free.

But those who resist God will find themselves in a pretty lonely place.

Everyone on earth, no matter who you are, or where you live . . . sing God's praises!

God, you led your people through the desert. The earth shook like crazy, and the skies opened up and rained hard because you were there.

Then you sent good and gentle rain where it was needed. And the dry, tired land came back to life.

Everyone on earth, no matter who you are, or where you live . . . sing God's praises.

Your people found themselves in your goodness. And in you they were home.

You make sure the poor are cared for.

Everyone on earth, no matter who you are, or where you live . . . sing God's praises!

Your home is in the ancient heavens, and your powerful voice is heard throughout the world.

Your strength is in the skies and his holy places.

You give strength and power to your people. Bless you, God.

Everyone on earth, no matter who you are, or where you live . . . sing God's praises!

A Reading from the First Letter of Peter [4:12–14; 5:6–11]

My dear friends, don't be surprised at how difficult life can be as a follower of Jesus. Think of it as sharing your suffering with Jesus, and then you can shout for joy when his glory is finally revealed. God's Spirit is resting on you, even when people make fun of you because you believe in Jesus. It's not so bad to be humble now, because God will lift you up later.

Let God carry your burden of worries for you, because God really cares about you. Don't let yourselves lose control. Pay attention to what you're doing and what's going on around you. You could easily be caught up in something that's wrong, or could hurt you. Don't do things that hurt people. Be steady in the faith you have. There are plenty of brothers and sisters of faith throughout the world who know what you're going through and suffer for Jesus' sake themselves.

Your troubles won't last forever. God's grace will support you, strengthen you, and lift you up and finally take you to be with God and Jesus forever.

The Word of the Lord.

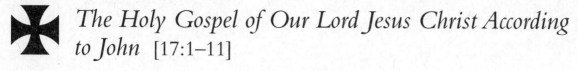

✠ *The Holy Gospel of Our Lord Jesus Christ According to John* [17:1–11]

Jesus looked up to heaven and prayed to God:

I know my time has come. Give me your glory so that I may show your glory to everyone who sees me. I ache to give these people eternal life—that means knowing you deeply. I'm done now with the work you gave me. I've made your name known, and people know that you and I have been working together. Take me again to yourself. And when I leave them soon, I ask you to please, please protect them. Help them to work together just as you and I work together.

The Gospel of the Lord.

The Day of Pentecost

A Reading from the Acts of the Apostles [2:1–21]

On Pentecost, everyone was together. All of a sudden, there was a noisy rush of wind from the sky and it filled the whole house where they were. Then little flames appeared on the tops of each of their heads! Everyone was filled with the Holy Spirit, and the Spirit helped them talk in different languages so everyone could understand what was being said.

Faithful Jews from all over the world were living in Jerusalem at that time. A crowd gathered around the house. They were curious because although they were from other places, they could hear their own languages spoken. They were astonished. "How can these people from Galilee know how to speak my language? Or your language? How are they doing that? They're talking about God's power and we understand what they're saying. What is going on?"

Some people who heard them thought they were talking crazy talk, like they were drunk. Peter was with the other eleven apostles, and he stood up and said, "Listen to what I have to say. It may sound like we're drunk, but we're not. It's only nine o'clock in the morning. Remember the prophet Joel said that in the last days, God would pour out the Spirit on everyone and you will hear about what is to come and what is real. On that day, everyone who turns to me will be saved. Today is that day."

The Word of the Lord.

Psalm 104

Good God, you do so many wonderful things! In your wisdom you have made everything that is.
The earth is full of your creatures.
There's the great and wide sea full of living things we couldn't count even if we could catch them, big ones and little ones, too.

Breathe your Spirit upon us and all of creation.

The ships move on the seas, and underneath them is the sea monster,
which you made just for the fun of it.
And, all of them, big and little animals, on the land and under the sea,
look to you to provide them with food when they need it.
And you come through for them.
You open up your hands and they are filled with good things.

Breathe your Spirit upon us and all of creation.

When you look away from them, they are terrified;
you snatch their breath away, creatures die and turn to dust.
You breathe your Spirit and new things are created, and that's how the earth is replenished.

Breathe your Spirit upon us and on all of creation.

May your glory always be before us. May you be happy in everything you make.
You look at the earth and it shakes. You touch the mountaintops and they smoke.
I will sing to you as long as I live. I will praise you as long as I have breath to sing.

Breathe your Spirit upon us and on all of creation.

May these words of mine please you. I will rejoice in you, God. Bless the Lord, my soul. Hallelujah.

Breathe your Spirit upon us and on all of creation.

A Reading from the First Letter of Paul to the Corinthians [12:3b–13]

You can't say, "Jesus is Lord," unless the Holy Spirit helps you say it. There are lots of different gifts, but we share the same Spirit. There are lots of different kinds of work to do, but we all work for the same God. There are lots of ways to serve, but God is the one who motivates us to do all of them. Each of us is given a gift from the Spirit for the good of us all. Somebody might be especially wise, another knows about a lot of different things. One might have great faith, and another can heal. Someone might be able to do great things in God's name, and another is good at figuring out God's will. Someone might be able to speak a different language, and another can translate. All of those gifts are energized by the same Spirit who determines who gets what gift.

Just like your body is in one piece but has different parts, all of us are the different parts that make up the body of Christ, which is the church. We were all baptized into this body, no matter who we are or where we came from, and we all are bathed in the same Spirit.

The Word of the Lord.

✠ *The Holy Gospel of Our Savior Jesus Christ According to John* [20:19–23]

The disciples were together behind locked doors that first Easter evening. They were frightened of the church authorities after Jesus had been put to death and then was raised. All of a sudden Jesus was standing in the middle of them all and said, "Peace, everybody." Then he showed them the wounds on his hands and side so they would know it was him. They were thrilled to see Jesus. Again Jesus said, "Peace. Just as my Father sent me, I'm about to send you." When he said this, he breathed on them and said, "Here's the Holy Spirit for you. You have the power to forgive sins or not forgive. Use that power well."

The Gospel of the Lord.

Trinity Sunday

A Reading from the Book of Genesis [1:1–2:4]
(see the Great Vigil of Easter, Year A, p. 94)

Psalm 8

God, you are in charge of everything. How great is that?
Even babies and little children praise you and your name.
You have drawn a line in the sand, and your enemies have
    backed off.
When I look up at the night sky, and see the heavens,
I am in awe of what you have made.
The moon and the stars . . . you formed them
and placed them right where they need to be in the sky.

God, you are in charge of everything. How great is that?

I feel so small when I see all the stars.
How could you possibly take notice of us?
Why do you bother to chase after us and give us good things?
    We're almost like angels, but not quite.
You've given us honor and glory to wear like jewelry.

God, you are in charge of everything. How great is that?

You have given us the job of taking care of all that you
    have made.
We're responsible for the ground on which we walk.
We must care for the sheep and cows,
    even the wild animals that roam outside any fences
    we've built;
the birds that fly, the fish that swim,
    and whatsoever lives on the ocean floor that we can't see.

All of them are awesome.
All of them deserve our respect.

God, you are in charge of everything. How great is that?

A Reading from the Second Letter of Paul to the Corinthians [13:11–13]

Now finally, brothers and sisters, I think that's all I have to say. Keep things together. And for God's sake, get along with each other! Love one another and the God of love and peace will be with you. Greet one another with a holy kiss. All your friends here say hello.

May all of you feel the grace of the Lord Jesus Christ, the love of God, and the warm embrace of the Holy Spirit.

The Word of the Lord.

✠ *The Holy Gospel of Our Lord Jesus Christ According to Matthew* [28:16–20]

The eleven disciples went to Galilee, to the mountain where Jesus had told them to meet. When they saw him, they worshiped him; but some still weren't sure that he was God's Son. Jesus said to them, "God has told me to tell you, don't ever stand still. Go and help people to become disciples. All of them, no matter where they live. Baptize them in the name of the Father and of the Son and of the Holy Spirit, and teach them the new way of living I introduced to you. And don't you ever, ever forget this: I am with you always. Always."

The Gospel of the Lord.

Proper 1 (see The Sixth Sunday after the Epiphany, Year A, p. 42)

Proper 2 (see The Seventh Sunday after the Epiphany, Year A, p. 45)

Proper 3 (see The Eighth Sunday after Epiphany, Year A p. 48)

Proper 4

A Reading from the Book of Genesis [6:9–22, 7:24; 8:14–19]

Noah was a good man with three sons. God was very pleased with Noah because he was the best there was. Everyone else was filled with anger and violence, and they were ruining the world. God said to Noah, "I'm going to wipe everything clean and start all over. Here's what I want you to do. Make a huge boat that can float on water for a very long time. I'm going to make the water flood the earth and all the people will be destroyed except for you and your family. Make the boat big enough to hold two of every living thing. You will need to bring a male and a female of every kind of bird and animal on the boat, so when this is over they can start families. You'll need enough food for your family and all the animals." Noah did everything God asked him to do. The waters rose and they floated a very long time. Finally it was dry. So Noah and his family walked off the boat and the birds flew out, and the snakes slithered out, and the cheetahs bolted off the boat to start God's plan of beginning again.

The Word of the Lord.

Psalm 46 (see The Great Vigil of Easter, p. 98)

A Reading from the Letter of Paul to the Romans [1:16–17; 3:22b–28]

I will not hide my love of God's Good News, because it has the power to save those who believe, no matter who they are. God's goodness is revealed through faith in Jesus. We're all in the same boat. We've all sinned and don't even come close to what God had planned for us to be. But all of us are made right with God with God's gift of grace; Jesus gave his lifeblood for us. And now our sins don't matter to God. We matter instead because Jesus matters to us.

Do we have anything to brag about? Hardly. Would following the law save us? Nope. Would trying to be good save us? Nope. We have been made right with God not by what we have done or will do, but by faith in Jesus.

The Word of the Lord.

✠ *The Holy Gospel of Our Lord Jesus Christ According to Matthew* [7:21–29]

Just because you use my name, does it mean you are part of God's kingdom? Doing the will of my Father shows that you are kingdom material. It's not the talk that counts. You also have to walk the walk. Otherwise I won't recognize you as one of my own.

If you hear what I say and act on what I've said, you will be like the smart man who built his house on solid rock. When the rain came, and the flood waters rose, and the winds howled, the house stood strong against the storm.

But if you have heard what I say and don't act on my words, you'll be like the fool who built his house on sand. When the rains pounded it, and the floodwaters poured through the windows, the winds pushed it from side to side and it fell with a great thud.

When Jesus had finished talking, the crowds were amazed at his teaching. It was like he knew what he was talking about, and they had never heard anything like it from their own teachers.

The Word of the Lord.

Proper 5

A Reading from the Book of Genesis [12:1–9]

God was talking to Abram and said, "Leave everything you know behind; your country, your cousins, the home you grew up in, and go to the place I will show you. You are going to be something special. I will bless you so that you can bless others. I will be on your side—those who are good to you, I will be good to them. But those who cause you trouble will find themselves in more trouble than they can imagine." So Abram packed up his things and left, just as God told him to do. He took with him his wife and nephew, and the helpers in their household, and came to the land of Canaan. There, God appeared to Abram and said, "I will give this land to your family." Abram built an altar there to worship God. He kept going, step by step, building altars, and worshipping God as he moved toward the Negeb.

The Word of the Lord.

Psalm 33:1–12

Good people, praise God.
Pick up your harps and your violins and guitars.
Make beautiful melodies.
Sing God a new song with loud voices.

The whole world is filled with God's love.

God's word is real
and can be trusted.
God loves goodness and justice.

The whole world is filled with God's love.

God spoke the skies into being
and with one breath the angels were made.

God holds the waters of the sea in a bottle
and stores the depths of the oceans in his closet.
The whole world is filled with God's love.

Everyone in the whole world,
get down on your knees in respect and wonder!
One word from God and everything was created.
God tells the earth to stop spinning and it stops.
The whole world is filled with God's love.

The nations of the world plot and plan
but they can do nothing like God can do.
The thoughts of God's heart last forever.
God's plans are wise and good.
Happy are the people who belong to God and follow God.
The whole world is filled with God's love.

A Reading from the Letter of Paul to the Romans [4:13–18]

God promised Abraham he'd be the father of us all, not because he followed the law, but because he was faithful. If only perfect people who follow the law perfectly will realize God's promise, then we might as well call the whole deal off because the promise will mean nothing. The law is hurtful. But if there is no law, you can't break it.

It's faith that matters. God's promise is pure grace, and flows to those who keep the law and who share the faith of Abraham. The God of Abraham gives life to the dead and "calls into existence things that don't exist." Abraham had no reason to hope he would become a father of many nations, but he believed. And it happened.

The Word of the Lord.

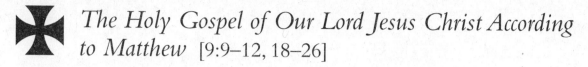

✠ *The Holy Gospel of Our Lord Jesus Christ According to Matthew* [9:9–12, 18–26]

As Jesus was walking, he saw a man named Matthew collecting taxes at a booth. (People didn't like tax collectors because some tax collectors were cheaters.) Jesus said, "Follow me," and Matthew got up and followed him. As they were eating dinner that night, there were other tax collectors and sinners around the table with Jesus and his disciples. When the church authorities saw this, they said to the disciples, "Why does your teacher eat with tax collectors and sinners?"

When Jesus heard them say this he said, "It's the sick people who need a doctor, not the healthy ones."

While Jesus was speaking to them, a church leader came and knelt in front of him, saying, "My daughter has just died. I know if you lay your hands on her, she'll live." So Jesus and his disciples got up and went with him. While they were on their way, a woman who had been suffering for twelve years snuck up behind Jesus and touched the hem of his robe. She thought, "If I only touch his robe I'll be healed."

When Jesus turned and saw her, he said, "What courage you have! Your faith has healed you." And the woman was healed from that time on.

When Jesus got into the leader's house, it was full of people crying over the dead girl. He told them to go away, because she wasn't dead, but asleep. They laughed at him. When they were all gone, Jesus went into her room, took her hand and she sat up. News of Jesus bringing the dead girl to life spread like wildfire around the countryside.

The Gospel of the Lord.

Proper 6

A Reading from the Book of Genesis [18:1–15]

God appeared to Abraham one hot day as he was sitting near his tent. Abraham looked up and saw three men coming toward him. He got up to meet them, saying, "Please, stay here a little while and rest. Let me bring you water to wash your feet, and offer you some good food." So they said, "Thank you. That would be very nice." Abraham ran into the tent and told Sarah to make some cake. He told his servant to prepare an excellent meal. They all sat down together in the shade of the tree and ate together.

One of them asked, "Where is your wife, Sarah?" Abraham said, "She's there in the tent." The man replied, "I'll be back this way this time next year. She'll have a son in her arms when I come back." Sarah was listening to this from the tent.

Abraham and Sarah were way too old to have children. So when Sarah heard this, she laughed to herself, thinking, "Really? Now that I'm old and my husband is even older, *now* I'm going to have a baby?"

The man asked Abraham, "Why did Sarah laugh at what I said? Is anything too difficult for God? I tell you, by the time I come back next year, she will have had a son."

Sarah said, "I didn't laugh."

The man said, "Oh yes you did. I heard you. You laughed."

The Word of the Lord.

Psalm 116:1, 10–17 (see Maundy Thursday, Year A, p. 83)

A Reading from the Letter of Paul to the Romans [5:1–8]

Since we are right with God through faith in Jesus, we have peace. We are surrounded by grace now. And we are confident that we will share in God's glory. We can also say that the trouble we've had has made us stronger and produces character and hope. We are not discouraged because God's love has been poured into our hearts opened by the Holy Spirit.

Jesus died for us at just the right time. God loves us and Jesus gave his lifeblood for us, even though we were sinners.

The Word of the Lord.

✠ *The Holy Gospel of Our Lord Jesus Christ According to Matthew* [9:35—10:8]

Jesus went all over the place proclaiming God's Good News and curing sick people. When he saw the crowds of people, his heart went out to them, because they were anxious and helpless, like sheep who have no shepherd to guide them. "So much work to do, so few workers. Let's ask God for more helpers."

Jesus sent out his twelve disciples with the power to cure sick people and cast out demons. Here are the names of his disciples: Simon Peter and his brother Andrew; James and John, sons of Zebedee; Philip and Bartholomew, Thomas, and Matthew the tax collector; James and Thaddaeus; Simon and Judas, the one who betrayed him.

Jesus sent them out with these marching orders: "First, go to your own people. As you go, tell people the Good News about the kingdom of heaven being near. Cure sick people. Raise dead people. Make the lepers whole again. Cast out demons. Give much, as you have been given much."

The Gospel of the Lord.

Proper 7

A Reading from the Book of Genesis [21:8–21]

Isaac was a happy boy and loved by his parents. When his mom Sarah saw that Isaac and Ishmael were playing together (Ishmael was Isaac's half brother; his mother was Hagar, Sarah's slave) she wasn't at all happy. She told Abraham to get rid of Ishmael and his mother. Abraham was really upset about this, but God told him not to worry. Each of his sons, Isaac and Ishmael, would be the "father of a nation."

So Abraham gave Hagar food and water and sent her and Ishmael out of the house and into the desert. When their water was gone she thought they would probably die out there in the wilderness. God heard Ishmael crying, and God's angel called to Hagar from heaven, "Don't be afraid! God has heard you crying. He will come to help you." Then, Hagar found a well and was able to get water for the both of them.

God was with Ishmael, and he grew up to be strong.

The Word of the Lord.

Psalm 86:1–10, 16–17

Bend down close to me, God, so you can hear me.
I am absolutely miserable.
Watch out for me. I trust you can take care of me.

Be kind and gentle with me today, God.
Make my soul smile again.

I know you are good and kind. I'm counting on your kindness.
And by the way, I need some forgiveness too.

Listen to me when I call out for you. Sometimes no one else will listen.

Be kind and gentle with me today, God.
Make my soul smile again.

There is nobody like you, God. And nothing like the things you do.
You make the whole world wonder and worship.

Be kind and gentle with me today, God.
Make my soul smile again.

Turn my way, and give me a dose of your strength.
Smile on me so that everyone can see
that I am the one you've helped.

Be kind and gentle with me today, God.
Make my soul smile again.

A Reading from the Letter of Paul to the Romans [6:1b–11]

So to get more grace should we sin even more? Heavens, no. That makes no sense. You know, don't you, that all of us who have been baptized, have been baptized into Jesus' death? Our old selves have been buried with him, so that just as Jesus was brought back to life by the glory of the Father, we too can have a brand new life. Our old self died with him, so that sin isn't our master anymore. We know that Christ will never die again. Death has no power over him. When he died, sin died with him. The life he lives now, he lives for God. You too are dead to sin and alive to God in Christ Jesus. Remember that.

The Word of the Lord.

✠ *The Holy Gospel of Our Lord Jesus Christ According to Matthew* [10:24–39]

A student doesn't deserve more respect than his teacher, a servant doesn't deserve more than his master, but they might be treated the same way. I'm telling you, if they call me the devil there's no telling what they're going to call you! But don't be afraid of what they say about you. Everything will be clear in the end. I've told you some secrets that I want you to tell everyone. The things you haven't talked about before, go up to the rooftops and shout about them. Don't be afraid of people who can hurt your body; they can't touch your soul. Instead, be concerned about God, who holds your soul in his hand. You can buy two tiny birds for a dime, right? Yet God knows everything they do. And did you know that God knows exactly how many hairs are on your head? Don't worry. God values you more than a thousand tiny birds.

If you stand up for me, I will stand up for you before my Father. But if you ignore me, don't count on me to be on your side.

Don't think this is going to be easy. Things will fall apart before there is peace. You might have to choose between your family and me. If you choose me, it will be worth it. I want all you are and all you have to give, or don't follow me at all. You may lose your body for my sake, but find your life in me.

The Gospel of the Lord.

Proper 8

A Reading from the Book of Genesis [22:1–14]
(see Easter Vigil, Year A, p. 99)

Psalm 13

How long, God, do I have to wait to see your face?
Have you forgotten about me?
How long must I wrestle with my thoughts and every day
feel so sad?
I think about you all the time.
How long will others push me around?
Please listen to me and answer me, God.
I don't want to be so sad anymore.
Don't let anyone push me around and tell me that you
don't love me.
I know you love me more than anything
and you make my heart happy and my eyes twinkle.
You make me want to sing because you have been so good
to me.

A Reading from the Letter of Paul to the Romans [6:12–23]

Don't give up on being good. You may think about doing bad things, but that doesn't mean you have to give in and do them! Instead, stand before God as somebody who is alive after being dead, and your body parts are your tools to do good. God's grace is what motivates you now; not sin. Does that mean, you can sin as much as you want because God's grace has you covered? I don't think so! Whatever makes you tick is your master. Sin used to be your master. But now, your master is God. God has made you holy—not perfect, but holy. Which means that the new life

God has given you is an eternal kind of life, not one that brings about brokenness and death.

The Word of the Lord.

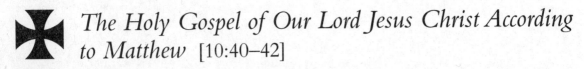

✠ *The Holy Gospel of Our Lord Jesus Christ According to Matthew* [10:40–42]

Jesus said this:

Whoever welcomes me, welcomes the one who sent me. (He meant God the Father.) And whoever offers a cup of cold water to someone who is thirsty, as my follower, he or she will be rewarded.

The Gospel of the Lord.

Proper 9

A Reading from the Book of Genesis [24:34–38, 42–49, 58–67]

Abraham's servant went to Laban and said, "I'm looking for a wife for Abraham's son Isaac. God has been very good to Abraham; he has lots of camels and donkeys and sheep. A woman would live a good life if she married his son. Here's how I'm going to pick a wife for him. I'll stand by the spring of water and if a woman comes to the spring, I'll ask her to give me some water. If she replies, 'Here, have some water. Let me get some water for your camels, too,' that woman will be Isaac's wife."

And that's exactly what happened. Rebekah was the one who came to the spring and offered him water. He said, "I think God has chosen you to marry Isaac!" She said, "I will," and she packed her stuff so she could go with him. It took some time to get to where Isaac lived. As they got close to Isaac's home, they saw he was out in the field. Rebekah asked, "Who is that man who is coming to meet us?"

"Why that's Isaac, the man who will be your husband." Isaac brought her into his mother's home, and married and loved her. Isaac was happy his wife Rebekah was there to comfort him when his mother died.

The Word of the Lord.

Psalm 45:11–18

Listen closely to me, girls.
Leave your family and your father's house.
Come and live with the king
who will honor you and your beauty.
You will wear beautiful gowns made of gold.

You will be glorious in the king's court.
There will be maids to attend to your needs.
It will be a wonderful life.
King, you will have many sons and I will make your name famous in every generation.

A Reading from the Letter of Paul to the Romans [7:15–25a]

I don't "get" me. I end up doing exactly what I don't want to do! That's how I know there's sin inside me. I can want to do what's right, but sometimes I just can't do it. I want to do the good thing, but I don't, and the evil thing is what I actually do. It's like I'm stuck in a loop of sin. I really want to follow God's way and do the right thing. I do. Sometimes it's like there's a war going on inside me. It really gets me down. Who can save them from this battle going on in me? Jesus can! That's who! Thanks be to God.

The Word of the Lord.

✠ *The Holy Gospel of Our Lord Jesus Christ According to Matthew* [11:16–19, 25–30]

Jesus told the crowd: I'm trying to figure out how to describe this generation of people. They're like kids who yell at each other in the middle of town and say, "Why should I bother playing music for you if you're not going to dance. I give you everything, and you give me nothing back."

John didn't eat fancy food or drink wine, and people said, "He's crazy and possessed by a devil." I came and ate dinner with you, and drank your wine, and they say, "Wow. He sure eats and drinks a lot, and hangs out with sinners, too!"

And yet, you know what they say, the proof of the pudding is in the eating.

Then Jesus turned to talk to God: Thanks, Father, for showing the truth to the simple people and hiding it from the people who think they're so smart. You have given me everything I need. And I follow your direction.

Here's what I want people to know, "You can come to me, people. I know you are tired from carrying heavy loads. Come to me and I will give you rest. If you carry my load, and learn from my example, you will also be gentle and humble in your heart. Come; find rest. I will share your burden."

The Gospel of the Lord.

Proper 10

A Reading from the Book of Genesis [25:19–34]

Abraham was Isaac's father. Isaac was forty years old when he married Rebekah and he asked God for children. Finally, when he was sixty, Rebekah became pregnant. She was so miserable she said, "If this is what motherhood is like, why should I bother?" God said to her, "The reason you are miserable is because you've got two babies, not just one. And you'll see, they'll be as different as two separate nations."

When they were born, one baby was all hairy and red and they named him Esau. The second was born holding on to his brother's foot. They named him Jacob. When they grew up Esau was a hunter and Jacob was more of a homebody. Esau was Abraham's favorite, and Rebekah preferred Jacob.

Jacob was cooking stew once, when his brother came in from the field, starving. He begged his brother for some stew. Jacob said, "You can have some, but first you have to sell me your birthright." (That means that the oldest child always inherited the father's goods, and Esau was the oldest.) Esau was so hungry all he could think about was food. He said, "I'm about to die of hunger, what do I care about my birthright? You can have it. Just give me some stew."

Jacob put the stew in a bowl, but before he gave it to Esau he said, "Swear that it's mine."

Esau said, "Yes, it's yours. Now give me that stew."

Jacob gave him bread and kept filling his brother's bowl with stew. When Esau was finally full, he got up and walked away.

And that's how Esau lost his birthright.

The Word of the Lord.

Psalm 119:105–112

God, I read your word and suddenly I can see where I'm going.
It's like suddenly the sun came up, and it's not dark anymore.
I know I always do the right thing when I follow your ways.
So I'll keep following them no matter what.

Your word is a lantern to my feet, God,
and a light so I can see where I'm going.

Sometimes I get really frustrated.
Keep me going, God; keep me strong.
It makes me happy to praise your name
and I want to learn more about you.

Your word is a lantern to my feet, God,
and a light so I can see where I'm going.

I know I've got lots of choices to make. It's up to me to make good ones.
I'll remember what you've taught me.
Sometimes people want me to do things I know I shouldn't
but I'll remember what you've taught me.

Your word is a lantern to my feet, God,
and a light so I can see where I'm going.

I know I will be the best I can be if I follow your way.
I know I'll be a happier person if I follow your way.
I'll set my heart on doing good things for people
and make sure I keep walking your way always.

Your word is a lantern to my feet, God,
and a light so I can see where I'm going.

A Reading from the Letter of Paul to the Romans [8:1–11]

If you believe in Jesus Christ, you don't need to worry. For Jesus has set you free from the law and sin and death. God has done for you what the law could never do for you.

If you live as if the law means everything, that's where your mind will be. But if you want to live according to the Spirit, set your mind on the Spirit who is life and peace. Then your life will please God.

God lives inside of you. No matter what happens to you and your body, Christ is in you. The same Spirit who raised Jesus from the dead, will give you life as well.

The Word of the Lord.

✠ *The Holy Gospel of Our Lord Jesus Christ According to Matthew* [13:1–9, 18–23]

Jesus was sitting beside the sea. So many people crowded around him that he finally got into a boat and pushed off into the water, just so he could have some space to himself.

From the boat, he told people stories.

A farmer went into his field to scatter seed. Some seeds fell on the hard path and the birds came and ate it right up. Other seeds fell on the rocky soil. The seeds started to grow but since their roots weren't very deep, when the sun came up, they got scorched and withered up.

Other seeds fell in the thorns, which choked them.

But some seeds fell on really good soil and produced lots of grain.

Here's what that story means:

If you hear but don't understand God's Word to you, you are like seeds on the pathway. Nothing starts to grow inside of you.

If you joyfully hear God's Word but your joy lasts only a little while, and when trouble comes you forget all about it, you're like the seeds that fell on soil full of rocks.

If you hear the word, but all your worries choke what God says, you're like the seeds that fell in the thorns.

But, if you hear and understand God's Word, if you make it real in your life by what you do, you are like the seeds that fell on good ground, and produced good strong plants.

The Gospel of the Lord.

Proper 11

A Reading from the Book of Genesis [28:10–19a]

Jacob set up camp for the night as the sun was setting. He found a stone and used it for a pillow. He dreamed that there was a ladder so tall that it reached up to heaven. Angels of God were using the ladder to go up to heaven and back. Then God stood right next to him and said, "Hi Jacob. I'm God, the God of Abraham and Isaac. I will give you and your children the land you're sleeping on right now. You will have so many children they will live as far as the eye can see—to the west and to the east and to the north and to the south. Because of you, all the families on earth will be blessed. That's my promise." Jacob woke up all excited. He said, "Wow. I had no idea God was here! How awesome this place is." He was afraid when he realized what he just dreamed. "This is really the house of God and the gate of heaven."

He got up early in the morning, took the stone he used for a pillow, and made it into an altar. He poured oil on the stone and called it Beth-el, which means House of God.

The Word of the Lord.

Psalm 139:1–11, 22–23

God, you know me better than anyone, even myself.
You know what I'm doing, you even know what I'm thinking.
When I move around or when I lay down,
when I walk or sit still, you always know where I am.
There's nothing I say that you haven't already figured I'm going to say.

God, you know me inside and out.

You are in front of me to guide me,
behind me to protect me,
and I feel your hand on my shoulder, so I know I'm not alone.
It's almost too good to be true.
Is there anywhere I can go where you are NOT?
Not any place that I know.
Can I run fast enough to get away from your Spirit?

God, you know me inside and out.

If I soar into the sky, you're there.
If I lay down in the dirt, you are there too.
If I fly like a bird to the middle of the biggest ocean,
and then dive down into the waters,
I wouldn't be surprised that you're there, too, to guide me.

God, you know me inside and out.

If I say, oh my God, I feel like it's the darkest night even in the middle of the day,
I'm so sad . . . you tell me, it's alright.
Dark or day, I am with you.
Figure out who I am, God. Then let me know.
Look into my deepest thoughts.
I'm glad to have you here with me, to help me and lead me back to you.

God, you know me inside and out.

A Reading from the Letter of Paul to the Romans [8:12–25]

So, brothers and sisters, we owe it to God to live according to God's ways, rather than by every desire of our hearts. Those of us who are led by God's Spirit are children of God.

God has adopted us so we shouldn't act like slaves to sin and fear. When we cry, "Abba! Father!" it is the Spirit telling our hearts that we are children of God and will receive every good thing God wants to give us. If our faith in God causes us trouble, we know that we will also end up receiving his glory.

Nothing horrible that happens to us here compares to the glory God will show us. All of creation aches for God, and God's children and creation will be set free and eventually receive God's glory as well.

We groan along with creation as we wait for our hope to be realized. That hope will save us. Even if we can't see what we wait for, we wait for it with patience.

The Word of the Lord.

✠ *The Holy Gospel of Our Lord Jesus Christ According to Matthew* [13:24–30, 36–43]

Jesus told the crowd another story:

God's kingdom is like someone who planted good seeds in his field. While everyone was sleeping, someone came and planted weeds in the wheat and snuck off. When the plants grew, the weeds grew as well. The workers came to the owner of the field and said, "We thought you planted good seeds. Where did all these weeds come from?"

"It must be my enemy who did this," he said. The workers asked if he wanted them to pull out the weeds. The owner said, "No, because if you pull the weeds up, the wheat would get pulled up too, and it's not ready. Just let them both grow together until harvest time. Then I'll have you collect the weeds to be burned, and gather the wheat into the barn."

Jesus left the crowds wondering what that meant, and went into the house. His disciples caught up with him and asked him to explain what he was talking about.

Here's what he said:

The one who planted the good seeds is the Son of Man. The field is the world and the good seeds are the children of God's kingdom. The weeds are the children of the evil one who planted them. The harvest will come at the end of the age, when the angels gather up the crop. At the end, the angels will gather up the evil and throw it into the fire. And the harvest of the children of the kingdom will shine like the sun. Better pay attention to what I'm saying!

The Gospel of the Lord.

Proper 12

A Reading from the Book of Genesis [19:15–28]

In the morning, angels woke Lot up and told him to grab his wife and daughters and get them out of the city, because it was going to be destroyed. He dawdled, so an angel took them by the hand, because God is good, and made sure they were safely outside the city, saying, "Run for your life, and don't look back or stop or else you will be in danger." But Lot said, "I appreciate you saving our lives, but I won't run into the hills, because I am afraid we'll all die there. Why don't we go to that little town there instead and we'll be safe." The angels said, "Okay, but hurry to that town so the city you left can be destroyed."

Fire rained down on the cities and everyone in them and all the grass was burned up too. Lot's wife couldn't help herself from looking back, and she turned into a pillar of salt. Abraham got up early in the morning to see what had happened to the cities of Sodom and Gomorrah, which were destroyed. All he could see was smoke rising from the place they used to be.

The Word of the Lord.

Psalm 105:1–11, 45b

We'll thank you, God, whenever we pray.
We'll let everyone know what good you have done.
We'll sing songs of praise when we tell each other the stories.
We are glad we turned our hearts toward you.
We always turn toward you and your strength
and look for your face wherever we are.

Don't forget what God has done.
Tell the stories of God's goodness.

You are part of God's family—
children of Abraham and children of Jacob
God, you are our God
and you decide what will happen.

Don't forget what God has done.
Tell the stories of God's goodness.

You never forget the promise you made to your people,
the promise you made for thousands of generations of families.
The promise you made with Abraham,
and then again with Isaac,
and again with Jacob.
It's an everlasting promise with God's people:
"I promise I will give you the land I said I would give you."

Don't forget what God has done.
Tell the stories of God's goodness.
Hallelujah.

A Reading from the Letter of Paul to the Romans [8:26–39]

God's Spirit helps us when we're weak. When we don't know how to pray, the Spirit fills in those prayer gaps in our hearts with sighs too deep for words. God is always looking in our hearts and knows the Spirit is in us working and praying on our behalf.

We know that everything works together for good in the end for those of us who love God and work with his purpose. God shaped us in the image of his Son. God's family is huge, and Jesus is God's firstborn. We were called to be part of God's family, and God made us right with himself and will also share glory with us.

So what is there to worry about? If God is on our side, how can we lose? Who can stand against God? If God gave his very own Son for us, don't we already have everything we need? No one can hurt us. God is the one who makes us right. No one can condemn us. Christ Jesus himself sits at God's side and represents us and brings us into God's family. Is there anything or anyone who can separate us from the love of Christ? Anything? No! Nothing can! Absolutely nothing! Because he loves us, we always win. I am absolutely sure that death itself can't tear us from God. And neither can angels, or kings, or anything on earth now or in the future, or anything in all of God's universe. Nothing can separate us from God's love that we have in Christ Jesus our Lord.

The Word of the Lord.

✠ *The Holy Gospel of Our Lord Jesus Christ According to Matthew* [13:31–33, 44–52]

Jesus told the crowds another story:

God's kingdom is like the littlest seed there is. When it grows into the biggest tree, all the birds want to come and build their nests in it.

Let me put it another way. God's kingdom is like yeast. When you mix a tiny bit of yeast in flour, all of it is leavened and the dough rises into bread.

Or, how about this? God's kingdom is like someone who collects pearls. When he finds the most beautiful pearl of all in the market, he gets so excited that he sells everything he has so he can buy it.

Or this—God's kingdom is like hidden treasure, buried in a field. You would be happy to sell what you have so you could buy the field with the treasure in it.

Or this—God's kingdom is like a net thrown into the sea that catches all kinds of fish. When the net is full, you put the good fish in one basket and throw out the rest. That's what will happen at the end of the world. Angels will come to sort the bad from the good.

"Do you understand what I'm talking about?" Jesus asked his disciples. "Of course we do," they replied. (Even though they didn't.) And Jesus said, "Everyone fit for God's kingdom is like the owner of a store who has a cupboard full of new and old treasures."

The Gospel of the Lord.

Proper 13

A Reading from the Book of Genesis [32:22–31]

Jacob took his whole family across the river with him, but slept alone on the other side. In the middle of the night a man wrestled with him until the early morning and injured Jacob's hip. Finally the man said to Jacob, "Let go of me, the sun is coming up." Jacob said, "I won't let you go until you give me your blessing." When the man asked his name, Jacob said, "My name is Jacob." Then the man said, "From now on your name will be Israel, because you've been fighting all your life with people and with God, and you always win." Then Jacob asked him, "Tell me who you are." The man wouldn't tell him but he blessed him. So Jacob said, "This is unbelievable. I have seen God face to face, and yet I'm still alive." And the sun came up, but Jacob was left with a limp because his hip had been injured.

The Word of the Lord.

Psalm 17:1–7

You have to listen to me, God!
I need someone to listen to me.
I'm not lying.
I know you can see inside my heart
and your ears can hear what I say.
You dig deep inside me and you'll see I've got nothing to hide.
There isn't any wickedness in me.
I stay away from people who will get me into trouble.
I walk in the right direction—your direction—
and I haven't fallen down yet.
I know you will answer me.

That's why I call out your name.
I know you will show me only kindness.
You are the one who will save me from those who want
to hurt me.

A Reading from the Letter of Paul to the Romans [9:1–5]

I'm telling you the truth. My heart is breaking. If I could take on your troubles, I would. If I could trade places with my people so that they would come to know Christ, I would do that. They are Israelites, God's people, and their history includes the adoption, the glory, the covenants, the giving of the law, worship, and the promises; to them belong the patriarchs, and they are the family into which Jesus Christ was born. God be blessed forever. Amen.

The Word of the Lord.

✠ *The Holy Gospel of Our Lord Jesus Christ According to Matthew* [14:13–21]

Jesus took a boat to his favorite place where he could be by himself for a while. When the crowds found out where he was, they ran from the towns to see him when he came ashore. When he got off the boat, and saw the huge crowds, his heart ached for them. So he stayed with them and cured the sick people in the crowd.

When it got to be evening, the disciples came to Jesus and said, "We're in the middle of nowhere. It's late. Send all those people away so they can go into town and buy themselves some supper."

Jesus said, "We're not going to send them away. Give them something to eat."

"Something to eat? All we have is five loaves of bread and two little fish!"

Jesus said, "Bring me what you've got." Jesus told the crowds to sit down on the grass. He took the five loaves and two fish, and blessed the bread as he looked up to heaven. Then he broke the loaves into little pieces, gave them to the disciples, and the disciples gave them to the crowds. Everybody ate their fill; they filled up twelve baskets full of the leftovers. There were about five thousand hungry men there that day, not counting the women and the children that were with them. And everyone of them had more than enough to eat.

The Gospel of the Lord.

Proper 14

A Reading from the Book of Genesis [37:1–4, 12–28]

This is the story of Jacob and his family. When Joseph was seven years old, he was in the field with the sheep and his brothers. Joseph told their father some of the bad things the brothers were doing. That didn't make the brothers happy at all. Jacob loved Joseph more than any of his other children. He had made him a beautiful long robe. His brothers knew their father loved Joseph the best and they hated him for it. They couldn't even be nice to him.

The brothers were in the field with the flock one day when Jacob sent Joseph to check on them. They could see him coming, and thought they might get away with killing him by saying a wild animal had eaten him. Reuben heard their plan and said, "Don't kill him. Just throw him in this pit instead." Reuben thought he'd come back later and rescue Joseph and get in good with their father for being a hero. The brothers stripped the robe off Joseph and threw him in the pit, which was empty and dry. When they sat down to eat, a caravan on camels came near on their way to Egypt. Judah had an idea. He said, "What's the point of killing Joseph if we could sell him for some money instead?" All the brothers agreed. So when some traders from Midian came by, they sold Joseph to them for twenty pieces of silver. And the caravan took Joseph into Egypt.

The Word of the Lord.

Psalm 105:1–6, 16–22, 45b

I am so thankful for all the good things in my life.
I'm going to thank God and tell everybody.

In fact, I might sing I'm so thankful
and tell everyone how good God is to me.

Don't forget what God has done.

Everyone who wants to know God or comes to know God
should live happy lives.
Go find God—you don't have to look very hard.
His face is in the faces of those he loves.
If you look at them with God's eyes, you'll see God's face too.

Don't forget what God has done.

Don't ever forget how good God is, all the miracles and
the great stories. I know I won't.
We're all children of Abraham, children of Jacob.
When people were hungry, God sent them someone
to help feed them, Joseph. But they put him in jail
because he scared them with his dreams.

Don't forget what God has done.

The king let him go, and Joseph was able to help feed everyone.
God worked through him to feed hungry people.

Don't forget what God has done.

A Reading from the Letter of Paul to the Romans [10:5–15]

Moses preached that the law would save people. But what does faith tell us? "The Word is so close to you, it's on your lips and inside your heart." That's faith. Saying out loud that Jesus is Lord, and believing it in your heart—you're saved. Make those words real in your life. Welcome God's work in your heart and your life and God will be there for you, making your life new. God promises to be there for everyone who wants God in his or her life. Doesn't matter who you are. Ask God into your heart. Ask God to save you and you're already right with God.

But how can you ask God into your heart if you've never heard of God? How can people hear unless we are willing to tell people about Jesus? "How beautiful are the feet of those who bring good news." Let's all be people with beautiful feet!

The Word of the Lord.

✠ *The Holy Gospel of Our Lord Jesus Christ According to Matthew* [14:22–33]

Jesus got rid of the crowds and made the disciples get into a boat and go to the other side of the lake. When he was finally alone, he went up the mountain to pray. He was still there when it got dark. By this time, a storm had come up on the lake and the boat the disciples were in was being battered by the waves. Early in the morning, Jesus came walking on the sea toward the boat. They thought they were seeing a ghost and they were all screaming in fear. Jesus yelled to them, "It's just me. Don't be afraid." Peter said, "If it's you, make me walk on water toward you." Jesus said, "Okay. Come." Peter got out of the boat, and started walking on the water toward Jesus. He noticed how strong the wind was and got scared and began to sink. "Jesus, save me," Peter said. Jesus reached out his hand and grabbed him. "Peter, why did you doubt you could do it? Have you so little faith in me?" The two of them got in the boat with the rest of the disciples and the wind stopped right away. Everyone in the boat worshipped Jesus, saying, "You really are the Son of God, aren't you?"

The Gospel of the Lord.

Proper 15

A Reading from the Book of Genesis [45:1–15]

There was a famine in the land and people from all around the area came to Egypt in search of food. They would come before Joseph, who was in charge of distributing the grain. A group of men came before Joseph one day and Joseph realized the men were his brothers who had sold him into slavery years before. But his brothers didn't know it was Joseph in front of them. Joseph was overcome with emotion and told everyone to leave him alone with these men who were his brothers. He started crying so loudly that everyone in the palace heard him.

"Look. It's me. It's Joseph! Tell me, is our father still alive?"

The brothers were so surprised they couldn't even talk. And they were ashamed as well, because they had treated Joseph so poorly, and thought he'd been dead for years. Yet he was standing right in front of them, as a leader in Egypt!

Joseph said, "Come closer to me, brothers." And they did. "Yes, I'm the one you sold to people in Egypt so you could get rid of me. There is no reason to beat yourselves up over that though, because God had a bigger purpose for me. Here I am, in a position where I can help you and your families. The crops have failed and your people are hungry. God has made me a ruler here in Egypt. I have grain to give you and it will keep you alive. It wasn't you who sent me here. It was God. Go home and tell our father that I am alive and bring him back here. Tell him the whole story. Hurry up. Bring all your families back with you, too, and all your animals. I will provide for all of you here."

Then Joseph collapsed in the arms of his brother Benjamin and cried and cried. He kissed all of his brothers and they all cried together and talked together for hours.

The Word of the Lord.

Psalm 133

Yes, it is a very good thing when brothers and sisters can get along with each other.
It's like having beautiful rich oil poured on your head when your skin is dry.

It is a good thing when we can all get along.

It's like having dew provide moisture in the desert.
That's what the Lord's blessing feels like; life forever more.

It is a good thing when we can all get along.

A Reading from the Letter of Paul to the Romans [11:1–2a, 29–32]

So, has God rejected the people whom he brought out of slavery in Egypt? No way! Once God blesses you, you always belong to God. Even though you reject God, God is merciful. All those who reject God can also receive God's mercy.

The Word of the Lord.

✠ *The Holy Gospel of Our Lord Jesus Christ According to Matthew* [15:21–28]

Jesus walked to a place called Tyre and Sidon. A woman who was not a believer ran toward him and shouted, "Show me some mercy, Lord, Son of David. My daughter is tormented by a demon."

Jesus kept on walking without even looking at her or answering her. His disciples asked him to send her away because she was bugging them. Jesus said to the woman, "I was sent only to God's people of Israel, not people in Canaan." That didn't discourage her. She knelt at Jesus feet saying, "Please, Lord, help me. I really need your help."

Jesus said, "Do you think it's fair to take food meant for the children and give it to the dogs?"

The woman said, "I get that, Lord. But the dogs have to eat too. And they will eat the crumbs that fall from the table if they have to."

Jesus was shocked by how strong she was and how much she kept pushing him to help her daughter. He said, "Woman, your faith is incredible! Your prayer will be answered as you wish." And her daughter was healed that very moment.

The Gospel of the Lord.

Proper 16

A Reading from the Book of Exodus [1:8–2:10]

A new king was on the throne of Egypt and he didn't know Joseph's story. The king (whom they called Pharaoh) noticed that there were more Israelite people than ever and they were stronger too. He thought, "We'd better pay attention to them, or if there's a war they might sign up with our enemies against us. And maybe escape." So Pharaoh put bosses over them to make them slaves. The Israelites built cities for Pharaoh. The harder the Egyptians made them work, the more kids they had. The Egyptians hated the Israelites and made their lives bitter and miserable.

Pharaoh said to the Hebrew midwives, "Here's what I want you to do: When you are at the birth of a Hebrew baby, if a boy is born, kill him; but if it is a girl, let her live." But the midwives loved God; they decided not to do what Pharaoh wanted them to do. They let the boys live. Pharaoh demanded to know why they weren't killing the boys as he'd told them to. They lied and said, "Those Hebrew women are stronger than Egyptian woman. Their babies are born before we even get there!" God was very pleased with those midwives and blessed them with big families; and the Hebrew people multiplied and became very strong. So Pharaoh commanded all the Egyptians, "If you see a Hebrew baby boy, throw it into the Nile, but let the girls live."

A baby boy was born and his mother hid him for three months. After a while she couldn't hide him any more. So she made a basket that would float on water, placed him in the basket, and put it in the river. She had his sister watch to see what would happen to him. Pharaoh's daughter came to bathe in the river. She found the basket and opened it and saw the beautiful baby crying inside.

Her heart sank. "This must be one of the Hebrews' children," she said. Then the baby's sister, who had been watching from a distance, came closer and said, "I'll find a Hebrew nurse for the baby if you want." Pharaoh's daughter said, "Would you do that for me? That would be great." The girl went back to her mother and told her what happened. So the Pharaoh's daughter actually paid the baby's mom to nurse her own child! When the baby grew up, she took him back to the Pharaoh's daughter, who raised him as her son. She named him Moses, which means "taken from the water."

The Word of the Lord.

Psalm 124

If God hadn't been on our side
when we were attacked by our enemies,
we would have been swallowed alive
and the flood would have swept us away.
Blessed be God who didn't let us be eaten up or drowned!

We have flown away like a bird escaping from a cage
and who is never captured.
Our help comes from God's hands
who made the heaven and earth
and all that is in them.

A Reading from the Letter of Paul to the Romans [12:1–8]

I'm asking you, brothers and sisters, because God is so merciful and good to you, to offer your very selves to God as a living sacrifice. Don't get sucked in by this world. Be transformed instead, by being open to new ways of thinking. That way you'll be able to figure out what God wants, and what is good and holy. Don't think you're more special than you are, or that you can get out of doing the right things. God has given each of you faith. Use that faith and use the brains God gave you to think clearly. Just as our bodies have many different kinds of parts, we are a body, a Christian body; and we're different parts connected together. Each of us has a different gift that we're supposed to use for the good of everyone. Some of us can see clearly what's going on. Others of us are good teachers. Kind leaders. Generous helpers. Cheerful cheerleaders.

The Word of the Lord.

✠ *The Holy Gospel of Our Lord Jesus Christ According to Matthew* [16:13–20]

Jesus asked his disciples, "Who do people think I am? What are they saying about me?" "Well, some of them say you're John the Baptist, or Elijah, or one of the prophets," said the disciples. Jesus asked them, "And who do you say I am?" Peter said, "I think you are the Messiah, God's Son." Jesus said, "God bless you, Simon! You didn't come to this idea on your own; my Father put it in your head. I tell you, I'm going to build my church on what you just said. Here are the keys to heaven; God will respect what you do here on earth." Then Jesus warned the disciples they'd better not tell anyone he was the Messiah.

The Gospel of the Lord.

Proper 17

A Reading from the Book of Exodus [3:1–15]

Moses had run away from Egypt out in to the desert. He was living a quiet life there. He'd gotten married and had a job tending the sheep that belonged to his father-in-law, Jethro, the priest of Midian. One day he took them way out past the wilderness where they could find something to eat. They settled down by Horeb, which was called the mountain of God. The sheep were happily munching away when Moses noticed that a bush was on fire. It seemed kind of strange to him, and he had this feeling that he should go see what had caused the fire. He looked at the bush. There was flame but no smoke. And it kept burning, but not burning up. "What is up with that?" Moses said to himself. It was an angel, a messenger trying to tell him something from God! It sure grabbed his attention.

Then Moses heard someone call him by name. Out there, in the middle of the desert! It was God himself talking to him, "Moses, Moses!" All Moses could say was, "I'm here."

Then God said, "Don't get any closer than you already are. And you should really take your shoes off, because this place where you are standing is holy ground. I'll bet you are wondering who I am, Moses. I am the God of your father, the God of Abraham, the God of Isaac, and the God of Jacob." When Moses heard this, he hid his face in his arms and wrapped his sleeve around his head, because he was afraid to look at God.

Then God said, "I have seen how my people who are slaves in Egypt are hurting. They cry themselves to sleep at night because their masters are mean to them and beat them, and give them no rest. Their cries make my heart hurt. I have a plan to get them out of Egypt and to show them their own place to live, a good place that is full of good things. I know what awful things are going on in Egypt. You are part of my plan. You are going to go to Pharaoh and march the people out of Egypt right under the nose of Pharaoh."

But Moses said to God, "Me? Are you kidding? You want to send me? Why would you think I could do this?"

"Don't worry, Moses," said God. "I will be with you the whole time. And when you and all the people get out of Egypt, then you can bring them here to this mountain and worship me."

But Moses said to God, "I'm not very popular with the Hebrew people or Pharaoh right now. What if I go to the Hebrews and say to them, 'The God whom your fathers knew has sent me to you to help you out of Egypt. Let's go.' What if they say, 'What God? What's his name?' What am I going to say then?"

"Tell them this, Moses," God says. "I AM Who I AM. That's all you have to say. 'I AM has sent me to you.'" God also said to Moses, "And tell them, 'The Lord, the God of your ancestors, the God of Abraham, the God of Isaac, and the God of Jacob, has sent me to you.'

"This is my name forever. Go tell them that."

The Word of the Lord.

Psalm 105:1–6, 23–26

We'll thank you, God, whenever we pray.
We'll let everyone know what good you have done.
We'll sing songs of praise when we tell each other the stories.
We are glad we turned our hearts toward you.
We always turn toward you and your strength,
and look for your face wherever we are.

Don't forget what God has done.
Tell the stories of God's goodness.

You are part of God's family—
children of Abraham and children of Jacob.
Everyone who wants to know God or comes to know God
should live happy lives.
Go find God; you don't have to look very hard.
God's face is in the faces of those he loves.
Look at them with God's eyes and you'll see God's face.

Don't forget what God has done.

Remember what God has done for you, the children of Jacob
and Israel.
God brought you into Egypt and made you more powerful than
your enemies.
God sent Moses and his brother Aaron to lead you to freedom.

Don't forget what God has done.

A Reading from the Letter of Paul to the Romans [12:9–21]

Let your love be real; hate what is evil, hold on tight to what is good; love each other; outdo one another in showing honor. Don't be lazy. Be enthusiastic. Be a good helper. Rejoice in hope. Be patient when you have troubles. Don't forget to pray. Give money or time to your brothers or sisters who need it. Welcome strangers with open arms. Instead of cursing people who hurt you, bless them. Be happy when other people are happy, and cry with them when they're sad.

Get along with each other. Don't think you're so special. Be kind to people who have less than you. And don't think you're so smart, either. Give up the idea of getting even. Instead, do what is right, and don't worry about making sure the other guy gets what he's got coming. Do whatever you have to do to live peacefully. Revenge is not your business. If there are scores to settle, let God do that.

Instead . . . if your enemies are hungry, give them something to eat. If they're thirsty, give them water. They'll wonder what you're up to when you treat them so well! Don't be overcome with evil; instead overcome evil with good.

The Word of the Lord.

✠ *The Holy Gospel of Our Lord Jesus Christ According to Matthew* [16:21–28]

Jesus started to tell his disciples what was going to happen. How he would soon go to Jerusalem and things would get ugly; he would be executed, and three days later he would be raised. Peter didn't like hearing that at all. "Stop talking like that, Jesus. We won't let this happen to you."

Jesus turned and said to Peter, "Get out of my way, Satan. You're not thinking about God's big picture, but only about what makes you feel better right now." Turning to the rest of the disciples, he said, "If you want to follow me, you'll forget about just what you want, and carry the burden of the cross alongside me. If you only think of yourself, you'll lose everything. But if you give up your life, you will gain it all. The Son of Man will come with his angels at the end and everyone will get what they deserve. Some of you in front of me will still be alive when the kingdom of God comes."

The Gospel of the Lord.

Proper 18

A Reading from the Book of Exodus [12:1–14]
(see Maundy Thursday, Year A, p. 83)

Psalm 149

God's people should sing their Creator's praise.
God's people should be full of joy.

Hallelujah. I've got a new song to sing to God.
Let's sing this new song together.

We can praise God by dancing a happy dance.
We can praise God by using a tambourine.
It makes God happy to see us so happy.

Hallelujah. I've got a new song to sing to God.
Let's sing this new song together.

Even people who never catch a break can be happy, because God is with them.
We can be happy when we're awake or when we're sleeping.
With God on our side, how can we lose?
Hallelujah. I've got a new song to sing to God.
Let's sing this new song together.

A Reading from the Letter of Paul to the Romans [13:8–14]

Don't owe anyone anything, except love. If you really love, you have already fulfilled the law. All God's commandments—Don't murder, don't steal, don't be unfaithful, don't want more than your fair share—they're all summed up in this commandment: Love your neighbor as you love yourself. Love doesn't hurt other people; so if you love, you have followed the law.

It's time to wake up, people. Salvation is nearer to us now than it has ever been. Our long dark night is almost over. It's almost day. So let's put on the armor of light. Let's give up the partying and fighting and jealousy, and live with integrity. Let's put on Jesus Christ as we put on our clothes each morning, and not bother with anything else.

The Word of the Lord.

✠ *The Holy Gospel of Our Lord Jesus Christ According to Matthew* [18:15–20]

If you have a problem with another member of the church, talk to them about it when the two of you are alone. If that person listens to you, that's great; if they don't listen, find one or two other people to go with you to talk, so you have witnesses. If the other person still refuses to listen, let the church know. And if even that doesn't work, just let them go.

God will honor what you do here on earth if you do it in Jesus' name, like putting things together or taking them apart. If you ask for something, God will do it for you. Know that whenever two or three of you are together in my name, I will be right there with you.

The Gospel of the Lord.

Proper 19

A Reading from the Book of Exodus [14:19–31]

When the people of God were on the move in the desert, God sent an angel to push them from behind. And a pillar made of cloud moved behind them as well. In the dark the cloud lit up the night, and kept the Egyptians and the people of God apart.

Moses raised his hand over the sea in front of them. God had separated the waters with a strong wind all night long, and it was like the sea had a dry pathway right through the middle of it with walls made of water to their left and to their right.

The Egyptians saw them walking through the sea and came after them, with their horses and chariots and those driving the chariots. The pillar of fire and cloud, which was separating them from the people of God, threw the Egyptians into a panic. The wheels of their chariots failed and got stuck in the mud. They looked at each other and said, "We'd better get out of here, because it looks like God is on their side."

God said to Moses, "Put your hand over the sea again," and in the morning, the sea returned to normal. The walls of water came down on every single Egyptian and their horses and chariots.

But the people of God kept on walking on dry ground, between the walls of water that God had made for them.

On that day, God saved Israel from the Egyptians who were after them. All the people of Israel knew that God had rescued them. So the people believed in God and in God's servant Moses.

The Word of the Lord.

Psalm 114

Hallelujah! When Israel came out of Egypt, where they lived
as strangers,
Judah became the place where God lived and Israel became
God's kingdom.
Even the sea could see it was in God's presence, and the waters
ran away.
The Jordan River saw God coming and turned around and went
the other way.

All the earth is in awe in God's presence.

The mountains were skipping and hopping like rams
and the little hills were frolicking like lambs.
What got into you, O sea, that you ran away from God?
And you, Jordan, why did you turn around?
Why were you skipping and hopping like rams, you mountains?
And you lambs, what were you frolicking about?

All the earth is in awe in God's presence.

All the earth is shaking in awe of God's power
and at the presence of the God of Jacob.
It was God who turned the hard rock into a pool of water
and stone into a spring of flowing water.

All the earth is in awe in God's presence.

A Reading from the Book of Romans [14:1–12]

Make sure you welcome people whose faith is not as strong as yours, but not so you can argue with them about what is right and what isn't. Different people have different opinions. Some people believe it's okay to eat anything they want. Other people think they should eat only vegetables. But you shouldn't judge each other by what you're eating. Some people think a holiday should be observed on a certain day, and others think it should be observed on a different day. What does it matter? God welcomes everyone into the household of God, so who are you to judge? Let God deal with people, and you leave them alone.

Whatever you eat, whatever day you observe, do those things in God's honor and give thanks to God when you do. Whatever you don't eat, or whatever day you don't observe, do *that* in God's honor, too.

You don't just live for yourself, or die for yourself. If you live or die, live or die for God. Because you belong to God, dead or alive. That's why Christ lived and died and lived again—so that he would be Lord of all.

Don't judge each other or mock each other. We are brothers and sisters before God, and we should stand next to each other when we answer for ourselves to God.

The Word of the Lord.

✠ *The Holy Gospel of Our Lord Jesus Christ According to Matthew* [18:21–35]

Peter had another question for Jesus. "If someone at my church hurts my feelings, how often do I have to forgive him? Is seven times enough?"

Jesus laughed at Peter, "Seven times? You've got to be kidding! More like seventy-seven times, I'd say. Let me tell you a story about forgiveness."

Jesus continued: There was a king whose slaves owed him some money. One who owed him $10,000 came to the king and told him he had no money to pay him back. So the king said he'd have to be sold, along with his family and everything he owned, to make up for his debt. But his debt of money had been forgiven.

That same slave whose debt had been forgiven ran into a fellow slave who owed him $100. He grabbed him by the throat and said, "You pay me what you owe me or else."

His fellow slave fell down on the ground and pleaded with him, "Please have patience with me. I promise I will pay you. Give me some more time."

But the first slave refused and threw his fellow into prison until he could pay the debt.

All the other slaves were very upset when they saw this because they knew that the first man had been unfair. The owner said, "When I knew you couldn't pay me what you owed, I listened to your story and forgave you. Shouldn't you have done the same when someone owed you money? You make me so angry, get out of my sight."

God, your heavenly Father, wants you to forgive from your heart, even as you have been forgiven.

The Gospel of the Lord.

Proper 20

A Reading from the Book of Exodus [16:2–15]

Everyone was whining to Moses and Aaron, "If only we'd stayed in Egypt. Even if we died there, at least we had food to eat. You brought us to the wilderness to starve us all." Then God said to Moses, "I am going to rain bread from heaven for you, and each day the people will gather enough for that day. We'll see if they can follow this set of instructions. Every sixth day, they can bring in enough for two days, so they can take a day off." So Moses and Aaron said to everyone, "God heard your complaint. In the morning, you will see bread that God will provide in the wilderness. There is no point in complaining or thanking us—it's all God's doing." In the evening, God provided quails so that the people could eat meat. In the morning, they saw bread called manna for them to gather. They weren't sure what it was. Moses told them, "That's the bread God said he would send you." God said, "Now you'll know that I'm God."

The Word of the Lord.

Psalm 105:1–6, 37–45

We'll thank you, God, whenever we pray.
We'll let everyone know what good you have done.
We'll sing songs of praise when we tell each other the stories.
We are glad we turned our hearts toward you.
We always turn toward you and your strength,
and look for your face wherever we are.

Don't forget what God has done. Tell the stories of God's goodness.

You are part of God's family—
children of Abraham and children of Jacob.
You brought your children out of Egypt.
The Egyptians handed over their silver and gold,
and celebrated when they left
because they were scared of you, God.
You hid your children and led them with lightning.
They asked you for meat to eat and you sent them quail.
You filled them full with bread from heaven.

Don't forget what God has done. Tell the stories of God's goodness.

You made water gush out of a rock,
and it flowed through the desert like a river.
You have never forgotten your promise to Abraham.
You led your people to freedom shouting yelps of joy through the desert.
You gave them land and wealth
so they followed your law.
At least they tried. Hallelujah.

Don't forget what God has done. Tell the stories of God's goodness.

A Reading from the Letter of Paul to the Philippians [1:21–30]

Either way, living or dying, I am with Christ. So I don't worry, but I know it is good for me to be here with you in the flesh. I do my best to help you in your growing faith. Live your life so that it's worthy of Christ's gospel. I want to know that you are working side by side with each other in faith, and are not intimidated by your enemies. You may be suffering, but remember you are suffering for Christ in whom you believe.

The Word of the Lord.

✠ *The Holy Gospel of Our Lord Jesus Christ According to Matthew* [20:1–16]

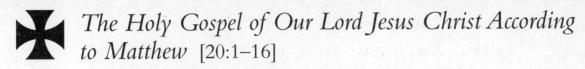

Jesus said the kingdom of heaven is like a man who owned a vineyard and found some people to work in the field for him. They agreed on their daily pay and they were sent to work. Three hours later the vineyard owner went and found more workers, and then again three hours after that, and at the end of the day he hired some, too. When evening came, they all lined up to get their pay. Those hired at the end of the day got a certain amount. Then the ones who'd worked all day long came and saw that they got the same as those who worked only an hour. They were really angry. The owner said, "But you and I agreed on your pay, and you did the work I asked you to do. Can't I pay people what I want to pay them? Do you hate me because I'm generous? Get used to it. The last will be first and the first will be last."

The Gospel of the Lord.

Proper 21

A Reading from the Book of Exodus [17:1–17]

The children of Israel were marching through the desert as God commanded. At one camp, they found no water at all to drink and they whined to Moses about it. Moses said, "Why are you whining to me? Don't you think God grows tired of your whining like I have?" "We can't believe you brought us out of Egypt to let us and our cows die of thirst out here in the desert. We're not sure if God is with us any more or not," replied the people.

Moses went to talk to God: "I don't know what to do with these people. They're ready to stone me because they are so thirsty."

"Okay," God said. "Take some of your best people with you, along with the staff I gave you. I will be standing on the rock at Horeb. Hit it with your staff and water will come out of it and all the people can drink." So Moses did it and all the people had water to drink.

The Word of the Lord.

Psalm 78:1–4, 12–16

Listen to me, people. Be quiet long enough to hear what I have
to say.
I will tell you stories of how things are,
and tell you stories of days long ago.

We will tell each other the stories of God's power.

I will pass along what our fathers knew.
In the years to come, we will tell each other
the stories of God's power and the amazing things God has done.

God divided the sea in two, made the water stand up like walls,
and let the people walk on dry land.

We will tell each other the stories of God's power.

God led the people with a cloud during the day and by night
with a glow of fire.
God split rocks open in the desert and water poured out.
Streams broke through the cliffs
and the waters gushed like raging rivers.

We will tell each other the stories of God's power.

A Reading from the Letter of Paul to the Philippians [2:1–13]

I hope you are encouraged in Christ, are sharing the Spirit with each other, and are full of compassion and sympathy. If you are, then I am a happy man. Walk in the same direction with each other, agreeing about things that matter. Don't be selfish or too full of yourselves, but remember who you are and honor others first. Don't just think about yourselves, but keep each other in mind. Allow yourselves to think and be like Jesus. Jesus didn't take advantage of his position as God, but emptied himself for our sake, being born as one of us. He humbled himself, and was obedient, even when it came to dying on the cross. Because of this, God lifted him up and gave him a name that is above every other name. Everyone should kneel when they hear Jesus' name, everyone in heaven and everything on earth and under the earth. Every tongue should be saying that Jesus Christ is Lord of all, to the glory of God our Father.

Therefore, my dear friends, just as you have always obeyed me, keep working on your salvation, being in awe of God who is working hard in you, helping you to do God's will and please God.

The Word of the Lord.

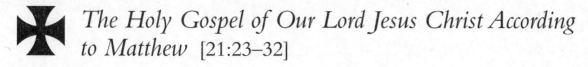

The Holy Gospel of Our Lord Jesus Christ According to Matthew [21:23–32]

When Jesus entered the temple, the priests came while he was teaching and said, "Who gave you the authority to do what you're doing?" Jesus said, "Let me ask you this question. If you know the answer, then I'll answer your question. Did the baptism that John the Baptist did come from heaven or did he do that all by himself?" They argued with each other. "If we say 'from heaven,' then he'll say, 'Then why didn't you believe him?' But if we say, 'of human origin,' we'll be in trouble with the people because they believed John was a prophet." So they said, "We don't know." Jesus said, "Then I'm not going to tell you by what authority I do what I do.

"What do you think about this? A man had two sons; he went to the first and said, 'Son, go and work in the vineyard today.' The son said, 'No, I don't want to go.' But later he changed his mind and went to work. The father told the second son to go work in the vineyard. That son said, 'Sure, I'll go,' but then he didn't. So which of the two did what the father wanted?"

They said, "The first." Jesus said to them, "Truly I tell you, the sinners are closer to the kingdom of God than you are. John the Baptist came to you and you did not believe him, but people you call sinners believed him. Even when you saw how they were changed, you didn't bother changing your minds to believe."

The Gospel of the Lord.

Proper 22

A Reading from the Book of Exodus [20:1–4, 7–9]

God laid out these rules for treating each other well and living a good life.

"Don't forget this: I am your God, the one who brought you out of Egypt where you were slaves. Don't put anything or anybody ahead of me in your lives. Don't use my name for anything but praise and prayer. I deserve your respect and so does my name. I made the Sabbath day so you could rest. Keep the Sabbath day holy and for me. Honor your parents who raised you. Do not commit murder or be unfaithful to those you love. Don't lie. Don't figure out how to get things that belong to your neighbor. Be happy with what you have."

Moses was on the mountaintop talking to God. The people were below, and they saw the thunder and lightning and smoke coming from the mountain, and they heard the trumpet sound. They told Moses they were glad he was talking to God, but they didn't want to talk to God themselves. And they were scared to death. "You don't need to be afraid," said Moses. "God wants you to listen and follow the right path. I'll talk to him for you."

The Word of the Lord.

Psalm 19

Look up to the skies and you'll see God's glory and the work that
God has done.
The days tell stories to each other and the nights tell each other
the news.

They can't use words like we do, but they still speak. They leave us messages everywhere.

You are my strength, God. You're the one who makes me whole.

When we see a sunrise over the sea, it's like God put it to bed beneath the waters, and it makes its entrance in the morning from the deep like a runner ready for a marathon.
The sun fills every corner of the sky at noon and heats up all you can see.
God's words are just what I need. They give me reason to get up in the morning.

You are my strength, God. You're the one who makes me whole.

God's words for me put light in my eyes and clear my head in the morning.
God's words are precious to me, and like honey on my lips.
They are wise and make my heart glad.

You are my strength, God. You're the one who makes me whole.

If I can follow them, I know I'll be a better person and a better friend to all.
God, keep speaking to me in ways that make me a better person.
Help me pay more attention to your words than I do my own thinking, and I will be whole.
Let the words on my heart and in my mouth be good ones, God.

You are my strength, God. You're the one who makes me whole.

A Reading from the Letter of Paul to the Philippians [3:4b–14]

If anyone thinks they are something special, let me tell you, I'm even more special. I've done everything right. I'm one of the people of Israel, from the tribe of Benjamin, born to the right people. I'm a Pharisee, someone who studies God's law. I was the most enthusiastic anti-Christian there is. And no one can pin any crime on me.

But whatever I've done right, whatever reward I have for doing the right things—none of that compares to knowing Christ Jesus. I have lost everything from my former life for his sake but those riches are garbage to me now. Based on faith, not whatever good I do or whatever great person I think I am, I am considered holy in God's eyes, because I know Christ and the power of his new life. I may get myself in all kinds of trouble because I talk about him all the time, but it's worth it. I know I will be with him in the resurrection.

I have a long way to go. I keep working at it, though. Jesus Christ has made me his own. It doesn't get any better than that! Dear friends, I haven't made it on my own. I have done this only with God's help; I forget what I've left behind and push forward to what lies ahead, which is where Christ Jesus is.

The Word of the Lord.

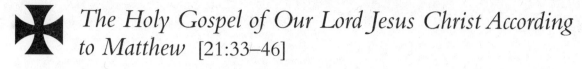

✠ *The Holy Gospel of Our Lord Jesus Christ According to Matthew* [21:33–46]

Jesus said: Here's another story for you.

A landowner planted a vineyard, put a fence around it, and made a wine press and watchtower. He left the country and leased the vineyard to people while he was gone. When it came time, he sent his people to collect the results of the harvest. But the tenants beat up one of his people and killed and stoned the others. So the landowner sent more servants, and they treated them the same way. Finally he decided to send his own son, thinking, "They'll have more respect for my son." When the son came to the vineyard, the tenants thought to themselves, "He's the heir to this whole operation. Let's kill him and get his inheritance." And they killed him.

Jesus then asked, "When the owner himself comes, what do you think he should do to those tenants?" They replied, "We think he should put those miserable crooks to death and lease the vineyard to others who will produce the harvest he expected."

Jesus said to them, "Haven't you read in the scriptures: 'The stone that the builders rejected has become the cornerstone; this was the Lord's doing, and it is amazing in our eyes'? I'm telling you, the kingdom of God will be taken away from you and given to those that actually produce fruits of the kingdom. You'd better watch out."

When the chief priests and the Pharisees heard the stories he was telling, they realized that Jesus was talking about them. They wanted to arrest him, but they were afraid of the crowds of people who believed Jesus was a prophet.

The Gospel of the Lord.

Proper 23

A Reading from the Book of Exodus [32:1–14]

Moses was spending a long, long time on the mountain talking with God. The people went to Aaron and asked him to make a god for them to help them get out of the desert, because they didn't think they would ever see Moses again. So Aaron said, "Okay, take off all your gold jewelry and I will make a statue that looks like a cow, and we can ask it to help us." The people were delighted with their new god and brought it offerings and danced around it and sang praises to it.

God saw this, and sent Moses down the mountain at once. "Wow. They were sure quick to turn the other way once you were gone. They're worshipping a golden cow already! I won't tolerate this. They're a bunch of whiners. After all I've done for them. . . . Move aside so I can be done with them. You're the one I want to deal with and I will have you start a new people for me."

Moses begged God to spare these people. "Don't let the Egyptians see how angry you are. Change your mind. Calm down. Don't bring disaster on your people. Remember the promise you gave Abraham and Isaac and Israel; you promised to give land to your people and they would be in that land forever."

So God's mind was changed about the disaster that was going to take place because of what Moses said.

The Word of the Lord.

Psalm 106:1–6, 19–23

Hallelujah!
We give you thanks, God, because you are good and you never run out of mercy.
Who can remember all of your mighty acts
or praise you as they should?
Happy are you if you treat others with justice
and always do what is right.

Thanks, God, for being good and never running out of mercy.

Include me when you are doing great things for your people.
Make sure I get a dose of your saving help.
I want some of the good things you've promised
and I will be glad to rejoice with your people,
and inherit what you have planned for us.

Thanks, God, for being good and never running out of mercy.

Just as our fathers and mothers sinned, we have sinned too.
We've made poor choices that have hurt you and other people.
The people of Israel decided to worship a golden statue instead of you,
and they exchanged your glory for a statue of a cow that eats grass.

Thanks, God, for being good and never running out of mercy.

They forgot that you were their Savior,
who had done great things in Egypt, and awesome things at the Red Sea.

You might have destroyed them if Moses hadn't stood up
for them.
You changed your mind and turned away your anger.

Thanks, God, for being good and never running out of mercy.

A Reading from the Letter of Paul to the Philippians [4:1–9]

My brothers and sisters, whom I love so much, stand firm in the Lord in this way: Help the women who are fighting with each other to see that they can agree about the Lord. They have struggled with me in the work of the Gospel along with my other coworkers. They are good people; they just need some guidance.

Rejoice in the Lord always; again I will say, Rejoice. Be famous for your gentleness. God is near. Don't be overcome with worry. In fact, don't worry about anything. Instead go to God with things that concern you. Let God know what is bothering you. And the peace of God, which is beyond anything we can understand, will guard your hearts and your minds in Christ Jesus.

Finally, dear ones, whatever is true and honorable, whatever is just and pure, if you can find the good, that's what you should focus on. Keep on doing what I've taught you, and God's peace will always be with you.

The Word of the Lord.

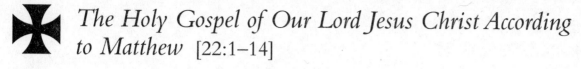

✠ *The Holy Gospel of Our Lord Jesus Christ According to Matthew* [22:1–14]

Here's another one of Jesus' stories:

The kingdom of heaven is like a king who gave a wedding party for his son. He sent his servants to call those who had received invitations to the party, but they wouldn't come. He tried again to get them to come into the party, saying, "Tell them that I've prepared an awesome dinner for them. Everything is ready for them. Tell them to come and enjoy the banquet." But those who had been invited had other things on their minds and other things to do. And one even beat up the servant who was sent to invite him! The king was outraged. He sent his troops to destroy those murderers. Then he turned to his servants and said, "Our wedding party is ready but we need guests. Go into the streets of the city and invite everyone you see to the banquet." So they went out, and gathered everyone they could find, good people and bad people both. And the wedding hall was filled with guests. The king arrived at the party and noticed a man there who wasn't dressed for the party. He asked "Hi, how did you get in here dressed like that?" He had nothing to say. The king said, "Throw him out." Many are called, few are chosen.

The Gospel of the Lord.

Proper 24

A Reading from the Book of Exodus [33:12–23]

Moses was talking with God. "You told me to lead these people, but I can't do this alone. If you care about me the way you say you do, please, give me some direction, so that I might know you as well as you know me and that these people can know you too." God said, "I will go with you. I will give you support and let you rest." "Good," said Moses. "These people will be special; your chosen people. Will you show me your glory?" God said, "I will make sure you can see all of my goodness. I will be gracious to whom I will be gracious, and kind to whom I will be kind. But you can't see my face and live. How about this? Go stand on that rock, and while my goodness and glory pass by there, I will put you in a crack in the rock and cover you with my hand until I've passed. Then I will take my hand away. You can see my back, but you won't see my face."

The Word of the Lord.

Psalm 99

You are the best, God. You are the King.
See the people shake with excitement and fear.
Watch the ground tremble and hear it rumble.

You are the best and all the people know it.
Can you hear them speak your powerful name with wonder?

We will let everyone know that you are a great God.
We will climb your holy hill to worship you.

Here is what the people say to you,
"O mighty King, you treat us fairly,

And everyone comes before you as equals."
We recognize how great you are
and give ourselves to serve you.
You are holy and you amaze us.

**We will let everyone know that you are a great God.
We will climb your holy hill to worship you.**

Moses and Aaron are your priests,
Samuel was too.
When they called your name, you answered them.
You talked to them from the pillar made of cloud.
And they walked behind you and followed your path.
You answered their questions; you forgave them,
but made them accountable for the wrong they had done.

**We will let everyone know that you are a great God.
We will climb your holy hill to worship you.**

A Reading from the First Letter of Paul to the Thessalonians [1:1–10]

Here's a letter from Paul and Silvanus and Timothy:

Grace, everyone at the church in Thessalonica! We are always thanking God for you, and praying for you, remembering your faith and hard work of love. God has chosen you, and given you the gospel and the Holy Spirit along with it. We hope you know that we have worked hard to support you. You have used us as examples to follow how we love the Lord. In spite of being pushed around by people due to your faith, you have been strong and joyful and the Holy Spirit has allowed you to be a good example for others. People all over have heard all about your faith, and about how you welcomed us and are serving a living God, and waiting for God's Son Jesus to return to us.

The Word of the Lord.

✠ *The Holy Gospel of Our Lord Jesus Christ According to Matthew* [22:15–22]

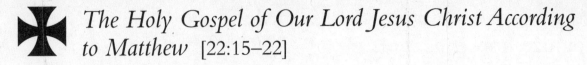

The Pharisees wanted to trap Jesus into saying something they didn't like. They sent some of their people to follow him. "Teacher," they said, "We know you are a sincere follower of God. Tell us this, then: is it against God's law to pay taxes to the emperor of Rome?" Jesus knew they were out to get him. He said, "Why are you setting me up, you hypocrites?" They gave him a coin that he asked to see. He showed it to them and said, "Whose head is this on the coin, and what is his title?" They answered, "It's the emperor's head on that coin." So Jesus said, "So give to the emperor the things that are his. Give to God the things that belong to God."

"Wow—I guess he told us, didn't he?" They were amazed, had nothing to say after that, and they left him.

The Gospel of the Lord.

Proper 25

A Reading from the Book of Deuteronomy [34:1–12]

Moses hiked up to the top of Mount Nebo and God showed him the land of Canaan. It stretched as far as Moses could see. God said, "This is the land I promised to Abraham and Isaac and Jacob and all their descendants. I've shown it to you, but you won't ever step foot in it." Moses died there and was buried in the land of Moab, but nobody knows where. He was strong until the day he died, when he was a hundred and twenty years old. The Israelites mourned for Moses for thirty days. God chose Joshua to replace Moses, and he was full of the spirit of wisdom. The Israelites obeyed him just as they had Moses.

No one could ever equal Moses, though. He did incredible signs and wonders that God sent him to perform. Moses knew God face to face.

The Word of the Lord.

Psalm 90:1–6, 13–17

God, you've been our help
from way back: my great-grandparents, my grandparents,
  and my mom and dad.
Before the mountains were formed,
before the earth was created,
you were God.
You made us from dust and that's where we will return.

May God be gracious to us
and bless all that we are
and all that we do.

We are children of the dirt.
A thousand years are nothing to you!
They go by like a couple of hours.

We are like a dream or a thought that fades during the day.
We wither like the grass.
In the morning we grow strong and tall,
and by suppertime, we're all dried up.

May God be gracious to us
and bless all that we are
and all that we do.

Be kind to us, God.
Don't take too long to come to us.
We need your kindness first thing in the morning
so we can be happy all day long.
Make us glad for the same amount of time that we had troubles.
Show us your goodness, God
and we'll pass it along.

May God be gracious to us
and bless all that we are
and all that we do.

A Reading from the First Letter of Paul to the Thessalonians [2:1–8]

Brothers and sisters, we're so glad we were able to be with you and we hope you found it productive, as well. When we came to you, we'd been beaten up in Philippi, and I have to say, it took a lot of courage to keep preaching the Good News. You know we don't do this to please ourselves, or even to please you, but to please God and to tell everyone his Good News. We tried to be humble and gentle with you. We care about you so deeply, and shared the gospel with you and also our hearts. You have become very special to us.

The Word of the Lord.

✠ *The Holy Gospel of Our Lord Jesus Christ According to Matthew* [22:34–46]

When the Pharisees heard that Jesus had bested the Sadducees, they sent a lawyer to ask Jesus this question: "Teacher, which commandment is the greatest one of all?" Jesus said, "Love the Lord your God with all your soul and with all your heart and with all your mind. That is the first commandment and the greatest one there is. And there's another that goes along with it, love your neighbor as yourself. All the other commandments are built on these."

Then Jesus asked them a question: "So, what do you think about the Messiah? Whose son is he?" They said, "He's the son of David." Jesus said, "How can David call him Lord if he's David's son, like it says in the scriptures?" No one was able to give him an answer. After that they didn't bother to ask Jesus any more questions.

The Gospel of the Lord.

Proper 26

A Reading from the Book of Joshua [3:7–17]

God said to Joshua, "Today I'm going to let everyone know that I am with you just as I was with Moses. You'll be in charge of the ark of the covenant." Joshua brought all the people together to tell them what God had said to him. "Here's how you know that the living God is with you: God will clear the land before us so we can live there. The ark of the covenant will go into the land first, before any of us. Let's pick twelve men, one from each tribe of Israel. And they will stop in the river, and the water will dry up. That will allow us to walk on dry land." The men who held the ark of the covenant stood there, on dry ground in the middle of the river, while the whole nation of Israel crossed into the promised land.

The Word of the Lord.

Psalm 107:1–7, 33–37

I can't say this often enough.
We have you to thank, God, for everything good we have. You are good.

God is really good. God's kindness never ends.

You look for ways to be good to us, and you're always calling us to come to you.
We run away, wander in the desert, and forget about you.
Then we wonder why we're thirsty and hungry, like there's a big hole in us.

God is really good. God's kindness never ends.

Then we go whining to you because we're hungry and thirsty.
You feed us and give us water.
You listen to us and hug us because you love us.

God is really good. God's kindness never ends.

You pick us up by the scruff of the neck and plop us on the right path.
You place our feet on the ground and then give us a nudge in the right direction,
again and again.

God is really good. God's kindness never ends.

So let's all be thankful for what God does for us,
even when we don't know it's God who's doing it.
When we're thirsty, God leads us to water.
When we're hungry, God gives us plenty to eat

God is really good. God's kindness never ends.

If we were smart, we'd remember this:
That God is good. All the time.
God is good to us.

God is really good. And God's kindness never ends.

A Reading from the First Letter of Paul to the Thessalonians [2:9–13]

I hope you remember how hard we worked, so that we wouldn't be a burden to you while we were with you preaching the gospel. We did our best to love you and encourage you, pleading that you live your lives the way that would make God happy. We thank God that you accepted the gospel not as our own words, but as the words right from God's mouth. God's Word is at work in you. We just know it.

The Word of the Lord.

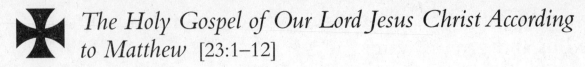

✠ *The Holy Gospel of Our Lord Jesus Christ According to Matthew* [23:1–12]

Then Jesus said to his disciples and the people who were following them around:

The scribes and the Pharisees teach you what Moses taught. Do what they teach you, but don't do what they do. They don't practice what they preach. They lay heavy burdens on the shoulders of others; but they themselves don't bother lifting a finger to help. They make sure their good deeds are seen by others. They love to sit at the head tables at banquets and they have the best seats at church. They expect to be greeted with respect when you see them at the market and be called "rabbi." Or teacher. Don't bother calling each other teacher, because all of you are students of the Messiah. And don't look to others as your father, because you all have one father, the one in heaven. The greatest among you will be your servant. All who puff themselves up will be humbled, and all who humble themselves will be honored.

The Gospel of the Lord.

Proper 27

A Reading from the Book of Joshua [24:1–3a, 14–25]

Joshua got everybody together so he could talk with them before God. He said, "This is what God wants us to remember: Long, long ago your people lived far away and served gods other than me. So I led Abraham to a new place and gave him many children."

Joshua went on, "We need to put away the gods that our fathers served, and serve our God with all that we have. Each of you needs to decide whom you will serve, our God or the god of the people of this land. I just know that my house and I will be serving our God."

The people answered, "We won't abandon the LORD our God to serve other gods. God led our people out of slavery and did great things for us, protecting us from other people along the way. Therefore we will serve the LORD, for he is our God."

But Joshua said to the people, "You know the LORD our God is holy. God wants every part of you, and requires you to follow him. This is a very big decision." The people said, "Yes, we know." "You can't change your mind, and serve the other gods from time to time," Joshua reminded them. And the people said to Joshua, "No, we will serve the LORD!" He said, "Then put away the other gods, and turn your hearts to the God of Israel." The people committed themselves to God that day, and Joshua wrote it all down so that they would remember.

The Word of the Lord.

Psalm 78:1–7

Listen to me, people.
Move closer to me so you can hear what I'm saying.
I will tell you stories and reveal the mysteries of times past.

Tell us stories of God's power; all the great things God has done.

Children need to hear about their fathers and mothers
and grandfathers and grandmothers. Nothing is secret.
They need to hear stories about God's power and
all the great things God did for them.
God set up laws for Jacob to teach the children of Israel
how to live and trust each other and God.

Tell us stories of God's power; all the great things God has done.

Each generation needs to know these things
and teach their children well.
And people will put their trust in God
when they hear these stories and keep God's commandments.

Tell us stories of God's power; all the great things God has done.

A Reading from the Letter of Paul to the Thessalonians [4:13–18]

Brothers and sisters, we want to make sure you know what's going on with your loved ones who have died. You have hope because we believe that Jesus died, but rose again. And we know that those who die will be raised again too, through Jesus. Jesus himself, along with the archangel's trumpet, will come down from heaven and all who died believing in Jesus will be raised. The rest of us who are still alive will join them in meeting Jesus and we will be together forever. Isn't that encouraging? Spread this news around.

The Word of the Lord.

✠ *The Holy Gospel of Our Lord Jesus Christ According to Matthew* [25:1–13]

Jesus said:

God's kingdom is like this: Ten bridesmaids took their lamps and went to meet the bridegroom. There were five smart girls, and five foolish girls. The foolish ones took their lamps but no oil to put in them! The smart girls took oil so they could light their lamps. The night was long, and the bridegroom wasn't showing up, so they all fell asleep. At midnight, he finally showed up. The girls without oil said to the smart girls, "Give us some of your oil so we can see!" But the smart girls replied, "No! There isn't enough for all of us. Go get some for yourselves from the dealers." While the foolish ones were buying the oil they should have brought with them, the bridegroom came and took the smart girls into the wedding, and then shut the door. Finally the foolish girls got some oil and came back to the wedding. They knocked on the door and said, "Let us in." But they heard in reply, "Sorry. Too late."

The point of this story is that you need to be prepared and you need to stay awake. Because you just don't know what will happen or when it's going to happen.

The Gospel of the Lord.

Proper 28

A Reading from the Book of Judges [4:1–7]

Once again God's people did something evil and they ended up as subjects to some else's king who treated them badly. They cried out to God to help them. Deborah was serving as a judge at that time. She used to sit under a palm tree and people would come to her and ask for her opinion about things. She sent word to Barak, "God wants you to go with many soldiers to Mount Tabor, and there God will give you the victory over your oppressors and you will win your freedom."

The Word of the Lord.

Psalm 123

I'm looking to you, God!
I am looking to you for help and guidance.
I am looking to you for mercy.
    Have mercy on us, God.
We have done wrong and we have had more than enough
    trouble in our hearts.
We have had plenty of hatred from those around us.
We don't need any more.
I'm looking to you, God!
I am looking to you for help and guidance.
I am looking to you for mercy.

A Reading from the First Letter of Paul to the Thessalonians [5:1–11]

I know you want to know the exact time these things will happen and when Jesus will come back for us. But brothers and sisters, it will be like a thief coming in the night. Just when you think everything is secure, suddenly your house is broken into. And just like a woman in labor, once it starts, there's no turning back. Thank God you are not in the dark, my friends, and you have no reason to be afraid. You are children of God, children of the light. Let's be alert and sober, and put on faith and love like a protective coating. And wear the hope of our salvation like a helmet on our heads. God has made us for salvation, so that no matter if we're alive or if we've already died, we may be alive with him. Keep encouraging each other, as I know you are.

The Word of the Lord.

✠ *The Holy Gospel of Our Lord Jesus Christ According to Matthew* [25:14–30]

Jesus said: Here's another story about the kingdom for you:

A man was heading out of town, and he wanted his servants to take care of his money while he was gone. To one servant he gave $5,000, to another $2,000, and to the last one $1,000. After the man had left, the first servant invested his money and doubled what he'd been given. So did the servant who had been given $2,000. But the last guy dug a hole in his yard and buried his $1,000 in the dirt. After a long time, the man came back and wanted to see how they'd done with what they'd been given. The first servant said proudly, "Look. You gave me $5,000 and I've made another $5,000 for you."

"Excellent!" said the man. "I will promote you because you've been so good with my money." The same thing happened with the servant who had turned $2,000 into $4,000. Then the last man, who had hid his $1,000 in the ground said, "I was too scared to do anything with your money so I hid it in my yard. But it was safe. So here's your $1,000." The man said, "Are you kidding? Why didn't you at least give my money to someone who would know what do to with it? Let me have that so I can give it to someone else. The only way to make more, is to do more with what you have. If you do nothing, you will have nothing. Take this worthless servant out of my sight."

The Gospel of the Lord.

Proper 29

A Reading from the Book of Ezekiel [34:11–16, 20–24]

God says:

I will look for my sheep and find them, just as a shepherd does. I will rescue them from all the dangerous situations they've gotten themselves into. I will bring them into their own land and feed them on the mountains of home, close to water. I'll make sure they have good, rich pasture. I will be their shepherd and I'll make them lie down and rest. I will care for the injured and make the weak ones strong again. I'll get rid of the fat, mean ones and I won't let them hurt the others. David is the one I've chosen to serve as their shepherd for me. He will feed them and take care of them. And I will be their God.

The Word of the Lord.

Psalm 100

Be happy in God, everyone.
With joy in your hearts, serve God and
sing as you serve God.
Know this: The Lord is God.
You made us, God, and we belong to you.
We are your people. We are the sheep in your pasture.
We will sing your praise whenever we come before you.
You are good, God, and your mercy never ends.
You will be faithful year after year after year.

A Reading from the Letter of Paul to the Ephesians [1:15–23]

I've heard about your faith in Jesus and your love toward each other. It makes me so happy when I hear these things, and I thank God for you. I pray that God will give you a spirit of wisdom as you grow in your faith, so that with the eyes of your heart wide open, you will know hope. And you will know the riches of what God has given you, and the greatness of God's power. God put this power to work in Christ when he raised him from the dead and seated him at his right hand in the heavenly places, far above all authority on earth, and above every name that is named, not only now, but forever. And God has made Jesus the head over the church, which is his body, the fullness of him who is with us in everything we do.

The Word of the Lord.

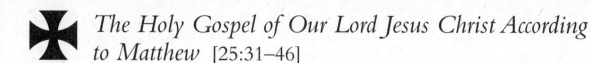

✠ *The Holy Gospel of Our Lord Jesus Christ According to Matthew* [25:31–46]

Jesus said, "When the Son of Man comes again with all the angels, then he will sit on the throne of his glory. Everyone on earth will stand before him. And he'll separate them from each other like a shepherd separates the sheep from the goats. Then he'll say, 'The kingdom is yours. Come. When I was hungry, you fed me. And when I was thirsty, you gave me a drink of water. You welcomed me when I didn't know anyone. When I needed clothing, you gave me some. You took care of me when I was sick and visited me in prison.' They'll answer him, 'Lord, we never saw you. When did we see you hungry or thirsty? And when did we see you were a stranger or needed clothes? And when were you sick or in prison? When did we see you and help you?' And he will answer them, 'I'm telling you, when you helped the very least of my people, you helped me.' Then he will say to the others, 'Get out of my sight; when I was hungry and thirsty, you gave me nothing to eat or drink. When I was a stranger, you turned your head the other way, and didn't make sure I had clothing. You didn't visit me when I was sick or in prison.' Just like the others, they asked, 'When did we see you hungry or thirsty, or alone or naked or sick and in prison? When did we NOT help you?' And the Son of Man will answer them, 'This is what it comes down to—when you didn't help one of my people, you did not help me. Those who did will live forever, but you will be gone from my sight.'"

The Gospel of the Lord.

Year B

The First Sunday of Advent

A Reading from the Book of Isaiah [64:1–9]

I wish you would rip the heavens open and come down to us, so that the mountains would shake because you are near. Be like a spark that ignites a pile of twigs, or fire that makes water boil—then your enemies would know who you are, and they would shake just like the mountains. No one has ever seen or heard any god like you, who works in the lives of people. You touch our lives. But we build barriers between you and us, God. Then you get angry, and we sin all the more because we forget that we belong to you. Then we can't seem to do anything right. And our lives are as dirty as a filthy cloth. Our lives have no substance and when the wind blows, our sins carry us away. It seems you have hidden your face from us, because no one can feel your presence anymore. We are obsessed with our own sinful ways. Yet we know you are our Father. We are clay and you are the potter. You can shape us and make us yours. Please don't be angry with us, God. Do not remember how sinful we can be. Remember instead that we are all yours.

The Word of the Lord.

Psalm 80:1–7, 16–18 (see Advent 4, Year A, p. 10)

A Reading from the First Letter of Paul to the Corinthians [1:3–9]

With this letter I send you grace and peace from God our Father and the Lord Jesus Christ. I always thank God for you because of the grace that God has poured into your lives through Jesus. For I can see your lives are richer in every way because you can speak from your heart about God. As you wait for him to be with us again, you have everything you need. God has called you into relationship with Jesus and will give you strength.

The Word of the Lord.

✠ *The Holy Gospel of Our Lord Jesus Christ According to Mark* [13:24–37]

Jesus said, "One day soon the sun will go dark, the moonlight will be turned off, the stars will fall out of the sky, and the heavens will shake. Then the Son of Man will come through the clouds with power and glory. And he will send his angels to every corner of the earth to gather up his people. The fig tree has this lesson to teach us: When there is a tiny leaf, you can tell that summer is coming. Just like that leaf, when you see the signs in the heavens, you'll know the Son of Man is close. Heaven and earth will pass away, but my words won't. No one knows when this will happen—not the angels, not even me. Only the Father. So make sure you stay awake, because you don't know when this will happen either. If you were going on a trip, you'd put someone in charge to watch your house. That's what you need to do. Keep watch, because you don't want to be surprised or asleep when he comes. STAY AWAKE."

The Gospel of the Lord.

The Second Sunday of Advent

A Reading from the Book of Isaiah [40:1–11]

God says, "Isaiah, I want you to comfort my people, please. Speak softly and tenderly to the people of Jerusalem and tell them that the hard times are over, and all is right with God again. Listen, you can hear a voice crying in the desert, "Make things ready for God. Prepare a highway right through the middle of the wilderness." And just watch; the valleys will all be lifted up, and the mountains and hills will be made low. The uneven and rough places will be smoothed out. And then God's glory will be revealed and everyone, everywhere will see it.

All people are like grass or like flowers. They wither and fade, and when God's breath blows, they can barely stand up against it. Well, the grass may wither, and flowers may fade, but the word that God speaks will last forever.

Get up on the highest mountain, lift up your voice and make it strong. Don't be afraid but shout out, "Here is your God!"

God is powerful. And yet tender like a shepherd holding little lambs in his arms and carrying them home, with the mother sheep following behind.

The Word of the Lord.

Psalm 85

You have been so good to us, God.
You smiled on us and made us happy again.
You wiped our record clean
and pardoned what we have done wrong.

Keep showing us mercy, God,
and be with us always.

I always want to listen to you
because you speak about peace
to those of us who listen
and open our hearts to you.

Keep showing us mercy, God,
and be with us always.

It's true that you are very close
to those of us who believe in you
if we only open our eyes.

Keep showing us mercy, God,
and be with us always.

Mercy and truth will talk and laugh with each other.
Love and loyalty will be best friends forever.
Faithfulness will sprout like a plant reaching up for the sky.
Truth will bubble up from the ground
like cool water on a really hot day.
And goodness feels like the sun smiling down on me when I'm cold.

Keep showing us mercy, God,
and be with us always.

I know you want all the best for us, God:
good food, lots of money and plenty of time to spend it, lots and lots of friends.
But most of all, you want us to follow kindness down the path
and live with each other without fighting.

Keep showing us mercy, God,
and be with us always.

A Reading from the Second Letter of Peter [3:8–15a]

You can't ignore this fact: God has a different sense of time than we do. One day to God is like a thousand years to us. And a thousand years is like one day. God's promises may seem slow in coming, but God's day will come. Be patient. God wants all of you to come back to him.

God's day will sneak up on us, and then everything we know will be dissolved. While you wait, lead lives you can be proud of, and that would please God. When the old things pass away, a new earth and a new heaven will be formed. That's where goodness will live. Until then, work at being peaceful, and be thankful that God is patient with us.

The Word of the Lord.

✠ *The Holy Gospel of Our Lord Jesus Christ According to Mark* [1:1–8]

This is the beginning of the story of the Good News in Jesus, who is the Son of God.

Just as it was written in the book of the prophet Isaiah, a voice was in the desert crying, and preparing the way of the Lord. John the baptizer appeared in the desert, shouting to people that they needed to turn their lives around and be made clean. People from all over were coming to see him, and be baptized by him, confessing their sinfulness. John used to wear camel's hair for clothes, and he would eat grasshoppers and wild honey.

"I'm nobody," he would say. "I'm just here to tell you that someone more powerful is coming. And I've been baptizing you with water, but he will baptize you with the Holy Spirit."

The Gospel of the Lord.

The Third Sunday of Advent

A Reading from the Book of Isaiah [61:1–4, 8–11]

God has anointed me with the Holy Spirit and sent me to bring good news to people who need it most. God sent me to mend people whose hearts are broken, to let prisoners know they are free people, to release people from whatever is holding them back. I'm here to let them know that this time is God's time. God will provide comfort to those who are crying, and decorate their lives with gladness instead of dark ashes and sadness.

God's people should stand up straight like tall oaks that are planted to display God's glory. They should repair their ruined cities.

God says, "I hate robbery and bad behavior. But I love it when people treat each other well. Tell the people I will make a deal with them that will last forever; they will be my people and all the nations of the world will see that they and their children are blessed by me."

At this news, all of me broke out in songs of gladness. I feel like I've been wrapped in God's salvation, and covered with God's goodness. Just as the earth in the springtime sends up shoots of beautiful new plants, and gardens produce green things to eat, God has sown the seeds of goodness and praise, which will grow strong and tall so that everyone will see.

The Word of the Lord.

Psalm 126

We thought we'd died and gone to heaven when we saw God
 had put Zion back together.
We were so happy we couldn't stop laughing. And when we
 weren't laughing we were singing.

God has done great things for us and we are so happy.

Everyone was telling each other how good God was.
Bring us back to health, God.
Build up the places that were torn down.

God has done great things for us and we are so happy.

Those of us who cried all those many long nights, will wake up with joy in our hearts for sure.
And those who went out into the field while they were crying will come back home happy

God has done great things for us and we are so happy.

A Reading from the First Letter of Paul to the Thessalonians [5:16–24]

Rejoice every minute of the day. Never stop praying. And always, always give thanks to God. This is what God wants for you in Jesus Christ. Don't throw water on the Holy Spirit in your lives. Don't mock the words of the prophets, but hold on to the good things you've been given. Stay away from every form of evil. May our God of peace make you holy. And may your spirit and soul and body be ready for the time when Jesus comes again. God is faithful and God will help you be faithful, too.

The Word of the Lord.

✠ *The Holy Gospel of Our Lord Jesus Christ According to John* [1:6–8, 19–28]

John was a man sent by God to testify to the light, so that everyone would believe through him. He himself wasn't the light, but he pointed to the light. Some people came by to ask John if he was the Messiah. He told them he was not.

"Well, then, who are you? Are you Elijah?"

"No," said John.

"Are you the prophet?"

"No," said John.

"We need to know who you are so we have an answer for those who sent us here to ask you."

John said, "I am the voice crying in the desert that the prophet Isaiah talked about." The people wanted to know why he was baptizing if he wasn't the Messiah. John explained that he baptized with water. And that soon, someone much more important would be here.

The Gospel of the Lord.

The Fourth Sunday of Advent

A Reading from the Second Book of Samuel [7:1–11, 16]

King David said to Nathan, the prophet, "I'm living in a house made of wood, but the ark of God lives in a tent."

Nathan told the king to do what he had in mind, because God would always be with him. That very night Nathan had a dream. In the dream, God said, "Go ask David if he is ready to build me a place to live. I've been moving around in a tent ever since I led the people out of Egypt. I've wanted a house made of cedar wood. Tell David that I've been with him since I plucked him out of the sheep pasture and made him king. I've made a place for the people to call their own and their enemies have finally left them alone. If you make a house for God, God will establish a kingdom born from your family."

The Word of the Lord.

Canticle 15 [Luke 1:46–55]

My soul sings out with joy
and my spirit proclaims God's goodness
for God has made me feel special.
From now on, everyone will see that I have been blessed.
The Almighty has done great things for me, and God's name
is holy.
God is merciful to those who seek guidance.
Everyone sees how strong God is.
God breaks up the groups who think they are stronger than
he is.
God throws dictators off their thrones and gives confidence and
pride to the lowest of the low.

The hungry people are filled with good things to eat because
of God
and those who already have more than they need get sent on
their way hungry.
God has come to rescue the people.
God remembers the promise of mercy
that was made to our fathers and mothers.

A Reading from the Letter of Paul to the Romans [16:25–27]

God is able to make you strong and has given you the good news about Jesus being God's very self, come among us. Now this good news is available to everyone so that we all might be faithful and obedient. Praise God for his wisdom and openness through Jesus Christ. Amen.

The Word of the Lord.

✠ *The Holy Gospel of Our Lord Jesus Christ According to Luke* [1:26–38]

God sent an angel named Gabriel with a message for a young woman named Mary in Nazareth. She was engaged to Joseph, who was a descendant of King David.

Here was the message, "Greetings from God himself, Mary. You are special in God's eyes. And God holds you close to his heart." Mary couldn't figure out what was going on and what the angel could possibly mean by that. Gabriel told her not to be afraid, that God had only good things in mind. "Here is the plan, Mary. You will conceive a baby boy and name him Jesus when he's born. He will be great, the Son of the Most High, and he will reign over God's people like King David did, but his kingdom will never end."

Mary said, "But I'm not married. Why would you choose me to be Jesus' mother?"

Gabriel said, "The Holy Spirit will make this happen, and you will be surrounded by God's power as if it were incense. Your child will be holy. He will be called the Son of God. And guess what else? Your older cousin Elizabeth, who's never been able to have children, is already six months pregnant. So you see, nothing is impossible with God."

Then Mary said, "Okay. I am willing to work with God on this plan. I trust that God can do what he says he will do." And then the angel left her alone to think about things.

The Gospel of the Lord.

The Nativity of Our Lord Jesus Christ: Christmas Day (see Year A, p. 13)

The First Sunday after Christmas Day

(see Year A, p. 16)

The Second Sunday after Christmas Day

(see Year A, p. 20)

The First Sunday after the Epiphany

A Reading from the Book of Genesis [1:1–5]

In the very beginning, when God created the heavens and the earth, the earth had no shape or substance. Darkness covered everything there was, and God's breath blew over the deep waters. Then God said, "Let's have some light!" and there was light. God saw that light was good. Then he separated the light from the darkness. God named the light Day and the darkness he named Night. That was the first evening and the first morning there ever was.

The Word of the Lord.

Psalm 29 (see Epiphany 1, Year A, p. 26)

A Reading from the Acts of the Apostles [19:1–7]

Paul asked some disciples in Ephesus if they'd received the Holy Spirit when they became believers. They replied, "Holy Spirit? What Holy Spirit? We've never heard that there was a Holy

Spirit. We were baptized with water by John." Paul told them that John's baptism pointed to the one who would come after him—Jesus. Once they heard that, they wanted to be baptized in the name of Jesus. And Paul laid his hands on them and asked that the Holy Spirit would come upon them. And all twelve of them were filled with God's Spirit and spoke in tongues and were able to speak God's truth.

The Word of the Lord.

✠ *The Holy Gospel of Our Lord Jesus Christ According to Mark* [1:4–11]

John the baptizer was in the desert, shouting about being baptized, being forgiven, and turning your life toward God. People from all over came to hear him preach and be baptized in the Jordan River. John wore rough camel's hair and ate grasshoppers and wild honey. He kept pointing to the one who was to follow him. "I am not the One you're looking for," he would say. "He's coming after me and he will baptize you with the Holy Spirit. Get ready for him." Jesus himself came from Galilee to be baptized by John in the river. And just as he was coming up out of the water, he saw the heavens open and the Holy Spirit landed on him like a dove. And he heard a voice from heaven say, "You are my Son, whom I love so much; I am pleased with you."

The Gospel of the Lord.

The Second Sunday after the Epiphany

A Reading from the First Book of Samuel [3:1–10]

A boy named Samuel was working in the temple with the priest named Eli. In those days, people didn't hear from God very often, and they didn't receive dreams from God either. Samuel slept in the room where the ark of God was. Eli was an old man and didn't see very well. Eli slept in a room down the hall. Samuel woke up as he heard someone say, "Samuel! Samuel!" Thinking it was Eli, he popped out of bed and said, "Here I am. I'm coming." He ran to see what Eli might need. "I heard you call and I'm here. What can I do for you?" Eli said, "I didn't call for you. Go back to sleep."

So Samuel went back to bed. Samuel didn't know God yet and he didn't know that it was God who was calling him. He heard the voice again, "Samuel! Samuel!" and once again Samuel went to see what Eli needed. "I didn't call you, Samuel. Go back to bed." After Samuel got back to sleep, he heard the voice again for the third time, and went to help Eli. This time, Eli figured out that God was calling the boy. Eli told Samuel, "Next time, if you hear someone call you again, say, 'Talk to me, God. I am listening.'"

So Samuel went back to bed and this time God came and stood next to him and said "Samuel! Samuel!" Samuel did as Eli told him and said, "Talk to me, God. I am your servant and I am listening."

The Word of the Lord.

Psalm 139:1–5, 12–17

Lord, you know me better than anyone, even myself.
You know what I'm doing. You even know what I'm thinking.
When I move around or when I lay down,
when I walk or sit still, you always know where I am.
There's nothing I say that you haven't already figured I'm going to say.

God, you know me inside and out.

You are in front of me to guide me, behind me to protect me,
and I feel your hand on my shoulder, so I know I'm not alone.
That's almost too good to be true.

God, you know me inside and out.

You yourself created all my parts. You pieced me together in my mother's womb.
You did an excellent job making me, and I thank you for that.
You are amazing. That's for sure.

God, you know me inside and out.

You've known me forever.
Your eyes could see my arms and legs, even before they were fully formed.
Day by day I grew bigger until I was finally me with all my parts, ready to be born.

God, you know me inside and out.

I'm amazed by your deep thoughts, O God;
the number of them astounds me.
I couldn't possibly count them all,
because there are more of them than grains of sand on the shore.
If I were to count them it would take forever, and by then I'd be as old as you.

God, you know me inside and out.

A Reading from the First Letter of Paul to the Corinthians [6:12–20]

"I can do anything I want," but not everything is good to do. "I can do anything I want," but I will not let anything have power over me. Worrying about food, being unfaithful to my spouse . . . these are things that aren't meant for our bodies and us. Did you know that your body is part of the body of Christ himself? Would I take part of Christ's body and give it to a prostitute? I don't think so! So stay away from stuff like that. Remember that your body is the place where the Holy Spirit dwells. You are God's temple; you don't belong to yourself anymore. God paid dearly for you, and you belong to God. Therefore, use your body not to shame God but to glorify God.

The Word of the Lord.

✠ *The Holy Gospel of Our Lord Jesus Christ According to John* [1:43–51]

Jesus decided to go to Galilee one day. There he found a man named Philip and said to him, "Follow me. Let's go!" Philip was from Andrew and Peter's hometown. Then Philip found Nathaniel and said, "We've found the Messiah, the one Moses and the prophets wrote about. His name is Jesus and he's from Nazareth."

Nathaniel said, "Nazareth? You're kidding! I can't believe anything good can be from Nazareth."

Philip said, "Well, come with me and we'll find out." When Jesus saw Nathaniel coming toward him, he said, "Now there's a good man, that Israelite walking my way." Nathaniel said, "How did you know me?" Jesus said, "I saw you standing under the fig tree before Philip came and got you." Nathaniel was so impressed by this he said, "Wow. You must be God's Son! You are the King of Israel!"

Jesus laughed. "Do you believe in me because I told you I saw you under the fig tree? Believe me, there are bigger and better things to come! You will see heaven opened and angels dancing with the Son of Man."

The Gospel of the Lord.

The Third Sunday after Epiphany

A Reading from the Book of Jonah [3:1–5, 10]

The word of God came to Jonah again, saying, "Get up already! Go to the great city of Ninevah, and tell them what I want you to tell them." So Jonah got up and went to Ninevah, just like God asked him to. Ninevah was a really big city. It would take three whole days just to walk from one edge to another. Jonah walked into the center of the city and yelled, "You've only got forty days to turn yourselves around, people, or you will be destroyed!" The people of Ninevah believed what Jonah was saying. They changed their ways and turned toward God. When God saw this and how they'd abandoned their evil ways, he changed his mind and didn't punish them as he had originally planned.

The Word of the Lord.

Psalm 62:6–14

I sit here waiting, silently. I'm waiting and hoping for God.
Only God is my rock, my salvation, the one I can hold on to
without being shaken off.

God has told me again and again, power belongs to God.

God is my strong rock and a place for me to feel secure.
I would put your trust in God if I were you, people.
Go ahead and pour out your heart to God, your safe place.

God has told me again and again, power belongs to God.

People who think they're special are like a breath that comes
only once.
Even not so special people can't be trusted.
In fact, if you put all of them together on a scale, they would be
lighter than a breath!

Stay away from blackmail, and robbery.
And even if you come into a lot of money, don't get too attached to it.
God's love is steadfast. You can count on God's love.

God has told me again and again, power belongs to God.

A Reading from the First Letter of Paul to the Corinthians [7:29–31]

Time is running out, brothers and sisters. We need to live as if everything matters. Because it does. Your wife should no longer be your main focus. Your grief shouldn't distract you, even your joys, and business, and shopping are not the main things in your life. Everything is different now. And things are changing quickly.

The Word of the Lord.

✠ *The Holy Gospel of Our Lord Jesus Christ According to Mark* [1:14–20]

After his cousin John the Baptist was arrested and thrown in jail, Jesus came to Galilee and picked up where John left off, proclaiming the Good News of God: "The time is right, people, and the kingdom of God is near. Turn yourselves around and believe this good news." As he was walking along the Sea of Galilee one day, he saw two fishermen, Simon and his brother, Andrew, throwing their nets into the sea. Jesus said to them, "If you follow me I'll show you how to fish for people." So they dropped their nets and followed him. A little farther down the shore, he saw some other fishermen, James and John, mending their nets. He called out to them, too, to follow him. They left their nets, their boat, and their father, Zebedee, along with his hired men, and followed Jesus.

The Gospel of the Lord.

The Fourth Sunday after the Epiphany

A Reading from the Book of Deuteronomy [18:15–20]

Moses called all the people together and said, "God is going to give you a prophet like me, and he will be one of you. You need to listen to him. This is what I heard you say: 'We will die if we can't hear God's voice or see the fire that means that God is with us.' I told God you said that. He said, 'Okay. I'll give them a prophet and I will put my words in his mouth, and he'll tell them everything I say to them. I'll hold them accountable if they don't listen to him, though. Don't listen to anyone else who says they speak for me, just know that they don't.'"

The Word of the Lord.

Psalm 111

Hallelujah. I'm going to thank God with everything I have and
everything I am,
right here in the middle of this congregation.
God has done really great things! You would do well to pay
attention to them.
God's works are full of majesty and splendor and power and
God's goodness never ends.

Knowing God is the beginning of wisdom.

God, you are full of compassion and grace.
You give food to those who follow you. You never forget
your promises.
You show your people your power, by giving them the land they
live in.

Knowing God is the beginning of wisdom.

The things you do with your very own hands are full of
faithfulness and justice. What you say is true.
The things you do will hold up because you do them in truth
and you are always fair.

Knowing God is the beginning of wisdom.

You have taken back your people for yourself.
Your promises go on forever.
Your name is holy and everything about you is awesome.
Knowing you is the beginning of wisdom,
and we all would be wise to act according to your ways.

Knowing God is the beginning of wisdom.

A Reading from the First Letter of Paul to the Corinthians [8:1–13]

You asked about the food that was given as offerings to other gods. Let me say this about that. Yes, we know that we all know what's right. But we have to use our knowledge well. Knowledge can puff us up and make us think we're better than we are. Love builds us up, rather than puffs us up. We know there is only one God, who created everything, and we know there is only one Jesus Christ, through whom we exist. But not everybody knows that.

Some people have become used to having other gods, even though those gods have no power at all. Eating food offered to them doesn't really matter. You need to pay attention to the feelings of other people, however. You don't want to trip them up on their way to the one God.

That's why I say it would be better if you didn't eat food offered to idols, so they don't get the wrong idea about who God really is and what God wants from them. That's why I never eat meat offered to idols, because I don't want them to be confused, turning away from the true God I want them to know.

The Word of the Lord.

✠ *The Holy Gospel of Our Lord Jesus Christ According to Mark* [1:21–28]

Jesus and his followers went into the synagogue at Capernaum. Jesus started teaching the people there and they were astounded by how much he knew. A man who was mentally ill walked into the synagogue while he was teaching and yelled, "What are you doing here, Jesus? Have you come to destroy us? I know who you are. You're the holy one of God." Jesus told him to quiet down and told the illness to come out of him. Just then, he convulsed and screeched, and then was healed of his illness. Everyone was amazed. "Wow," they said. "Jesus must know what he's talking about, and has authority to cure people." Word got out about what Jesus had done and everyone in Galilee began to talk about him.

The Gospel of the Lord.

The Fifth Sunday after the Epiphany

A Reading from the Book of Isaiah [40:21–31]

Haven't you heard? Don't you understand? Isn't this what you've heard all your life? God sees the whole earth like a ball of dirt, and those of us who live here are like insects on it. God stretches out the heavens like a curtain across the sky, and opens them up like a tent to camp in. God is mightier than any prince or king on earth. They are like seeds, which haven't yet taken root. When God blows on them, they shrivel up and the wind carries them off like dust.

"Is there anyone like me?" says the Holy One. "Before you answer that question, look at the stars and the mountains and ask yourself, so who made these? I made all the mountains and all the stars and call each of them by name. Why do you think you can hide from me, Jacob? Or that I don't care about what you do, Israel?"

Don't you get it? God, the creator of every single thing, also created you. God never gets tired, and knows everything and everybody. God is the one who can give you the courage and strength to do what you need to do.

Young men will run out of energy before God does. But if you turn to God he will give you what you need. You will be like a mighty eagle with wings that will take you anywhere. You will be like a runner that never gets tired, and your journey will never get old.

The Word of the Lord.

Psalm 147:1–12, 21b

Hallelujah! It feels so good to sing God's praises. It just feels right to honor God with our songs.
God is building things up again that have been torn down.
He is gathering the people who got scattered, is healing broken hearts, and is taking care of people's wounds.
God counts the stars in the skies one by one and calls them each by name.
The Word actually became one of us, and lived among us.

Our God is so incredibly great.
There is no limit to his wisdom.
Our God picks up people whose spirits are low and throws the bad ones to the ground.
Sing a song of thanksgiving to God and make beautiful music on your harp.
The Word actually became one of us, and lived among us.

God is the one who covers the heavens with clouds and gets the rain ready to fall to the earth.
God makes grass grow up on the mountains,
and all the green things that are good for us to eat.
God makes sure that there is food in the pasture for our flocks of sheep and herds of goats,
and provides food for crying baby birds when they're hungry.
The Word actually became one of us, and lived among us.

There's no point in showing off your biggest horse
or your strongest bodybuilder; God's not impressed.
God is impressed with people who wait on him patiently with faith and trust.
Jerusalem, worship the Lord. Zion, praise your God.
The Word actually became one of us, and lived among us.

A Reading from the First Letter of Paul to the Corinthians [9:16–23]

Just because I talk about what Jesus has said and what he means to me, that doesn't mean I should brag about it. It's like I can't help but talk about it. God has been so good to me, it's the only choice I have. It's my job to give away the Good News to everyone.

I could do anything I wanted, you know, but in order to reach more people with God's Good News, I meet people where they are so that I can understand them better and how to talk with them. It makes more sense to learn someone else's language before expecting them to understand mine. By being able to connect with people, it's like I'm living the Good News as well as talking about it!

The Word of the Lord.

✠ *The Holy Gospel of our Lord Jesus Christ According to Mark* [1:29–39]

After teaching in the synagogue one day, Jesus, James, and John went over to Simon and Andrew's house. Simon's mother-in-law was really sick with a fever. Jesus sat next to her and took her by the hand. He helped her get up, and the fever was gone! After that, she felt so good she made them a big dinner.

Later that night, it seemed everyone in the city came to the house. There were people who were sick, and it seemed some were possessed by demons. Jesus spent the evening curing people, and freeing people from their demons so they could live good lives again.

In the morning, before the sun rose, he was able to sneak out of the house alone. He went to a quiet place and prayed. Meanwhile, Simon and his friend were franticly searching for him. They finally found him, and said, "We've been looking all over for you. Everyone wanted to know where you were."

Jesus said, "Today, we're moving on to the next town, so I can tell them about God's love as well. Because that's what I'm here to do!" They went to the little towns in Galilee, proclaiming God's love in the synagogues and freeing people from their demons.

The Gospel of the Lord.

The Sixth Sunday after the Epiphany

A Reading from the Second Book of Kings [5:1–14]

Naaman was a really great general in his king's army. But he had a nasty rash on his skin. His wife had a helper who suggested he go see a healer in Samaria, so his rash would clear up.

Now Naaman wasn't sure his king would let him go to another country for a cure. But the king said, "Sure, go. I'll even send you a letter from me, along with 750 pounds of silver and 150 pounds of gold—so they'll know that you are friendly."

When Naaman got there, he gave the king of Israel the letter. It said, "This is my man, Naaman. Please make his rash go away. Thanks, King Aram."

That set the king of Israel off. "What? How am I supposed to heal him? I don't take orders from anyone. King Aram is just trying to pick a fight with me. This must be a trick."

Meanwhile, Elisha the prophet heard that the king was upset. He sent word to the king, "What are you so upset about? Calm down already. Send Naaman to me and I'll do what I can. I'll ask God to heal him and then they'll know who God is. It'll be fine."

So Naaman went to Elisha's house and knocked on the door. A servant came to the door and said, "Elisha says go to the Jordan River and dip yourself under the water seven times. You'll be good as new. Goodbye."

Now Naaman was uspet. "Why didn't Elisha come talk to me himself?" he said. "I am a very important man, you know. I thought he'd come and call on God's name and wave his hand over me and heal me on the spot. I came all this way. The Jordan River is dirty. I've got better rivers than that back home. I could have stayed home and bathed in them and saved myself the trip. This is really insulting."

And he stomped off in a huff.

His servants ran after him to calm him down. They said to him, "You know, he could have made it very difficult, and you would have done what he said. This is a simple solution. Swallow your pride. Get over yourself and go to the river. Wash and be clean. It couldn't hurt, and it might even feel good."

So he did. He dipped himself under the water seven times, just like Elisha told him to do. And his rash cleared up—all of it!

He ran back to Elisha and said, "I was wrong and you were right. Now I know that God helps you and that your God is good. Your God cured me. Let me give you this silver and gold as a thank-you gift."

Elisha said, "No, thank you. I won't take your gift. It is enough for me to see you healed and to see that you believe in the one true God." Naaman said, "Well, if you won't take anything, let me ask you for something. Let me take a big pile of dirt from where you live, where your God helps you, and then I'll feel like I'm taking a piece of God back home with me. I will never worship another God again. This dirt will remind me of the good you and God did for me here."

The Word of the Lord.

Psalm 30 (see The Great Vigil of Easter, Year A, p. 105)

A Reading from the First Letter of Paul to the Corinthians [9:24–27]

You know that in a race, even though everybody in the race is running, only one is going to be first across the line and win first prize. Think about being in a race. Do everything you can to win first place. Train yourself well. Athletes train hard and they receive a bouquet of flowers that will just die soon. We're running a race and the prize for finishing is being with God forever! So I train hard and run well so that no one will disqualify me.

The Word of the Lord.

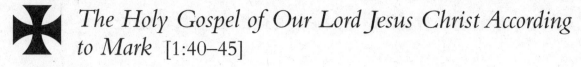

✠ *The Holy Gospel of Our Lord Jesus Christ According to Mark* [1:40–45]

A man with a skin disease came on his knees to Jesus, begging him, "I know if you want, you can heal me and I can get back to my life. People will consider me clean again." Jesus was moved with pity for this man. He stretched out his hand and touched him. "Of course I choose to heal you. Be healed. Be clean!" At once he was cured of his disease, and he was made clean. Jesus told him, "Don't say anything to anybody. But get yourself to the priest and show him that you're cured, because that's what Moses' law tells you to do."

The man didn't listen to him. He started telling everyone he saw about how Jesus had cured him. Then those people told other people and pretty soon Jesus couldn't go anywhere without people recognizing him. So he stayed in the countryside, where there were fewer people. But word got around, and people came looking for him from all over the country.

The Gospel of the Lord.

The Seventh Sunday after the Epiphany

A Reading from the Book of Isaiah [43:18–25]

"Forget what used to be. Don't get stuck in the past. Because I am about to do something brand new," says God. "It's on its way. Can you tell? I will make a road through the wilderness and rivers in the desert. The wild animals will bow down to me; even the jackrabbits and the ostriches because I make water flow in the wilderness, and rivers in the desert, to give drink to my people, so that I might hear them sing my praise. The animals love me, but you did not call upon me, Jacob; and you seem to be tired of me, Israel! You have not honored me with your sacrifices. What's going on with you?

You don't listen to me, but you expect me to listen to the endless stories of your sin. And you've got a lot to tell. I will erase the memory of all of them. I want to forget them so I will.

The Word of the Lord.

Psalm 41

God pays attention to you when you pay attention to those who are poor.
If you honor those who struggle to makes ends meet,
it will make you a better person. A happy person too.
God watches out for those who are compassionate.
You can count on God when you're in trouble or sick.
Don't be afraid to admit to God the things you have done wrong.
Ask God to be gracious to you. Tell God you know you need healing and that you count on it.
People who don't like you will always give you grief.
They whisper about you behind your back and mock you to your face.

They figure out how to make you look stupid.
Sometimes you can't even count on friends to be there for you.
But you, God, I expect you to be gracious and good to me.
Make me strong when people mock me.
Don't let them win.
You know that I walk with integrity
and want to be yours forever.
Bless you God. Bless you forever.
Amen.

A Reading from the Second Letter of Paul to the Corinthians [1:18–22]

God is faithful. God's Word for your lives is always YES. That is very clear. All of God's promises to you are good and every one of them is a YES because of Jesus. God's mark is on you, and you are anointed just as God anointed Jesus. We have the Holy Spirit in our hearts now, as the first payment on all of God's promises.

The Word of the Lord.

✠ *The Holy Gospel of Our Lord Jesus Christ According to Mark* [2:1–12]

Jesus was at home in Capernaum. Crowds gathered around, and blocked the door to the house because they wanted to listen to him teach. Four men tried to get through the door with their paralyzed friend, but couldn't make their way through the crowd. So they got up on the roof, made a hole in the roof, and lowered the man on a bed through the hole. He ended up right in front of Jesus! Jesus was amazed at the work they went to so they could help their friend, and their belief that Jesus could heal him. Jesus said to the man on the bed, "Son, your sins are forgiven. All is right with God."

Some people were wondering to themselves, "Who does this guy think he is, forgiving sins? That's God's job, and no one else. That's outrageous."

Jesus knew they were talking about him and he said to them, "What is your problem anyway? Which is easier, to say to a man who can't walk, 'Your sins are forgiven,' or to say, 'Stand up and pick up your mat and walk out of here'? But so that you can make the connection that the Son of Man (that's me) has authority on earth to forgive sins"—he said to the man who couldn't walk—"I say to you, get up, pick up your bed so no one trips on it, and go home." And the man stood up, immediately took his bed, and walked out right before them all. They were all shocked. They praised God, saying, "Can you believe what we just saw? Have you ever seen anything like that before?"

The Gospel of the Lord.

The Eighth Sunday after the Epiphany

A Reading from the Book of Hosea [2:14–20]

"I want to bring the one I love back to me. I want to give her hope and vineyards that will produce beautiful fruit. I want her to be the one I fell in love with so long ago." Just like a husband runs after his wife who has left him, and says, "Please come home, I love you," God says to us, "You are my people. I want you to be mine again. Please don't look for love any other place. I will promise to love you and I will end all the violence and let you rest without being scared. I will keep you as my own forever, and you will know how much I love you."

The Word of the Lord.

Psalm 103:1–13, 22

Bless God,
everything inside me, bless God's name.
Bless God,
and don't forget all that God has done for you.
God forgives all your sins.
God heals all your diseases.

God lifts you up when you're down,
and pours love and mercy all over you.

God gives you good things for as long as you live
so that you will be young and strong like an eagle flying overhead.
God works things out and wants justice for those who are under
someone else's thumb.

Moses came to know God
and the people who knew Moses knew God.

**God lifts you up when you're down,
and pours love and mercy all over you.**

God is kind and full of mercy and is patient with us.
God's heart overflows with love.
He doesn't always see the bad things we do
and doesn't stay angry with us for very long.
God doesn't give us the punishment we might deserve.

**God lifts you up when you're down,
and pours love and mercy all over you.**

As high as the highest heaven, that's how much God loves us.
As far as one end of the earth to the other, that's how far God throws our sin.
As much as a father loves his children, and will do anything for them, that's how much God cares for us.
So, bless you, God. Bless all that you do and all the places we find you.
Bless God, my soul.

**God lifts you up when you're down,
and pours love and mercy all over you.**

A Reading from the Second Letter of Paul to the Corinthians [3:1–6]

Do we have to reintroduce ourselves to you and prove who we are again? You are our letter of introduction. You are the proof that our message is from God and what we say is true. You are a letter from Christ, prepared by us but written on our hearts by God's Holy Spirit. God has given us this confidence. God has made us messengers of his promise as we carry God's

Spirit with us. God's Spirit brings new life wherever we deliver it like a letter.

The Word of the Lord.

✠ *The Holy Gospel of Our Lord Jesus Christ According to Mark* [2:13–22]

Jesus went out again beside the sea and was surrounded by a crowd of people as he taught. As he walked along he saw Levi, who collected taxes, sometimes taking more from people than he should have. Jesus said, "Come with me. Follow where I go." So Levi got up and followed Jesus. Jesus went to Levi's house and lots of tax collectors and sinners followed him there for dinner. When the church authorities found out, they were upset that he was eating with people known to be sinners.

When Jesus heard that they were upset with him, he said, "Listen, if you are perfectly healthy, you don't need a doctor, do you? But you really need a doctor when you're sick! That's what I'm doing here. I'm here to help sinners. They're the ones who need me. Not the perfect people."

Everyone was fasting (not eating in order to get closer to God). People came to Jesus and said, "So John's people fast, and the church authorities fast, why don't your followers fast?"

Jesus said, "Why would they need to get closer to God when I'm right here with them? I won't be here with them forever. If you're going to make some wine, you need new skins to put it in, because it will expand and burst old skins and then you won't have any wine at all. If you want new wine, find some new skins. You need to pay attention to how you do things as well as what you believe. What you do needs to match what you believe."

The Gospel of the Lord.

The Last Sunday after the Epiphany

A Reading from the Second Book of Kings [2:1–12]

God was planning on taking Elijah up to heaven by a whirlwind. Elijah and Elisha were walking together, when Elijah said, "You stay here, because you're not supposed to go any further. Let me go ahead." But Elisha said, "What? I'm not going anywhere without you. I'm not leaving you behind." So they kept on walking together. The prophets there came out to Elisha because they'd heard that Elijah was going to be taken to heaven by a whirlwind. "Elisha," they said, "Do you know that today God is going to take Elijah, your master, away from you?" Elisha told them to hush. He already knew.

Elijah said to him, "Elisha, stay here; God is sending me to Jericho." But Elisha said, "I told you, there's no way I am leaving you." So they went to Jericho together.

Once again the prophets came out to warn Elisha that God was going to take Elijah to himself in a whirlwind. And once again Elisha told them he knew, but they should keep quiet about it.

Then Elijah said, "Stay here; for now God is sending me to the Jordan." But Elisha said, "I'm not leaving you. Let's go to the Jordan." They started walking and fifty of the prophets went to see what was going to happen. They saw Elijah take off his cloak and roll it up and hit the water with it, and the water moved so that they could walk on dry land right through the middle of the river. (Just like the Israelites did in the Red Sea!)

On the other side of the river, Elijah said to Elisha, "Before God takes me, tell me what I can do for you." Elisha said, "The only thing I ask for is twice the amount of Holy Spirit that God has given you. That's the only thing I want." Elijah said, "That's a hard thing to give you! If you see me as God takes me to heaven, then you'll get what you ask for."

As they kept walking and talking, a chariot and horses made of fire came between the two of them, and Elijah went up into heaven in a whirlwind. Elisha kept watching and crying out, "Father, father! The chariots of Israel and its horsemen!" He saw it all. And when Elijah was gone he tore the clothes he was wearing, and began to cry.

The Word of the Lord.

Psalm 50:1–6

God, you're always talking to your creation!
You call to the sun to have it rise,
and then to put it to bed again at the end of the day.

God has spoken. God's glory is in creation for us to see.

When you come, you will not be quiet about it.
A bright flame will go before you and you'll be surrounded
by a raging thunderstorm.
You will call everyone and everything together to witness.
You call to the heavens and the earth from above.

God has spoken. God's glory is in creation for us to see.

We watch you deal with your people.
"I want to be surrounded by those who love me and have made
a commitment to me."
We can hear the heavens shouting that you are a fair judge
and that you always keep your word.

God has spoken. God's glory is in creation for us to see.

A Reading from the Second Letter of Paul to the Corinthians [4:3–6]

If you can't understand the good news we've brought you, it's not because we're hiding its meaning. You can't see very well because you live in the darkness. The Good News of Jesus is the light that will help you see. This is not about us. It's about Jesus. We will do what we can for you, so that you will be able to understand. God turned the light on in our hearts, so that when look at Jesus, we see the face of God.

The Word of the Lord.

✠ *The Holy Gospel of Our Lord Jesus Christ According to Mark* [9:2–9]

Jesus took Peter and James and John up the mountain with him one day. As they were looking at him, it seemed like he turned into a different person. His clothes were dazzling white and he was shining from the inside out. Then Moses and Elijah were there with him, and the three of them were talking together. Peter got really excited and said, "This is so good, I think I should build a house for each of you so we can always be here together." It was a stupid thing to say, but Peter always blurted out silly things when he was scared. They were all terrified at what was happening. A cloud came over them and a voice from inside the cloud said, "This is my Son, and I love him. Listen to him." Then, when they looked around, Elijah and Moses were gone. Only Jesus was with them. As they were coming down the mountain, Jesus told them not to say a word about what they had just seen, until after he had been raised from the dead.

The Gospel of the Lord.

Ash Wednesday (see Year A, p. 54)

The First Sunday in Lent

A Reading from the Book of Genesis [9:8–17]

After the floodwaters had gone away, God said to Noah and his sons, "Here's the deal. I'm establishing an agreement with you and your children and with every creature in that big boat. I will never again destroy the earth with floodwaters. Here's a sign of my commitment to you; I'm putting a rainbow in the clouds. Every time you see a rainbow, know that I remember the deal we've made, and the commitment I have to you and all the animals on the earth.

The Word of the Lord.

Psalm 25:1–9

My soul is in the palm of my hands, God,
and I'm lifting it up to give it to you. I trust you with it, God.
I trust that you won't let them make fun of me, or humiliate me.
Don't let those of us who count on you be put to shame.
Let the plans of the wicked, sneaky people fall to pieces.

Show me how to follow your path.
I want to walk in love and faithfulness.

Lead me in your truth and teach me.
You are the God who saves me. I've trusted you ever since
  I can remember.
Your compassion and love have no beginning and will have
  no end. They go on forever.
Don't remember the things I've done wrong.

Instead remember that you love me because you are kind and good.

Show me how to follow your path.
I want to walk in love and faithfulness.

God, you are gracious and the only one who can teach us the right way to live. You are willing to guide those who are willing to learn.
The paths that lead in your direction are love and faithfulness.
Those who are in relationship with you will always walk in your direction.

Show me how to follow your path.
I want to walk in love and faithfulness.

A Reading from the First Letter of Peter [3:18–22]

Christ became a man and suffered like a man for our sins—the sins of the righteous and the unrighteous, too—in order to bring us in relationship with God. Even though his body died, his spirit was made alive. After he died, he visited those who had died but were waiting for him. Baptism is important and saves you, not because it washes your body clean with water, but because it offers you to God with a clean spirit through Jesus, who is alive now, and in heaven sitting right next to God, surrounded by angels.

The Word of the Lord.

The Holy Gospel of Our Lord Jesus Christ According to Mark
[1:9–15]

Jesus came from Nazareth to the Jordan River to be baptized by his cousin John. Just as he was coming up out of the water, he saw the clouds ripped open and the Holy Spirit flew from heaven and landed on him like a dove. Then he heard this voice out of the clouds, "You, Jesus, are my Son, and I love you very much. I am so very pleased with you. Don't you forget that." Then the Spirit drove him right then into the wilderness, beyond where anyone lived. He was there for forty days, and was tempted by Satan himself. But he wasn't alone. He was with the wild beasts who became his friends. And angels came to care for him when he was sore and tired and hungry.

When he left the wilderness, he heard that John had been arrested for the things he was saying about the king. Jesus went to Galilee, where he was from, and he told people God's Good News. "The time has finally come, people," Jesus said, "and God's kingdom is so very close and real. Turn in God's direction, and believe in God's Good News."

The Gospel of the Lord.

The Second Sunday in Lent

A Reading from the Book of Genesis [17:1–7, 15–16]

When Abram was ninety-nine years old, God came to him said, "I am God Almighty. Come with me. Be holy. I will promise to always be your God, and I will make sure you have many children, and your children will have many children."

Abram was so surprised that he fell on his face when he heard this. God said, "Here's the agreement I'm making with you. You will be the ancestor of many, many different kinds of people. I'm going to call you Abraham, not Abram anymore. You will be blessed. Some of your children and grandchildren will be kings. And my promise will live on in all of them. I will always be your God and their God."

God said to Abraham, "And your wife, Sarai, I'm going to call her Sarah from now on. I will bless her, and she will have a son. She will be the mother of many people and kings as well."

The Word of the Lord.

Psalm 22:22–30

If you say you love God,
then you should start singing songs to God.
Because I think God is awesome
and you should too, all of you who've ever known God.
Everyone drop what you're doing and sing praises to God.

God does awesome things.
God pays attention to poor people when we don't.
And doesn't hide from poor people like we do.
God always hears them when they pray.
If you say you love God join me in singing praises loud and long whether you sing well or not.

God doesn't care if you can't sing
or even if you can.
You also praise God when you make sure
everyone has enough to eat.
Make sure everyone knows
how good God has been to you.

If you say you love God, sing God's praises with me.
God loves it when we sing.

Everyone, everywhere, has God in their heart.
Sometimes they don't even know.
God is everywhere, and for everyone.
Everyone who has ever lived owes their life to God.
Deep in my heart I give myself to God
and hope my kids and their kids do too.

Sing praises with me; God loves to hear us sing.

A Reading from the Letter of Paul to the Romans [4:13–25]

It wasn't the fact that he obeyed the law that made God promise Abraham he would be the father of many people, but because he was righteous. If it takes obedience to the law, then faith doesn't mean anything and the promise is no good. Promise depends on faith. We look to Abraham as a model for our faith. There was no reason for him to hope he would have a child with his wife, Sarah. But God had promised him he would be "the father of many nations." He was convinced that God would make good on his promise. And God did!

God rewarded Abraham's faith with a child. With millions of children! God will make good on the promise that our Lord Jesus has made us right with God through his death and resurrection.

The Word of the Lord.

✠ *The Holy Gospel of Our Lord Jesus Christ According to Mark* [8:31–38]

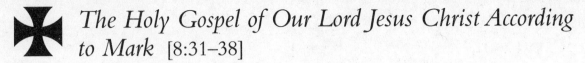

Jesus told his followers that soon he would suffer under the hands of the people in charge, that he would be rejected by them all and then killed. But that after three days he would come to life again. He didn't try to keep it a secret. Peter took him aside and jumped all over him for saying this. Jesus looked them all right in the eye and turned to Peter and said, "Get behind me, Satan! We're not talking about the same thing. Your thinking is about what humans want. My thinking is about what God wants." Then Jesus gathered the crowd around him and his followers, "If any of you really want to follow me, you have to put your own wants aside, and walk with me carrying your cross. If you mainly want to save your life, you'll end up losing it. Those who lose the life they're living on account of me and God's message of love, will save it. After all, what's the point of having everything in the world you could want, but then losing your life? Don't be ashamed of me and what I've taught you, and I won't be ashamed of you when I return in glory with the angels at the end."

The Gospel of the Lord.

The Third Sunday in Lent

A Reading from the Book of Exodus [20:1–7]

Moses was on Mount Sinai and here's what God said to him, "I'm the Lord your God who rescued you from slavery in Egypt; I'm the only God you should have. I'm the one you should teach your children to love and respect. Here are my guidelines for you to live with each other in peace. Don't use my name for your own purposes or to put on a show. Put aside one day especially for me, and keep it holy and restful. Give both your parents the honor they deserve. Don't kill. Don't be unfaithful to your husband or wife. Don't be greedy and want what your neighbor has."

The Word of the Lord.

Psalm 19 (see Proper 22, Year A, p. 192)

A Reading from the Second Letter of Paul to the Corinthians [1:18–25]

If you tell people about Jesus and how he died on the cross, it sounds ridiculous. But you and I get it. Jesus lived and died for us, and God's power is in that story! God's power makes us wise. So who's ridiculous now? God saves us even when we are ridiculous and then fills us with the power of Jesus' story. Ridiculous or not, God is wiser and more powerful than any human who ignores him.

The Word of the Lord.

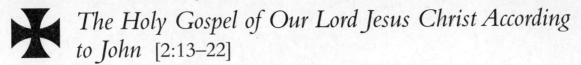

✠ *The Holy Gospel of Our Lord Jesus Christ According to John* [2:13–22]

Jesus was in Jerusalem at Passover time and he went to the temple. There he found people selling cows and sheep and doves for the temple sacrifice, and money exchangers. It made him angry. He took a whip and chased everyone out of the temple, with it, even the sheep and cows and doves. Then he went around and flipped over the tables that people were sitting at to exchange money. He shouted, "Why are you in my Father's house pretending it's a place to make money instead of seeing it as God's special place?"

"What do you think you're doing? Are you crazy?" said the Jews who saw all this.

Jesus said, "If you destroy this temple, I will put it back together in three days."

The Gospel of the Lord.

The Fourth Sunday in Lent

A Reading from the Book of Numbers [21:4–9]

God's people were on their way to the Red Sea. It was taking a really long time to get to the Promised Land and the people were getting cranky. They whined to Moses and to God, "Why, oh why did you take us out of Egypt and bring us here to the desert? So we could die out here? There's no food and no water, and besides that, the food we get is miserable."

Then things got even worse for them. Snakes started swirling around their feet and bit some people and they died. That got people thinking they had been wrong to complain. They said to Moses, "We're sorry we were grumbling to you and God. Please make the snakes go away." So Moses prayed and asked God to make the snakes go away.

God said, "Make a snake and put it on a pole for everyone to see. Then if they get bit, they can look at this snake on the pole, and they won't die." Moses made a snake out of brass and put it on a pole and sure enough, people didn't die when the snakes bit them.

The Word of the Lord.

Psalm 107:1–3, 17–22

If God has been good to you, you should talk about it.
God was good to our ancestors.
God rescued people from the most awful places all over the world.
Some of them were fools and didn't appreciate that
and turned away from the God who saved them.

Thanks, God; you are so good. There is no limit to your love!

Things didn't work out so well for them.
They grumbled about the food and wouldn't eat
and almost starved to death.
Then they turned back towards God and God came and saved them again.
God's Word healed them and put them back on their feet.
I hope they know what great things God has done for them and will thank God with prayers and shouts of joy.

Thanks, God; you are so good. There is no limit to your love!

A Reading from the Letter of Paul to the Ephesians [2:1–10]

The way you were living before you knew Jesus Christ was almost like you were dying inside. Just doing whatever feels good without thinking about anyone but yourself is not a good way to live. We all have a tendency to be that way. But God, whose love for us never ends no matter how we act, has made us alive again, together in Jesus. By God's grace we have been saved from ourselves! And we can be different now and live differently now. The way Jesus lived. Believing in God's goodness shows us the way to God and the way to walk with God in our hearts. Having God in our hearts is a gift. There's nothing we could do to earn it, and there's nothing we can do to make God go away. We are whom God has made us, and in Jesus Christ we can do great things for people in need, as God has always wanted us to do.

The Word of the Lord.

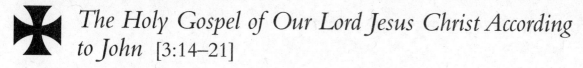

✠ *The Holy Gospel of Our Lord Jesus Christ According to John* [3:14–21]

Just as Moses put that snake on a pole in the desert for everyone to see and be saved, I will be lifted up so that everyone who looks at me and believes in me will have a life that never ends. God loved this world and everything and everyone in it so much, that he sent his only son—("That's me," Jesus said)—into the world. And everyone who believes in me can live an eternal life. I didn't come here to put you down, but to raise you up and save you from yourselves.

I am the light that has come into the world. Sometimes people would prefer darkness even when they could have light, so that no one sees what they're doing. But you don't need to be afraid of being in the light. It will show everyone that God is in your hearts and God is in the things you do.

The Gospel of the Lord.

The Fifth Sunday in Lent

A Reading from the Book of Jeremiah [31:31–34]

I tell you, very soon I will make a new agreement with you. It won't be like the agreement I made with your fathers, when I had to take them by the hand and lead them out of Egypt. They broke that agreement. Here's the new deal—I will put my word inside your hearts! And I will be your God and you will be my people. You won't even have to teach each other about me, because all of you will know me! Even the little kids. I will forget all that was wrong between us, and we'll start all over again.

The Word of the Lord.

Psalm 51:1–13

God, I know you are loving and kind. Now I need your mercy
and forgiveness.
Wipe away what I've done wrong.
Scrub me clean, God.
Wash the wickedness right off me.
I know what I've done. In fact, I can't get it off my mind.
You are the one I have hurt.
You know what I've done.

Scrub me clean, God.
Wash the wickedness right off me.

You are so right to call me out on my sin.
You see and tell the truth.
It seems I've never been able to walk the right path,
even before I was born!

Scrub me clean, God.
Wash the wickedness right off me.

You look deep inside me for the truth that's in there.
Make me understand the truth you find.
Clean the house of my soul, and it will be clean.
If you do the washing, I know I will sparkle inside.

Scrub me clean, God.
Wash the wickedness right off me.

Make me feel joy again. Let me hear happy songs
so that my sad, tired body can rejoice again.
Don't look at my sin. Turn your face away from me.
Make my sin go away.
Then there will be space inside for a brand new, clean heart.
Then my spirit can start all over again, the right way.

Scrub me clean, God.
Wash the wickedness right off me.

Don't send me away from you, wherever you are, God.
Don't take your special Holy Spirit away from me.
Once again, give me the great joy knowing that you are saving me.
Keep me going with that help that your Spirit never stops giving.

Scrub me clean, God.
Wash the wickedness right off me.

A Reading from the Letter to the Hebrews [5:5–10]

Jesus didn't make himself a priest. No, God appointed him. "You are my Son," said God. "You are a priest forever." Jesus was the best priest, offering prayers to God, pleading for us, and God heard him. He learned through Jesus' suffering. He became the one who leads us to our salvation.

The Word of the Lord.

✠ *The Holy Gospel of Our Lord Jesus Christ According to John* [12:20–33]

People from all over had gathered in Jerusalem for a festival. Some Greek people came up to Philip, one of Jesus' disciples, and said, "Sir, we would like to see Jesus." So Philip and his brother Andrew went to tell Jesus there were people to see him. Jesus said, "I think my time to be glorified has finally come. You know, one grain of wheat is just one grain of wheat, unless you bury it in the ground. Just when you think it's dead, it starts to grow and you have more and more wheat. That's how it is with your life. If you cling so closely to the life you know, you're going to lose it. But those who are ready to turn away from their life to follow me will have a life that is eternal. If you want to follow me, serve me wherever you find me. God will honor you.

"My soul is agitated. Do I dare say, 'Father, don't make me go through with this? Save me?' No, I won't do that. This is my purpose. Father, let me bring only glory to your name." All of a sudden a voice from heaven said, "I have glorified it and I will glorify it again."

The crowd couldn't believe what they just heard. "It must have been thunder," somebody said.

"No, I think it was an angel talking to him," somebody else said.

Jesus told them, "That voice was for your benefit, not mine. This will be a turning point for this world; when I am lifted up high above the earth, I will gather all people everywhere to myself." He said this because he knew he was about to die on the cross.

The Gospel of the Lord.

The Sunday of the Passion: Palm Sunday

At the Liturgy of the Palms

✠ *The Holy Gospel of Our Lord Jesus Christ According to Mark* [11:1–11]

Jesus and his disciples were getting close to Jerusalem. When they were near the Mount of Olives, Jesus sent two of the disciples into the village ahead. He told them, "Right as you get into the village, you'll find a donkey that has never been ridden before. Untie him and bring him back to me. Someone might ask what you think you're doing. Just tell them, 'The Lord needs it and we'll bring it back.'" So they went into the village and it happened just as Jesus had told them it would.

They brought the donkey to Jesus and put their coats on it for him to sit on. As Jesus rode into Jerusalem, people spread their coats on the road in front of him. Others laid down branches from the field. Everyone was shouting and singing, "Hosanna! Blessed is the one who comes in the name of the Lord. Blessed is the Son of David, Hosanna!"

Once he was in Jerusalem, he went to the temple. Then he saw it was getting late, so he went to Bethany with his twelve disciples.

The Gospel of the Lord.

At the Liturgy of the Word

A Reading from the Book of Isaiah [50:4–9a] (see Palm Sunday Year A, p. 79)

Psalm 31:9–16 (see Palm Sunday, Year A, p. 80)

A Reading from the Book of Philippians [2:5–11] (see Palm Sunday, Year A, p. 81)

✠ *The Holy Gospel of Our Lord Jesus Christ According to Mark* [14:1–15:47]

Two days before Passover, Jesus' enemies were trying to figure out how they could arrest Jesus and have him killed without causing the people to get too upset.

When Jesus was visiting friends in Bethany, as he was sitting at the dinner table, a woman came in with a beautiful jar of very expensive ointment. She broke the jar open and poured the ointment on his head. Some people in the room saw that and said, "Why would you spend so much money on this, when you might have given it to the poor instead?" Jesus told them to leave her alone, that she was doing what she could to honor him, and get him ready for what was to come. "Let me tell you, people are going to be talking for a very long time about what she did here for me tonight."

Judas Iscariot, one of Jesus' twelve disciples, told Jesus' enemies where they might find him and arrest him. They were thrilled to get this information from Judas and promised him money if he would deliver Jesus to them.

While they were eating their Passover dinner, Jesus said, "You know, one of you is going to hand me over to my enemies." That upset all of them. Jesus continued, "It's one of you who is eating with me tonight. It would have been better if that person had never been born."

As they were eating, Jesus picked up a loaf of bread, blessed it, broke it into pieces, and gave it to them, saying, "Eat this. It's my body." Then he picked up a cup of wine, thanked God for it, and had all of them drink from it. "This," he said, "is my blood, a new agreement with God and everyone. I won't share wine with you again until the kingdom of heaven comes to pass."

After dinner they sang songs, and then went to the Mount of Olives. Jesus told them there that they would all desert him just as the scriptures had said they would. "After I'm raised from the dead, I will meet you in Galilee." Peter said, "Even if everyone else leaves you, I would never leave you." Jesus replied, "Really? You won't even make it through this evening before denying you ever knew me. Before the rooster crows twice, you will say three times that you never knew me." Peter insisted that he would die before denying he knew Jesus. And all the disciples said the same.

Then they went to a garden called Gethsemane. Jesus told the disciples to sit and pray while he went farther ahead to be alone and pray. For hours he prayed that God would keep his arrest and death from happening. "It is up to you, Father," Jesus said. "I will do what you want me to do."

When he was done praying, he went back to find the disciples and they were fast asleep. "Peter," Jesus said, "couldn't you even stay awake for an hour while I prayed?"

Jesus returned to his quiet spot and kept on praying for strength for the dark hours ahead. When returning to the disciples, he found them sleepy again. He went back to pray a third time. After that, he woke up the disciples and told them the time to sleep was over. His time to be handed over to his enemies had come.

Just then, Judas Iscariot showed up with an army of men sent by Jesus' enemies with swords and clubs. Judas had told them that the man he would kiss would be Jesus. So Judas went up to Jesus, called him "Rabbi," and gave him a kiss. The soldiers arrested Jesus, knowing he was the one they were looking for.

One of the disciples took out his sword and cut off the ear of one of the slaves. Then Jesus said to soldiers, "Have you come out with swords and clubs to arrest me as though I were a thug?

I've been teaching in the temple every day. Why didn't you come and get me there? But this is the way the scriptures said it would be." And right then all the disciples ran away, leaving Jesus there by himself.

They took Jesus to the high priest where all the authorities were gathered. Peter followed at a distance, right into the courtyard of the high priest. He sat down next to the fire to warm himself alongside the guards.

Jesus' enemies were trying to find testimony against Jesus so they could put him to death, but they couldn't find any. Some people stood up to talk about Jesus, but their stories didn't match, so their testimony was thrown out.

Then the high priest asked Jesus, "Don't you have anything to say about these stories we hear about you?" Jesus said nothing. Again the high priest asked him, "Are you the Messiah, the Son of the Blessed One?" Jesus said, "I am; and

'you will see the Son of Man
seated at the right hand of the Power,'
and 'coming with the clouds of heaven.'"

Then the high priest said, "That's all I need to hear. It sure sounds like he thinks he's God's son and to say that is against our law!" All of them said Jesus deserved to die. Some began to spit on him, to blindfold him, and to strike him, saying to him, "Tell us more, prophet of God!" The guards took him away to beat him.

Meanwhile a servant girl saw Peter in the courtyard. She stared at him as if she recognized him. She said, "Hey, you. You were with Jesus, weren't you?" Peter said, "I don't know what you're talking about." Just then Peter heard the rooster crow.

The servant girl started telling people that Peter was one of Jesus' disciples. Again he said that he was not.

Peter tried to get away but others said to him, "Sure you are. You are from Galilee just like the rest of Jesus' followers." Peter starting cursing and swore to God, saying "I have no idea who this Jesus is that you're talking about." Just then the rooster crowed a second time, just like Jesus said it would. And Peter broke down and cried.

In the morning, the chief priests and the rest of them had a meeting. They tied Jesus' hands together, led him away, and took him to Pilate, a Roman governor.

Pilate asked him, "Are you the king of the Jews?" Jesus said, "You say so." The chief priests started listing all their charges against him. Pilate said, "Listen to all their accusations against you. What do you have to say for yourself?" Pilate was surprised that Jesus had nothing to say.

It was tradition to release a prisoner for the people during this Passover festival time. They could choose who they wanted released. Pilate asked the crowd of people, "Do you want me to release the King of the Jews?" The chief priests talked the people into asking that Barabbas, a murderer, be released instead of Jesus. Pilate asked them what they wanted him to do with Jesus, the King of the Jews. The crowd said, "Put him to death on a cross." Pilate asked them why he should do that, since he couldn't see that Jesus had done anything wrong. The crowd shouted, "We want you to crucify him!" Pilate wanted to keep the crowd happy, so he released the murderer Barabbas. He had Jesus whipped and sent him to be nailed to a cross.

The soldiers decided to have some fun with Jesus after they whipped him and beat him. The put a purple robe on him, made a fake crown of thorns and pushed it onto his head. They saluted him, saying, "Hail, King of the Jews." They spit on him. When they were done mocking him, they put his own clothes back on and took him to crucify him. Jesus was too weak to carry his own cross to the place where they crucified people, so they found Simon of Cyrene in the crowd and got him to carry the cross for Jesus. When they got to Golgotha, they offered Jesus some wine to ease his pain, but he refused it. They nailed him to the cross, and divided his clothes between themselves.

This happened at nine o'clock in the morning. A sign was hung over his head that read, "The King of the Jews." Two thugs were crucified right next to Jesus. People walked by and shouted to Jesus, "Save yourself if you're the Son of God. Fool." The chief priests mocked him too, saying, "He saved others but can't do anything to save himself." Even those on the crosses next to him made fun of him.

At noon, the whole world went dark until three o'clock in the afternoon. Jesus yelled out to God, "Why have you left me all alone? Where are you, God?" Someone got him a sponge full of sour wine for him to drink. Then Jesus cried out one last time and took his last breath. A Roman soldier who was at the foot of the cross and had seen and heard all of this, said, "Jesus really was God's Son."

Many women who supported Jesus were there watching from a distance: Mary Magdalene; Mary, mother of James; and a woman named Salome.

After Jesus died, a man named Joseph of Arimathea asked Pilate if he could take Jesus' body and bury it. He wrapped the body in a linen cloth and laid it in a grave that had been carved in the rock in the hillside. He rolled a stone against the door to the grave. Mary Magdalene and Mary the mother of Joses saw where Jesus' body was laid.

Maundy Thursday (See Maundy Thursday Year A, p. 83)

Good Friday (See Good Friday, Year A, p. 86)

The Great Vigil of Easter (see Year A, p. 94)

Easter Day

A Reading from the Acts of the Apostles [10: 34–43]
(see First Sunday after the Epiphany, Year A, p. 27)

Psalm 118:1–2, 14–24 (see Easter Day, Year A, p. 110)

A Reading from the First Letter of Paul to the Corinthians [15:1–11]

Remember, my friends, the Good News that I brought you, which is saving you—I hope you still remember it. I gave you all the Good News I could, that Jesus Christ died for our sins just like the scripture said, that he was raised on the third day and appeared to over five hundred people, most of whom are still alive. You can talk to them about it. Then he appeared to James and all the apostles. Finally, he appeared to me. I know I am the least likely apostle, because I tried to kill off the church of God. God's grace made me who I am today, and I'm not wasting that gift. I work as hard as any of the apostles, only because of God's grace. It doesn't matter who brought you the Good News, it only matters that you believe it.

The Word of the Lord.

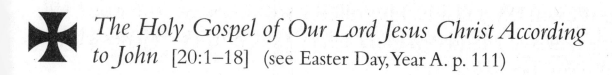

✠ *The Holy Gospel of Our Lord Jesus Christ According to John* [20:1–18] (see Easter Day, Year A. p. 111)

The Second Sunday of Easter

A Reading from the Acts of the Apostles [4:32–35]

All of the believers at that time were of one heart and soul, and no one claimed their own things only for themselves. Everything they had they shared with each other! The apostles powerfully witnessed to Jesus' resurrection, and all of them shared a great measure of grace. No one among them was poor, because those who owned land or houses sold them, and then gave the proceeds to the apostles to share with people who needed it most.

The Word of the Lord.

Psalm 133 (see Proper 15, Year A, p. 171)

A Reading from First Letter of John [1:1–2:2]

We've been telling you all along, this is what we have heard and seen with our very own eyes, what we actually touched with our hands. Life is eternal in God the Father. God has revealed this to us. We want you to join with us in this eternal life, just as we've joined with God. God is light. There is no darkness at all in God. If we walk in God's path we won't be walking in darkness either. If we think we don't sin though, if we think we don't put up any barriers between God and us, we're just fooling ourselves. However, if we admit who we are and what we do, God will forgive us and we can move on. Jesus talks to God on our behalf, and on behalf of everyone in the world. This is so that we all may be right with God.

The Word of the Lord.

✠ *The Holy Gospel of Our Lord Jesus Christ According to John* [20:19–31] (see Second Sunday of Easter, Year A, p. 114)

The Third Sunday of Easter

A Reading from the Acts of the Apostles [3:12–19]

Peter stood up to talk to the people, after making a lame man walk again:

People of Israel, why do you look at us as if we were able to make this man walk? You know that God—the God of your ancestors Abraham, Isaac, and Jacob—gave awesome powers to Jesus, who then died because of his convictions. He was the holy and righteous one, but you rejected him and sent him to his death.

But we believe in him and his name. It was through his name that we were able to make this man's legs strong again. Faith in Jesus has brought him to perfect health right in front of all of you.

Jesus suffered at your hands, just as prophets predicted would happen. But you can turn around, and turn to God. God will forgive.

The Word of the Lord.

Psalm 4

When I call you, please answer me, God.
I know you will back me up.
You have come to my rescue in tough times before.
Please listen to me now.

You have planted gladness in my heart, O God.

You people. What am I going to do with you?
How long will you mock me to my face?
How long will you follow things that have no substance whatsoever?

You have planted gladness in my heart, O God.

I know that the Lord does wonders for faithful people
And when I call upon God, he will hear me.

You have planted gladness in my heart, O God.

You should be very aware when you are in God's presence, and don't mess things up!
Calm your spirit when you lay down at night to sleep.
Do what you need to do, and count on God's goodness.

You have planted gladness in my heart, O God.

I know many people are whining that things couldn't get any worse,
and they wish things would get better quickly.
Lift up your face and have it shine on us, O Lord.

You have planted gladness in my heart, O God.

You have planted gladness in my heart.
I'm happier than when I have plenty to eat and drink.
I am at peace. When I lay my head down at night, I don't worry like I used to.
I fall asleep right away because I know that you, Lord, have my back.

You have planted gladness in my heart, O God.

A Reading from the First Letter of John [3:1–7]

Can you believe the love the Father has for us? He calls us children of God because that is what we are. That's hard for some to believe, because they don't know God like we do.

My dear ones, we are now God's children. Who knows what is next for us? We do know, however, that we are like God and we will someday see God face to face. This hope keeps us going.

In God there is no sin. There is sin in us, and we are guilty so often. But God removes our sin from us so that we are pure, like God is pure. Little children, do good, just as your Father does good.

The Word of the Lord.

✠ *The Holy Gospel of Our Lord Jesus Christ According to Luke* [24:36b–48]

All of a sudden Jesus was in the middle of his disciples and said, "Peace, brothers!" Instead of being peaceful, they were terrified and thought they were seeing a ghost.

Jesus said to them, "What are you scared of? Look, it's me, Jesus. See my hands and feet, still with the marks of nails. Go ahead and touch me. Ghosts don't have bones like I do." They were happy to see Jesus, but still weren't sure what was going on. Jesus said, "So, have you got something to eat here?" They gave him some broiled fish and watched him eat it.

Jesus said, "I told you when I was alive with you that everything written about me had to come true. Do you remember me saying that?" Then he opened their minds so they could understand what he was saying, and what the scriptures meant.

"It was written," Jesus said, "that the Messiah was to suffer and rise from the dead, and that in his name you should tell people about turning to God and having their sin forgiven. Remember that you heard me say this."

The Gospel of the Lord.

The Fourth Sunday of Easter

A Reading from the Acts of the Apostles [4: 5-12]

The church people were at a meeting in Jerusalem with Annas, and John and Alexander and a lot of other priests. Peter and some others were in jail, so they made the soldiers get them so they could talk to them. The church people asked them, "Who gave you the power to heal people? We want to know."

Then Peter filled up with the Holy Spirit and here's what he said to them: "If you really want to know. I'll tell you and everyone in Israel, that this man was healed by the name of Jesus Christ of Nazareth, the one you crucified, and the one God raised from the dead. Nobody else and no other name will bring you salvation."

The Word of the Lord.

Psalm 23

The Lord is my shepherd and I am the sheep.
I have everything I need.
He takes me to places where I can rest in peaceful, green pastures,
and lay down beside deep, still, soothing waters.
He puts new life back into me, and shows me the right ways to go.

The Lord is my shepherd and I am the sheep.
I have everything I need.

Even though I walk through the valley of the shadow of death,
I'm not scared because the Lord is with me.
And he carries a big stick to chase away wolves,
and a crook to grab me if I fall down a ravine . . . that makes me feel a lot better.

The Lord is my shepherd and I am the sheep.
I have everything I need.

When people who make fun of me are watching,
he spreads out a feast in front of them. A feast just for me.
And he anoints me just as a king would be anointed.
My cup is not only full, it is running over the top. My happiness is complete.

The Lord is my shepherd and I am the sheep.
I have everything I need.

There is nowhere I can go that the Lord's goodness and mercy isn't already there.
It's like living in the Lord's house.
And that's where I want to be forever.

The Lord is my shepherd and I am the sheep.
What more could I need or want?

A Reading from the First Letter of John [3:16-24]

This is how we know God loves us: Jesus made his whole life about us, and died for us. We ought to do the same for each other. How can God's love be in people who don't share themselves with those who need help? Little children, let's not just talk about love. Let's BE love and let's LIVE love. That way we will know God's love is in our hearts. Sometimes our hearts want to convince us that God won't love us. But that's just not true. God is greater than our hearts, so let's listen to him instead. Be bold before God. God loves it when we're bold. God will listen to our prayers and give us what we need. He asks this one thing of us; to believe in his son Jesus Christ and love one another. If we do that, God will be in our hearts. We know he's in our hearts by the Spirit that is between us.

The Word of the Lord.

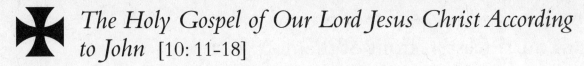

✠ *The Holy Gospel of Our Lord Jesus Christ According to John* [10: 11-18]

Jesus said, "I am the good shepherd who will do anything to keep his sheep safe. Shepherds who don't really care about their sheep see wolves coming for the sheep and they turn and run the other way. Not me. I am a good shepherd and I know every one of my sheep and they know me. I would lay my life down for my sheep. I've got other sheep that listen to my voice, and I hope to bring them to this sheepfold as well so we'll be one big flock with one shepherd. The Father loves me and I am willing to love my sheep and lay down my life for them."

The Gospel of the Lord.

The Fifth Sunday of Easter

A Reading from the Acts of the Apostles [8:26–40]

An angel who worked for God put an idea into Philip's head. "I want you to take a hike from Jerusalem to Gaza, where no one ever goes." So Philip got up and went. There he met a man who was going back to Ethiopia from Jerusalem. In Ethiopia the man worked for the queen. He was in charge of the treasury. When Philip ran into him, he was in his chariot reading the book of the prophet Isaiah.

Then the Spirit of God told Philip, "Go climb into that chariot and talk to that guy." So Philip ran alongside the chariot and asked him, "Do you know what you're reading?"

The man said, "Well, I'm reading it, but I sure could use some help understanding it. Get in this chariot and help me."

This was what he was reading:

As a sheep goes to slaughter, quiet as a lamb being sheared, he said nothing. He was mocked and humiliated and never got a fair trial. Who can claim him now, since he's no longer on earth?

When he read that, the man said to Philip, "Who is this talking about? Do you have any idea? Because I don't have a clue."

Philip took his chance to tell him about Jesus. The man was so excited about the Good News of God's love that when they came to a stream of water, he said, "Look, here's water and here's me. So why can't I be baptized right this very minute?" So Philip baptized him.

As soon as the man was baptized, the Spirit of God whisked Philip away, and that was the last the man from Ethiopia saw of him. But he didn't mind being alone on that road now, because he had Jesus in his heart, and he was as happy as could be.

Philip showed up north of there, and he preached about Jesus and God's love to all the villages along his way.

The Word of the Lord.

Psalm 22:24–30

I come to God's house to praise and serve God.
Here's what I will do.
I'll make sure the poor have something to eat,
and that they're not hungry all the time.
I'll make sure people know I do this because I love God,
and maybe they'll learn to love God too.

I come to God's house to praise and serve God.

If we all did the things that makes God happy,
like feeding the poor and take care of sick people
and making sure people aren't lonely,
then maybe everyone all over the world,
all the families from all the countries, would know God's love.

I come to God's house to praise and serve God.

God's love is for everyone in every place.
Everyone should know God, and worship him.
I plan to follow God all my life, and I hope my kids do too.
Then they can pass God's love on to their kids
and the kids their kids have.
They can pass on the stories of how God loved everyone in the whole world.

I come to God's house to praise and serve God.

A Reading from the First Letter of John [4:7–21]

Let's keep loving one another, because love comes from God. If you know how to love and actually love people, then you know God! If you don't love, then you don't know God. God. Is. Love. Here's how God showed his love for us—God sent his only son to live in the world, so that we might live through him. Since God loved us so much, we should love each other. No one has seen God or knows what God looks like, but if we love one another, God actually lives in us and when we love, then people will see God in us. God has given us his Spirit so that God's love in us might be real and perfect. Love is stronger than fear. We love because God loved us first. If you say you love God but hate your brother or sister, you're a liar. If you can't love someone you can see, how can you love God whom you can't see? Here're two things we all should do: Love God. Love our brothers and sisters.

The Word of the Lord.

✠ *The Holy Gospel of Our Lord Jesus Christ According to John* [15:1–8]

Jesus told his disciples this:

I'm like a vine and my Father is the vine grower. He snaps off the branches that aren't producing, and pinches the ones that are producing so they'll produce more fruit. The words I've spoken to you have washed over you and made you clean. You are a part of me, just as I am a part of you. Branches don't exist on their own. They have to be attached to the vine, don't they? If you stick with me and stay attached to me, all kinds of fruit will grow. Working together, we can do great things. If you follow me, God's power, which is in me, will be in you too.

The Gospel of the Lord.

The Sixth Sunday of Easter

A Reading from the Acts of the Apostles [10:44–48]

While Peter was preaching, the Holy Spirit overtook everyone who was listening to him. And the people who'd always been churchgoers were astounded that the gift of the Spirit had been poured out even on people who never went to church! You could hear them speaking in languages they didn't even know and praising God in all kinds of languages. Peter said, "There's nothing stopping us from baptizing these people who have received the Holy Spirit just like we have, is there?" And they were baptized in the name of Jesus Christ. The people invited Peter to stay with them to visit for a few days. And he did.

The Word of the Lord.

Psalm 126 (see Third Sunday of Advent, Year B, p. 224)

A Reading from the First Letter of John [5:1–6]

Everyone who believes that Jesus is the One, the Christ, is God's child. Here's how we know we're children of God, when we love God and do what God wants us to do. What God asks of us isn't too much for us, because God is on our side. Our faith always wins the day. God's Spirit is the one that leads to the truth, because the Spirit is truth.

The Word of the Lord.

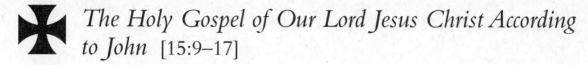

✠ *The Holy Gospel of Our Lord Jesus Christ According to John* [15:9–17]

Jesus told his disciples, "My Father loves me in the same way that I love you. Take in that love and rest in it. If you keep my commandments, you will show that you are 'in' my love, just as I do what my Father wants and I live in his love. I'm telling you this so you can feel joy, deep down and bubbling over. Here is my commandment for you. Love each other as I have loved you. This is the greatest love of all, to put aside your own wants for those of your friends. You are my friends if you love each other. You may think you chose me, but I really chose you. Now I'm choosing to send you out to go bear fruit, that is, to make something of this love that has been poured into you. If you need anything to do this job, just ask and my Father will give it to you."

The Gospel of the Lord.

The Seventh Sunday in Easter

A Reading from the Acts of the Apostles [1:15–17, 21–26]

Peter stood up to talk in the middle of all the believers (there were about one hundred twenty of them in all). He said, "Friends, Judas became a guide who led Jesus' enemies to him so they could arrest him. That was sad, because he was one of us. One of you who has been with us during Jesus' ministry from the time of his baptism until he went to heaven should become an apostle, a witness of Jesus' resurrection."

So they came up with two names: Joseph, called Barabbas, and Matthias. Then they prayed, saying, "Lord, you know everyone's heart. Show us which one of these you've already chosen to replace Judas in this ministry we share." Then they picked straws, and Matthias picked the short one. And he became the twelfth apostle.

The Word of the Lord.

Psalm 1

You're a happy one if you haven't fallen in with people who want to lead you in the wrong direction, or make fun of others, or think up ways to cause harm.

You're happy if God's Way has become your way,
and you know God's Word inside and out.

You're like a tree planted right by the water, and you grow a basketful of fruit at the right time of year, and your leaves are always green. It's like everything you do turns out right.

You're happy if God's Way has become your way,
and you know God's Word inside and out.

Not so with the troublemakers. They are more like chaff, the waste from ground wheat, which the wind just blows away. Nothing comes of what they do.

You're happy if God's Way has become your way,
and you know God's Word inside and out.

Those people will never be able to stand up straight in front of God.

God knows the ways of good people, but if you enjoy being wicked, your way is doomed to fail.

You're happy if God's Way has become your way,
and you know God's Word inside and out.

A Reading from the First Letter of John [5:9–13]

You can listen to humans talk and talk and talk, but God's talk is greater, because God testifies to Jesus being his Son. If you believe in the Son of God, you have that voice of God in your heart. And if you don't believe what God says about Jesus, you make God out to be a liar. Here's what God actually says about it: God gave us eternal life, and this eternal life is in God's Son. If you have the Son in your heart, you have life. And if you don't have him in your heart, then you don't have life. I write this to you who already believe, so that you'll know for sure that you have eternal life.

The Word of the Lord.

✠ *The Holy Gospel of Our Lord Jesus Christ According to John* [17:6–19]

Jesus was praying for his disciples and this is what he said to God: "I have done what you asked me to do, make your name known to the people you gave to me. They keep your word. Now they understand that everything I have you have given to me. I gave them the words you gave to me. They believe that you sent me. Now I'm asking you this on their behalf; you have glorified me in them. I am about to come to you, but they will still be here in this world. Protect them, Father, so that they may be one, just as you and I are one. I protected them while I was here with them. And now I'm leaving them. I want them to have complete joy in their hearts. Protect them from whoever wants to hurt them. Make them holy and true, just as your word is holy and true. Just as you sent me into the world, I'm about to send them, equipped with the truth."

The Gospel of the Lord.

The Day of Pentecost

A Reading from the Acts of the Apostles [2:1–21]
(see Pentecost A, p. 130)

Psalm 104:25–35, 37 (see Pentecost A, p. 131)

A Reading from the Letter of Paul to the Romans [8:22–27]

It's like the whole earth has been groaning until now, trying to give birth to something new. Not just the earth, but us too, who have been given God's good gifts, are anxiously waiting to be adopted, to be made new by God. That's our hope. And in that hope, God saves us. Hoping for something you can see right in front of you isn't really hope. Our hope is in something we can't see, but we wait patiently to be able to see it. The Holy Spirit helps us because we are weak. We don't always know how to pray or what to pray for. That's when the Spirit takes our sighs that are too deep to turn into words, and offers them to God for us. God searches our hearts and knows the mind of the Spirit within us.

The Word of the Lord.

✠ *The Holy Gospel of Our Lord Jesus Christ According to John* [15:26–27; 16:4b–15]

This is what Jesus said to his followers: "When the Spirit of truth comes to you from the Father, you will know me. Then you can tell others who I am, because you've always been with me. I'm going home to my Father. I know you will be sad and miss me when I leave. Here's the truth: It will be better for you if I go. Because when I go, I will send the Holy Spirit into your hearts.

And the Spirit will teach all of you the truth about what sin and being good and judgment are. I still have so much to teach you, but I know you can't take it all in right now. The Spirit of truth will lead the way into truth, and be there for you as you move into your future. The Spirit will show you the glory that the Father has given me.

The Gospel of the Lord.

Trinity Sunday

A Reading from the Book of Isaiah [6:1–8]

The year that King Uzziah died, I saw a vision of God sitting on a throne, way up high. The hem of God's robe filled the whole temple. Angels were all around. Each of them had six wings, two to cover their faces, two to cover their feet, and two to fly with. They were calling back and forth to each other, "Holy, holy, holy is the Lord of hosts. The whole earth is full of his glory." The doorways shook at their voices, and the place filled with smoke.

I was scared. "I am doomed," I cried. "For I'm a sinful person with unclean lips and yet I have seen the King, the Lord of hosts, with my very own eyes."

Then one of the angels flew over to me, holding a burning hot coal with a pair of tongs that he'd just taken from the altar in the temple. He touched my mouth with it and said, "Now that this has touched your lips, you're not sinful anymore."

Then I heard God ask, "Who can I get to do my work for me? Who should I send?"

I spoke up and said, "I'm the one you can send, God. Here I am. Send me."

The Word of the Lord.

Psalm 29 (see Epiphany 1, Year A, p. 26)

A Reading from the Letter of Paul to the Romans [8:12–17]

My brothers and sisters, we owe everything to God. So we shouldn't live just according to our own wants, because that will get us nowhere. But if we can live according to how God's Spirit wants us to live, then life will be amazing. Those of us who are led by God's Spirit are children of God. We don't live as slaves any longer. We're not slaves to fear. We've received a spirit of adoption. When we cry to God as our Father, it's the Spirit who helps us understand that we are truly God's children. And if we're God's children, then all that belongs to God becomes ours in Christ. When we suffer, even as God's children, we know we will also receive God's glory.

The Word of the Lord.

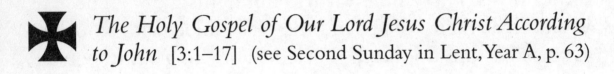

✠ *The Holy Gospel of Our Lord Jesus Christ According to John* [3:1–17] (see Second Sunday in Lent, Year A, p. 63)

Proper 1 (see the Sixth Sunday after the Epiphany, Year B, p. 245)

Proper 2 (see the Seventh Sunday after the Epiphany, Year B, p. 248)

Proper 3 (see the Eighth Sunday after the Epiphany, Year B, p. 251)

Proper 4B

A Reading from the First Book of Samuel [3:1–10] (see the Second Sunday after the Epiphany, Year B, p. 232)

Psalm 139:1–5, 12–17 (see the Second Sunday after the Epiphany, Year B, p. 233)

A Reading from The Second Letter of Paul to the Corinthians [4:5–12]

We're not making this up, or talking about ourselves. It's Jesus Christ as Lord that we're talking about. And we're his servants. God said, "Let light shine out of the darkness," and now that light shines in our hearts to let us see God's glory in Jesus' face.

We keep this treasure in a very special place in our hearts so that it's clear that all the power belongs to God and not to us. We have run into all kinds of trouble, but our spirits aren't crushed. It seems that we are carrying Jesus' death with us as well as his life, so that new life in him can be available to everyone.

The Word of the Lord.

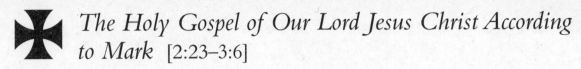

✠ *The Holy Gospel of Our Lord Jesus Christ According to Mark* [2:23–3:6]

On the Sabbath day, Jesus and his disciples were walking through the fields of grain. The authorities saw them pick the heads off the grain. "Did you see what they did? They can't do that on the Sabbath!" Jesus turned to them and said, "Did you ever read the story about King David and his friends, who went into the temple and ate the sacred bread because they were hungry? That was against the law, because only the priests were supposed to eat that bread. David gave some to his friends as well. The Sabbath was made for humans, not the other way around. And the Son of Man is in charge of the Sabbath."

Jesus went into the synagogue where there was a man with a crippled hand. The authorities thought he'd probably try to heal him, so they watched Jesus closely so they could catch him.

"Come here," Jesus said to the man. Turning to the authorities, he said, "So does the law say I can do good on the Sabbath or do harm, can I save a life or kill?" They had nothing to say to him. He was angry when he looked at them, and could see their hard, cold hearts. Jesus said to the man, "Stretch your hand out for me so I can heal it." And then he did. The authorities immediately went over to Herod's palace to figure out how they could work to destroy Jesus and all he was doing.

The Gospel of the Lord.

Proper 5

A Reading from the First Book of Samuel [8:4–11, 16–20]

Remember that God led the people of Israel out of Egypt, where they were slaves. Then they travelled around in the desert for forty years. Remember how God took care of them by sending them bread from heaven called manna? Remember when God gave them a new place to live, where they could build their own homes and plant gardens?

Remember how good God was to these people?

Well, apparently the people wanted more. More than freedom and their own land. More than just God taking care of them. They wanted a king, because the other countries had kings. They already had judges, who helped them decide what was right and what was wrong. They went to Samuel, who was a judge, and told him they wanted a king.

Samuel asked them, "Why do you want a king?"

"Well, we want to be like people in other countries. We want a king who will tell us exactly what to do."

Samuel said, "Do you know what else a king will do? Make your men leave their families and fight in his armies. The king will make the women work in his household. The kids will miss their moms and dads because they'll be off helping the king. Is that what you want? Are you sure?"

"Yes, we know," said the people. "We want a king. We want to fight other countries and to have other countries see how powerful we are." So Samuel talked to God about the people wanting a king.

God said, "They don't know what they're asking. This makes me unhappy, but give them a king. They'll have to see for themselves what a king is like."

So God helped Samuel choose a king for the people, and they chose Saul.

The people were happy. "Long live King Saul," they shouted. "Yay! Now we have a king, just like all the other countries."

The Word of the Lord.

Psalm 138

Everything in me thanks you, God, and I don't care who
hears me.
Thank you for your love for me.
Your name is sweeter to me than any name I know.
Your word is more precious to me than gold.
My soul will never forget the day when I was in deep trouble
and I called to you for help,
and you answered me.

Your love never ends. Don't leave me, God.
Don't ever leave me.

Everyone, even all the kings of the earth will praise you, God,
because they have heard your voice.
They will sing songs about you and how you are filled with glory.

Your love never ends. Don't leave me, God.
Don't ever leave me.

You may be God, but you pay attention to the little people.
You're not so impressed with people who are full of themselves.
And when trouble surrounds me on every side,
you keep me safe from people who want to hurt me.

Your love never ends. Don't leave me, God.
Don't ever leave me.

You stretch out your hand and pluck me out of the mud.
You have given me purpose and given me the ways I can fill that purpose.

Your love never ends. Don't leave me, God.
Don't ever leave me.

A Reading from the Second Letter of Paul to the Corinthians [4:13–5:1]

If we have faith in our hearts, we should have it on our lips as well. We know that Jesus is raised from the dead, and will raise us up too. And we'll all be with him someday together. We're working for you, so that grace can spread to more and more people, and they'll all have grateful hearts for God's goodness. Don't give up. I know it's hard. Even though your body gets tired, your spirit gets more and more enthusiastic every day. Whatever trouble we're going through now is getting us ready for what glory is to come. We can't see what it's going to be like. Because today we are temporary and what is to come is eternal. No matter what happens to our bodies or our houses here on earth, we know that God has built a house for us that is eternal, not made with hands, but made with God's love.

The Word of the Lord.

✠ *The Holy Gospel of Our Lord Jesus Christ According to Mark* [3:20–35]

Jesus and his disciples were so busy with all the crowds that they didn't even have time to eat. People were saying he was out of his mind, and when his family heard that, they went to see if they could grab Jesus and talk some sense into him. The authorities from the temple thought maybe Jesus had a demon in him.

But Jesus said to them, "How could a demon cast out another demon?" They thought his spirit might be unclean.

"Don't talk to me about the Holy Spirit," Jesus said. "I'm telling you, you can be forgiven for anything, but don't mess with the Holy Spirit. Because that's who forgives you."

Then his mother and his brothers sent for him. The crowd around Jesus said, "Your mother and your brothers and sisters are outside, asking for you." And he replied, "My mother and my brothers? I'm telling you, the people who are around me now, these are my mother and my brothers! Whoever does the will of God is my brother and sister and mother."

The Gospel of the Lord.

Proper 6

A Reading from the First Book of Samuel [15:34—16:13]

Saul the king gave Samuel no end of trouble. God was sorry he'd ever made Saul king. God said to Samuel, "Why do you let him get to you? Fill your oil flask and go find another to anoint king. Go to Jesse's house. He has many sons, and one of them will be the next king."

Samuel said, "But what if Saul hears about it? He'll kill me."

God said, "Do this. Take a heifer with you as if you're going to sacrifice it. Go invite Jesse to walk with you to the sacrifice and I'll show you which one of his sons I want to be king."

So Samuel went to Bethlehem, where Jesse lived, and invited Jesse and his sons to the sacrifice.

When Samuel saw Eliab, he said, "This man sure looks like a king to me. I'll bet he's the one God has chosen." But God told him, "Samuel, don't think the next king will be the most good-looking, or the tallest, or even the strongest. You humans are impressed by good looks, but not me. I look in their hearts."

Samuel looked over seven of Jesse's sons and God rejected each of them.

Samuel said to Jesse, "Are those all the boys you have?"

"Well," said Jesse, "I do have one more. He's my youngest and he's out watching the sheep."

"Go get him for me."

When David walked in, God whispered in Samuel's ear, "*This is the one.* Anoint him king now." David was made king in front of his brothers. And God's Spirit came down and filled David and stayed with him from then on. After he made David king, Samuel got his bags and hit the road.

The Word of the Lord.

Psalm 20

I hope that God always gets back to you when you're in trouble.
And that God always answers when you call.

God will send help and build you up until you're strong.

God will remember your efforts and your love.
I hope God grants you the deep desires of your heart
and makes all your plans work out for good.
We will all be happy when God supports and helps you succeed.
May God grant all your requests.

God will send help and build you up until you're strong.

Some people trust fancy cars and big bank accounts
but God's name is good enough for me.
Those people will learn someday, when everything falls apart
around them.
They will learn those things don't last.
but our God makes us stand up tall and confident.
God answers us when we call.

God will send help and build us up until we're strong.

A Reading from the Second Letter of Paul to the Corinthians
[5:6–10,14–17]

We are always sure of ourselves, even if we can't see the Lord any longer. Because now we walk forward by faith and not by sight. We would rather be with Jesus where he is now, full time, that's for sure. But whatever we're doing, wherever we are, we work at pleasing him. Jesus will see how we've done in the end. Christ's love inside us pushes us to do good. After all, he died for everyone, so that no one has to live just for now and just for themselves, but can live a life with purpose for the one who died and was raised for them. From now on, let's look at people through God's eyes. If anyone believes in Christ, he or she is a new creation. Everything about them has changed. Everything has become new.

The Word of the Lord.

✠ *The Holy Gospel of Our Lord Jesus Christ According to Mark* [4:26–34]

Jesus said, "Here's what God's kingdom is like. It's as if someone scatters seed all over, and watches and waits, and then sees the seeds grow. But he doesn't know how it happens, but he's sure glad it has. When the crop is ripe, he goes and harvests it."

"The kingdom is like a tiny seed, which you can hardly see because it's so small. And if it finds the right conditions it'll grow into the biggest of shrubs, and all the birds will want to make nests in its huge branches."

Jesus went on and on, telling stories like this to them. When he was with his disciples, he would explain what those stories meant.

The Gospel of the Lord.

Proper 7

A Reading from the First Book of Samuel [17:32–49]

David said to Saul, "Don't let that giant scare you. I will go and fight him." Saul tried to stop him, saying, "But you're just a kid and he has been a fighting man all his life."

David reminded Saul that he used to keep sheep for his father and had to fight lions and bears away. "I've rescued little lambs from the mouths of lions. I'll fight that Goliath just like I fought and killed those lions. God who saved me from those lions will save me from Goliath."

"Okay," Saul said. "God be with you!" Saul put his armor on David and strapped the sword onto him. But David couldn't even walk in the armor, much less fight! So he took the armor off. He picked up his walking stick and put five smooth stones from the river bed into his pouch. He had his slingshot in his hand and he went looking for Goliath.

When Goliath saw David, he laughed. "Who do you think I am, a dog? You brought a stick with you to fight me?" Goliath kept up the trash talk, "Bring it, boy. I will feed you to the vultures and let the hyenas eat your corpse."

David said, "It doesn't matter that you're bigger, and have swords and spears. I stand before you in the name of God. Today God is on my side. And I will triumph over you. And I will deliver you and your army to the vultures and the hyenas. And everyone will know there is a great God in Israel. And you will know that God doesn't fight. He hands you over to your enemy."

Goliath starting charging David. David picked up a stone from his pouch, and slung it right into Goliath's forehead. And Goliath fell face down on the ground and died.

The Word of the Lord.

Psalm 9:9–20

Anyone can come to God if they're in trouble,
especially those who are bullied and afraid.
God will never forget about them.
Sing God's praises, everyone.
Let everyone know what great things God does.

God won't ignore those who are crying.
Have pity on me, God.
So many people hate me.
Lift me out of the pit I'm in.
Sing God's praises, everyone.
Let everyone know what great things God does.

People who don't love you have fallen into their own pit,
the pit they dug for me.
And the trap they set has grabbed their own feet.
Sing God's praises, everyone.
Let everyone know what great things God does.

We all know you by your justice and mercy.
The wicked have trapped themselves in their own web.
They'll be sorry someday, along with everyone who
ignores God.
Sing God's praises, everyone.
Let everyone know what great things God does.

But the needy, the poor, will not be forgotten.
They have hope in their hearts that will never quit.
Make sure the wicked don't get away with their evil ways.
Stop them or catch them and throw them in prison.
Let them know who's Boss—that would be you.
Sing God's praises, everyone.
Let everyone know what great things God does.

A Reading from the Second Letter of Paul to the Corinthians [6:1–13]

I'm glad we're working together for Christ. You're not working so hard for nothing! God has poured grace on you. He said long ago, "At an acceptable time I have listened to you and on a day of salvation I have helped you." Well, guess what? NOW is that acceptable time, the day of salvation. We hope we're taking every obstacle out of the way so you can see God's goodness. We've been through a lot—prison, riots, beatings—but by God's power, and with love in our hearts and the Holy Spirit by our side, we are here to tell you all about it. We are alive, and joyful. We have made many people rich and although we have nothing, we have everything we could want or need.

Our hearts are wide open to you. There is no limit on our love for you. Keep your hearts open to us, please.

The Word of the Lord.

✠ *The Holy Gospel of Our Lord Jesus Christ According to Mark* [4:35–41]

When evening had come, Jesus said to his disciples, "Let's take this boat to the other side of the lake." And leaving the crowd behind, they all got in the boat. Suddenly the weather got bad and the wind howled and the waves tossed the boat in the air, and it was swamped with water. Jesus was sleeping on a pillow in the back through all this commotion! They screamed at him and woke him up, "We're all going to die. Don't you care?"

He woke up and scolded the wind, and said to the sea, "Peace! Stop already! Calm down!" Then the wind stopped, and it was as calm as it could be. He said to the disciples, "Why are you scared? Do you still not have faith?" And they were overflowing with amazement, and said to each other, "Did you see the wind and the sea obey him? Who is he, that he can control God's creation like that?"

The Gospel of the Lord.

Proper 8

A Reading from the Second Book of Samuel [1:17–27]

One day King Saul and Jonathan took all their soldiers to fight in a war. Both King Saul and Jonathan were killed. David loved King Saul and Jonathan very much, so when David heard that they were dead, he was very, very sad. He cried for a long time. Then he wrote a song, a sad song about how much he missed his friends.

> Oh, God, the people you loved are dead.
> They have been killed.
> These two strong men are lying on the ground.
> You mountains! And fields of wheat!
> You should be crying, too, because of my friends!
> You should cry too.
> Jonathan was so brave.
> He did not run away
> and Saul was very strong. He was afraid of nothing.
> O Saul and Jonathan, you loved each other so much,
> father and son.
> You were faster than eagles. You were stronger than lions.
> Jonathan, oh my friend, Jonathan. You are dead.
> I am crying for you, my brother Jonathan.
> I loved you, Jonathan.
> Your love for me was wonderful.
> O God, the people you loved are dead. They have been killed.
> These two strong men are lying on the ground.

The Word of the Lord.

Psalm 130 (see the Fifth Sunday in Lent, Year A, p. 75)

A Reading from the Second Letter of Paul to the Corinthians [8:7–15]

While you're working on your faith, speaking, knowing things, and love, why not work on this—being generous. It's a good test whether or not your love is real. You know how generous our Lord Jesus Christ is. He was king of all, and gave it all up so that by his poverty, you could become rich. In the same way, pay attention to those who have needs that you might be able to fill with your time, your money, your home. Wouldn't it be great if no one had too much, and no one had too little? Wouldn't it be great if everyone had just what each of them needed?

The Word of the Lord.

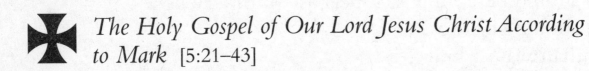

✠ *The Holy Gospel of Our Lord Jesus Christ According to Mark* [5:21–43]

Jesus got off a boat, and a big group of people surrounded him by the sea. One of the leaders of the local synagogue fell at Jesus' feet and begged him to heal his little girl, who was dying. "Come with me, Jesus. Lay your hands on her, and she will live." So Jesus pushed everyone aside and went with the man.

A large crowd followed him, and pushed him. A woman who had suffered for twelve years was in the crowd. She had seen many doctors but no one was able to help her. She'd heard about Jesus and thought, "If only I can touch his clothes, I'll be healed." So she snuck up behind him and touched the hem of his coat. Right that instant, she got better. And right that instant Jesus felt some power leave his body. He turned around and said, "Who touched my clothes?" The disciples said, "Jesus, look at all these people! They're ALL touching your clothes." Still he wanted to know who had touched him. The woman came up to him, expecting to be punished for touching him. She told him the whole truth. And Jesus said to her, "You have such a strong faith. You are healed. Go, be at peace and live a happy life."

While he was talking to her, people came from the synagogue leader's house to tell him his little girl had died. "Don't bother Jesus anymore. She's gone." Jesus heard that and said, "Don't be afraid. Believe instead." And Jesus took Peter, James, and John with him to the house, where they saw all kinds of people crying because the girl was dead. Jesus went in and said, "Why are you all crying? She's not dead. She's just sleeping." They laughed at him through their tears. He threw them all out of the house and took the little girl's parents with him into her room. People were stunned with amazement. He told them not to tell anybody about this, and then said, "Why don't you get her something to eat? She must be really hungry."

The Gospel of the Lord.

Proper 9

A Reading from the Second Book of Samuel [5:1–5, 9–10]

All the people came to see David. They said, "We are your family. You have been our shepherd and our leader, and now God has made you the king." They anointed him king when he was thirty years old and he was king for forty years. David named Jerusalem "the city of David." David was a really, really good king, because God was with him.

The Word of the Lord.

Psalm 48

God lives on a high mountain at the center of the world in a city
 fit for a king.
All the kings of the earth come to see God but they're scared
 when they catch a glimpse.
They shake with fear and scream like they're in pain.
They fall apart like a ship in a storm.

God will always guide us in the right direction.

We have waited quietly to feel God's loving-kindness.
The whole world knows about you, and your justice and goodness.
The mountains and the cities rejoice when they hear you speak.

God will always guide us in the right direction.

Explore the place where God lives. Walk around and get to
 know God.
Figure out how many towers are on the temple.
And then tell everyone that God is our God and will be forever.

God will always guide us in the right direction.

A Reading from the Second Letter of Paul to the Corinthians [12:2–10]

Someone I know who loves Jesus tells me he was "caught up in the third heaven." I'm not sure what that means. That's a great story to tell! But as for me, I won't tell of anything but my weaknesses. Don't get me wrong. I have a lot to be proud of. But I don't want people to think less of me or get tired of me. To keep me humble, I have a physical ailment, which torments me. I've begged God to heal me of it, but here's the answer I get: "You've got plenty of my grace. It's good enough for you. Power is perfected by weakness." So, I'm stuck with it. And I guess I will be proud of my weakness, because then I know that it is Christ who lives inside of me and makes me strong. I will put up with insults, and persecution, and all kinds of troubles for the sake of Jesus. For when I am weak, then I am strong.

The Word of the Lord.

✠ *The Holy Gospel of Our Lord Jesus Christ According to Mark* [6:1–13]

Jesus and his disciples came to his hometown so he could teach in the synagogue. The people in the congregation were astounded. "Where is he getting all this? How does he know all that? Have you seen the miracles he's done? Isn't he a carpenter, Mary's son? We know his whole family." At that point they began to be offended by him. Jesus said to them, "No prophet gets any respect from their hometown." He was amazed at how little they believed in him.

He went about the villages teaching. He needed some help to reach all the villages, so he sent out his disciples two by two and gave them authority to cast out unclean spirits. He told them to travel lightly, and depend on the kindness of the people they would meet. If they were invited to stay at someone's house, they should thank them for their generosity. He said, "Don't overstay your welcome or get pushy with people. If they don't want to talk to you, then move on." So they went and proclaimed the message Jesus had been proclaiming, that everyone should turn their lives around and follow God. They cast out demons, and healed people who were sick.

The Gospel of the Lord.

Proper 10

A Reading from the Second Letter of Samuel [6:1–5, 12b–19]

David got all the people together to reclaim the ark of God. They put it on a cart and brought it to a special place on the hill. And everyone was dancing with joy, singing, and playing their tambourines, harps, and cymbals. They danced and sang alongside the ark all the way to the Temple of God in the city of David.

As the ark came into the city, David's wife looked and saw her husband dancing like crazy. She thought he looked like a fool and she was embarrassed. They brought the ark to a special place and then David blessed the people in God's name and everyone took part in a big feast. Then all the people went back to their homes.

The Word of the Lord.

Psalm 24

The earth belongs to God, along with everything on it.
Every person, every animal, every plant.
God made the seas
and put the rivers in their banks.

Who is full of glory? The Lord our God, that's who.

So, who are we to think we can go to God's house?
Who are we to talk to God's face?
We have clean hands and pure hearts, and we tell the truth.
That's who can spend time with God.

Who is full of glory? The Lord our God, that's who.

God will bless us.
Open up your gates. Break down the doors.

Here comes God.
You ask, who is full of glory?
The Lord our God, that's who.
Open up your gates. Break down the doors.
Our God is full of glory.
Again you ask, who is it again?

Who is full of glory? The Lord our God is full of glory.

A Reading from the Letter of Paul to the Ephesians [1:3–14]

God is so good to us. When God blessed us with Christ, we received all kinds of spiritual blessings. Thank the heavens we were chosen to be part of God's love. Through grace, God wanted us and adopted us as children. Because of Christ and the grace God has poured into our lives, we are made right with God. We are forgiven for whatever wrong we've done. God's plan is to embrace everything, everything in heaven and everything on earth, in the fullness of time. In Christ we have been given everything according to God's purpose. We have been marked with the Holy Spirit just as God promised. We've been marked as God's very own.

The Word of the Lord.

✠ *The Holy Gospel of Our Lord Jesus Christ According to Mark* [6:14–29]

Herod the king heard that Jesus was casting demons out of people and curing people who were sick. Some people, including Herod, thought Jesus was really John the Baptizer who'd come back from the dead. Others thought he was Elijah or some other prophet. Herod had John arrested because John told him it wasn't right that he'd married his brother's wife. Herod really wanted to kill him, but didn't because John was known as a holy man. Herod actually liked a lot of what John had to say.

Then, at Herod's birthday party, his daughter danced for the partygoers and they were all so happy with her. King Herod said to her, "Tell me what you want and I'll give it to you. I swear, ask me for anything up to half my kingdom." She wasn't sure what to ask, so she went to ask her mother. Her mother told her to ask for the head of John the Baptizer on a platter.

That really upset the king, but he had promised. He sent a soldier to go get John's head. The soldier went to the prison, killed John, and brought his head on a platter and handed it to the girl who gave it to her mother. When John's disciples heard about it, they came and put his body in a tomb.

The Gospel of the Lord.

Proper 11

A Reading from the Second Book of Samuel [7:1–14a]

David was king and living in a comfortable house and his enemies were leaving him alone. He said to the prophet Nathan, "Wow, I'm living in a nice house, but God's ark is living in a tent. Maybe I should build God a house. What do you think?" Nathan said, "I think it's a great idea. Go for it. And God will bless it." That same night the word of the God came to Nathan, "Say to David, 'I have been moving around with the people of Israel ever since I took them from Egypt. And I've never complained that I didn't have a house to live in. I don't need a house.' I'll make David a house that his offspring can live in forever. I've turned David into prince out of a shepherd. I've been with him all the way, and turned his enemies away. When his days are over, he'll rest with his ancestors and his children will still sit on the throne of Israel."

The Word of the Lord.

Psalm 89:20–37

I've anointed David with holy oil.
I will make him strong and hold him in my hands.
The wicked won't have a chance against him.
His enemies will be sorry they tried to crush him.

God, you are my father, and the rock of my salvation.

His kingdom will be far and wide.
David will say to me,
"You are my father, my God, and the rock of my salvation."
I will make him my firstborn
    and higher than the kings of the earth.

I will keep my love for him forever,
    and I will always keep my promises.

God, you are my father, and the rock of my salvation.

His children will sit on his throne forever.
Unless they turn out to ignore me and my commandments:
then I will punish them, but I won't take my love away.

God, you are my father, and the rock of my salvation.

My word is good.
David's family tree will grow forever, as long as the sun is
    in the sky.
As long as the moon lights up the night.

God, you are my father, and the rock of my salvation.

A Reading from the Letter of Paul to the Ephesians [2:11–22]

Do you remember that you used to be strangers to God's promise, and without hope? Now because you have Christ Jesus in your hearts, God is very near. Jesus Christ is your peace. He has broken down the walls that divided people from each other because of where they were born, or what family they belong to. Christ Jesus got rid of the law, so that he could create a new group, which brings us all together. He preached peace. And through him all of us have access to God the Father.

So even if you used to be strangers, you're not anymore. You are members of God's family, descendants of the apostles and prophets, with Jesus being the foundation of it all. Through him we are all connected and we make up a place where God can live.

The Word of the Lord.

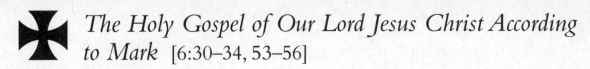

✠ *The Holy Gospel of Our Lord Jesus Christ According to Mark* [6:30–34, 53–56]

The apostles gathered around Jesus, and told him all that they had done and taught. He said to them, "You've been busy. Come away to a deserted place all by yourselves and have a rest."

They had been so busy, sometimes they forgot to eat. They got into a boat and found a place where there was no one else around. Or at least that's what they thought. Some people saw where the boat landed and ran from the towns just to see them. When Jesus saw how many people were there, hungry for God's Word and God's healing, his heart hurt for them. He could tell they were like sheep who didn't have a shepherd. So he sat down and began to teach them God's Word. People brought their sick friends on mats to wherever they heard Jesus was. Wherever he went, in cities, or on farms, or in marketplaces, people begged Jesus to touch them and heal them. All who touched the hem of his coat were healed.

The Gospel of the Lord.

Proper 12

A Reading from the Second Book of Samuel [11:1–15]

Israel was at war but David stayed in Jerusalem. One afternoon when David was walking around on the roof of his house, he saw a beautiful woman bathing at her house. He sent someone to see who she was. Her name was Bathsheba, and she was married to Uriah. David sent for her and took her to bed with him. She became pregnant. David wasn't sure what to do. Then he thought he should send for Uriah to come back from war to go sleep with his wife, so he would think the unborn child was his, rather than David's.

But Uriah did not want to desert his post and go back home, even for a night. David decided the best way to cover his misdeed was to have Uriah be on the front line of the most difficult battle so that he would certainly be killed. And he was.

The Word of the Lord.

Psalm 14

Foolish people tell themselves, "There is no God.
All of us do horrid things. None of us is good."
God sees all of us,
and wonders if any of us is wise.
Is there is even one of us who seeks God?

When will God's people be saved?

"Wicked people eat up my people like bread," God says,
"and don't bother turning in my direction."
They shake because they're afraid.

When will God's people be saved?

God is on the side of the good people and the evil people
know it.
They try to mess up the plans of those who follow God;
but God is where good people hide and find shelter.

When will God's people be saved?

When God restores the fortunes of his people,
I know that Jacob will rejoice.
And Israel will be delighted.

When will God's people be saved?

A Reading from the Letter of Paul to the Ephesians [3:14–21]

When I kneel before God to pray, I ask God to grant you strength deep inside through the power of the Spirit. I ask that Christ may find a place in your hearts and that you are planted in the soil of love. I pray that you may be filled with all the fullness of God, so you may know God. All glory be to God who is working with us and in us, accomplishing more than we could ever expect to do on our own.

The Word of the Lord.

✠ *The Holy Gospel of Our Lord Jesus Christ According to John* [6:1–21]

Jesus and his disciples found a place to be by themselves on the mountain for a bit. A huge crowd followed them because they had seen Jesus heal the sick. When Jesus saw the people coming toward him, he said to Philip, "Where are we going to get bread for these people to eat?" Jesus already had a plan in mind, but he wanted to hear what Philip would say. Philip said, "Six months' pay wouldn't buy enough bread for each of them to get a bite of bread." Then Andrew said, "Here's a boy who has five barley loaves and two fish. But that certainly won't feed all these people." Jesus said, "Make the people sit down on the grass." There were about five thousand people.

Then Jesus took the loaves, and when he had given thanks, he distributed them to those who were seated; then he did the same thing with the fish, and everyone had as much to eat as they wanted. When everyone was full, he told the disciples to clean up the leftovers, so no food would be wasted. When they got done, they had twelve baskets of leftover bread. And they started out with five loaves! When people realized what had happened, they said to each other, "This man is a prophet for sure, the one we were waiting for!"

Jesus could tell they were about to grab him and put him on their shoulders to make him king. So he snuck away and went to the mountaintop by himself.

When the sun was setting, the disciples got into a boat and started across the sea. Jesus was still on the mountain but it was dark. A storm came up while they were on the water and the sea got rough with a strong wind. They were in the middle of the lake when they saw Jesus walking toward them on the water. They were terrified. Then Jesus said, "Don't be afraid. It's me." They took him into the boat and immediately the boat reached land.

The Gospel of the Lord.

Proper 13

A Reading from the Second Book of Samuel [11:26–12:13a]

King David wanted to marry Uriah's wife, so he made sure Uriah was on the front line of the battle, and would most likely be killed. After Uriah died, King David married his widow and she bore David a son.

That didn't please God at all. God sent Nathan, a prophet, to tell David this story: "There was a rich man and a poor man. The rich man had many sheep, but the poor man had only one little lamb that he loved like a pet. At the rich man's house one day a visitor came. The rich man didn't want to prepare one of his own sheep for dinner, so he took the poor man's lamb and killed it and served it up to his guest."

King David was outraged. "That rich man deserves to die! Make him pay back the poor man four times over because he had no pity and no compassion."

Nathan turned to David and said, "YOU are the rich man. God anointed you as king and rescued you from Saul. God gave you this house, and wives, and you are king over all. If that was not enough, God would give you more. God says, 'Why have you done the awful thing you did, killing Uriah and then taking his wife? Trouble will always be in your family, because you have hated. There will be violence, and your wives will leave you. You did all this very secretly, but I will do this so everyone can see your shame.'"

And King David was sorry and admitted, "I have sinned against God."

The Word of the Lord.

Psalm 51:1–13 (see Fifth Sunday in Lent, Year B, p. 268)

A Reading from the Letter of Paul to the Ephesians [4:1–16]

From where I sit in prison, I beg you, please, lead a life that will reflect the life to which God called you. Be humble, gentle, patient, engaging each other with love, and always working toward peace. There is one body and one Spirit, just like there is one hope, one Lord, one faith, one baptism, one God and Father of all, who is above all and through all and in all. And God has distributed grace freely to all of us, through the gift that is Christ Jesus. Each of us has received a personalized, customized gift. Some of us are leaders, some can teach, others are kind and gentle pastors. All these gifts are to be used to build up Christ's body, and to nurture us so that we grow in faith.

We start out as children in faith, but we can't stay that way. We have to grow up and know where we stand so we don't get tricked. If you have to tell somebody something that is hard to hear, especially since it's the truth, be loving about it. That way we can all work together to become the body of Christ, building each other up in love.

The Word of the Lord.

✠ *The Holy Gospel of Our Lord Jesus Christ According to John* [6:24–35]

After Jesus had fed the five thousand people, the crowds looked around to find Jesus and his disciples. They found them on the other side of the sea. Jesus said to them. "You are looking for me because I filled your hungry bellies, not because you believe. Isn't that right? Look for the food that is eternal, which the Son of Man will give you. He's got God the Father's seal of approval. Don't just settle for food that grows stale after a day."

They asked him how they could perform God's work. Jesus told them, "The work of God you should do, is to believe in the one that God sent."

"What sign will you give us that you are the one? Why should we believe you?" they said. "God gave our ancestors in the wilderness bread from heaven to eat. What will you give us?"

Jesus said, "God is the one who gives you bread from heaven and it gives life to all the world."

They said, "That's the kind of bread we always want! Please, sir, give us this bread."

Jesus said, "I am the bread of life that God gives to you. If you follow me, your heart will never be hungry. If you believe in me, you will never be thirsty."

The Gospel of the Lord.

Proper 14

A Reading from the Second Book of Samuel [18:5–9, 15, 31–33]

David the king was dealing with people who wanted to overthrow him. He knew that his son Absalom was in on a plot. David ordered his army to go stop the rebellion, but deal gently with Absalom. There was a fierce battle and many were killed. Then David's men saw Absalom. He was riding his mule under some big branches hanging down from an oak tree, and he caught his head on the branches. The mule he was riding kept on running, and left Absalom hanging there. David's men surrounded him and killed him as he hung there, defenseless. They reported to King David the good news of their victory. The king wanted to know about his son. "Is he okay?" The leader of the army said, "All of your enemies who want to overthrow you should end up like Absalom." That's how King David knew his son was dead. He went to his room and cried loudly, because he loved his son Absalom, and now he was dead. "Oh, my son," David said, "I wish I could have died in your place. My dear, dear son."

The Word of the Lord.

Psalm 130 (see Fifth Sunday in Lent, Year A, p. 75)

A Reading from the Letter of Paul to the Ephesians [4:25–5:2]

Let's all stop lying and agree to speak the truth to each other. Because we belong to each other. You can be angry, but don't let it turn into sin. Don't let your anger come between you and God or your neighbor, because that lets room for the devil to sneak into your lives. Don't go to bed angry. Work things out between you.

And stop stealing from each other. Instead, work honestly and hard, so that you might have enough to share with those who are in need. Don't gossip about each other, or put each other down. Only say what will be helpful to building people up, rather than tearing people down. Let your words be filled with grace for those who hear them. Don't irritate God's Holy Spirit, because you carry the mark of the Holy Spirit from your baptism, remember? Put aside any resentment you may have, along with your anger, and any ideas you have to hurt each other.

Instead be kind to one another, and be gentle. Be ready to forgive each other, because you know that God has forgiven you. If you need to see an example of how to live, look to God. Imitate God! And live in love, as Christ loves us and gave himself for us, leaving a sweet smelling fragrance, which pleases the God who made us all.

The Word of the Lord.

✠ *The Holy Gospel of Our Lord Jesus Christ According to John* [6:35, 41–51]

Jesus said, "I am the bread of life that God gives to you. If you follow me, your heart will never be hungry. If you believe in me, you will never be thirsty."

Some people didn't like hearing him say that. They were stuck thinking about the Jesus they knew when he was growing up. "Who does he think he is, talking like that? Coming down from heaven? We know where he's from. He's from down the street, from Mary and Joseph's house." Jesus answered them, "I hear you talking about me and I know you don't like what I'm saying. The Father draws people to himself, and those who believe in me I will raise on the last day. I'm telling you, whoever believes already has eternal life.

"I am the bread of life. Remember that your ancestors who were hungry in the desert were given manna, a form of bread God sent from heaven? They ate that bread, but they died eventually like everyone else. But I am the bread of life that you will eat, and you will never die. You will live forever if I become part of you. The bread I give the world so that they may have life, that bread is my very life."

The Gospel of the Lord.

Proper 15

A Reading from the First Book of Kings [2:10–12; 3:3–14]

King David died after being king for forty years. Then his son Solomon became king. Solomon was a good king. He obeyed the laws his father set up and he loved and worshipped God. God said to him in a dream one night, "Tell me what you need and I will give it to you. Ask me for anything." Solomon replied, "God, you have been so good to my family. My father is gone, and I'm the king. And I feel like a little kid; I don't quite know what I'm doing. If you will give me anything, please give me wisdom so that I can do the job you've given me to do. Give me the ability to know between right and wrong."

That request pleased God to no end. God said, "Since you didn't ask anything for yourself like a long life or riches, or that your enemies die, I will grant your request. You will be the wisest king ever. And I will also give you what you didn't ask for—riches and honor. If you are a good king, and follow my direction as your father David did, I will also grant you a long life."

The Word of the Lord.

Psalm 111 (see Fourth Sunday after the Epiphany, Year B, p. 238)

A Reading from the Letter of Paul to the Ephesians [5:15–20]

Pay attention to the way you live your life. Make the most of the time God has given you, and don't be foolish and wasteful. Understand what it is God wants you to do. Don't drink too much, but drink your fill of the Spirit, and sing your hearts out in praise to God, giving thanks always for everything, in the name of Jesus our Lord.

The Word of the Lord.

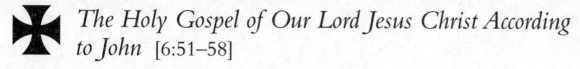

✠ *The Holy Gospel of Our Lord Jesus Christ According to John* [6:51–58]

Jesus said, "I am the living bread from heaven. If you take me into your life, you will live forever. The bread I give so that everyone will live is my very flesh, my very life."

The people listening said to each other, "How is this man going to give us his flesh to eat?" Jesus responded, "Believe me, unless you eat my flesh, and drink my blood, and take in my very life, you'll have no life in you at all. But if you do, you will have a life that is eternal, and I will raise you up on the last day. My flesh and body will transform you. I will be part of you if you are a part of me. The Father who lives sent me here, and I live because of him, so whoever partakes of me will live because of me."

"Remember that your ancestors who were hungry in the desert were given manna, a form of bread God sent from heaven? They ate that bread, but they died eventually like everyone else. But I am the bread from heaven that you will eat, and you will never die."

The Gospel of the Lord.

Proper 16

A Reading from the First Book of Kings [8:22–30, 41–43]

King Solomon gathered all the people and raised his hands to pray. He said, "God, you are the best. You have always kept your promises of steadfast love. You promised my father David that his children would always be the rulers of Israel if we walk the way you want us to go, am I right? Heaven cannot contain you, much less this beautiful temple I have built for you. Please accept this place as a house of worship, and hear your people's prayers. If someone who is not from the House of Israel hears about you and prays in this house, listen to them as well. We want all people to know you and know that this house of worship is also for them."

The Word of the Lord.

Psalm 84 (see Christmas 2, Year A, p. 20)

A Reading from the Letter of Paul to the Ephesians [6:10–20]

Be strong because you *are* strong. God has made you strong. Our enemy doesn't have a body. Our enemy is the power of darkness. Put on God like you put on a suit of armor, so you can stand against the enemy. And put on truth like you're putting on a pair of pants. Strap on goodness like a bulletproof jacket. Lace up shoes made of the gospel. Use your faith like a shield and salvation like a helmet. With the Spirit of God at your back, you will be covered!

Always remember to pray for strength. Be on alert. And pray for me while you're at it, so that I can be a good spokesman for the Good News, even if I am sitting in prison in chains. Pray that I can be confident and boldly declare God's word.

The Word of the Lord.

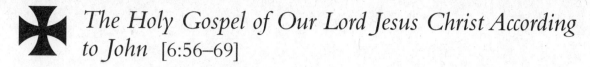

✠ *The Holy Gospel of Our Lord Jesus Christ According to John* [6:56–69]

Jesus kept talking about his body as bread. "Remember that your ancestors who were hungry in the desert were given manna, a form of bread God sent from heaven? They ate that bread, but they died eventually like everyone else. But I am the bread from heaven that you will eat, and you will never die. Just as the living Father sent me, and I live because of the Father, so whoever eats me will live because of me."

When he said these things in the synagogue, his disciples had a hard time hearing it. They didn't like Jesus talking about eating his flesh and blood. Jesus asked them, "Am I upsetting you? Would it upset you to see me ascend into heaven? I'm not talking about blood and flesh, you know. I'm talking about spirit and life! Think about that. Still, some of you won't believe. I know that God the Father has to open your heart before you come to me, believing."

Some of the disciples gave up on Jesus because they just couldn't understand. Jesus asked the twelve, "Do you want to leave me as well?" Peter said him, "Jesus, where would we go? Whom would we follow? You are the one with the words of eternal life. It may not seem like it sometimes, but we have come to know that you are God's Holy One."

The Gospel of the Lord.

Proper 17

A Reading from the Song of Solomon [2:8–13]

I hear the voice of the one I love. He's jumping over the mountaintop to be with me. He is graceful, like a gazelle. I can see him waiting for me, wanting to be with me. He's saying in his heart, "Come away with me. Winter is over and spring has sprung. Let me see your face and hear your voice surrounded by the wonders of God's creation. There's nothing that can disturb our joy. Come away with me."

The Word of the Lord.

Psalm 45:1–2, 7–10

My heart is bubbling over as I speak to the king.
You, O king, are the best man I know.
God has poured his grace all over you.
And you're not just good-looking; you are kind and good and
hate evil.
Wherever you go, you leave a fragrance of goodness.
Your palace is full of beautiful music. Listen to its beauty.

A Reading from the Letter of James [1:17–27]

Every good thing is a gift from God, who is the Father of Light. We are the firstborn of God's creatures and should reflect God's light. Try to follow these guidelines. Be quick to listen and slow to speak. And be *very* slow to anger. Clean up your act and make room for the word, which will save your soul. Don't just listen to God's Word. Act on it as well. That way when you look in a mirror you will see exactly who you are—a good person who hears what God has to say, and does what God has to say, too.

Watch your tongue. It can get you in a lot of trouble if you don't watch it.

If you want to do God's will, take care of orphans and widows who have no one to care for them but you. Don't let the world's bad habits creep into your life, like thinking only of yourself. That's a really bad habit.

The Word of the Lord.

✠ *The Holy Gospel of Our Lord Jesus Christ According to Mark* [7:1–8, 14–15, 21–23]

The church leaders were watching Jesus and they saw that some of his disciples didn't bother to wash their hands before they ate. (That is always a good idea as well as one of their rules.) So they asked Jesus, "Why do your disciples not follow the rules like they're supposed to?"

Jesus said, "Hmmm. I think Isaiah must have been thinking of you when he said, 'Some people honor me with their lips but their heart isn't even close to me.' You have abandoned God altogether, but hold on instead to the ways of men." Turning to the people, Jesus said, "I want you all to understand that there is nothing that will make you dirty from the outside. It's what's inside you that makes the difference. Evil deeds begin by being evil thoughts—like stealing, killing, cheating on your wife, lying—all these things make you unclean and they come from inside you."

The Gospel of the Lord.

Proper 18

A Reading from the Book of Proverbs [22:1–2, 8–9, 22–23]

Here are some wise sayings to think about:

Your good name and reputation are the most precious things you own and the hardest to replace if you lose them or if they're destroyed.

In God's eyes, there is no difference between a rich man and a poor man. God made them both.

If you do unfair things, they will come back to bite you. If you are generous with your food and share it, you will be blessed.

Don't kick someone if they are down on their luck, for God himself will be on their side, and you will lose in God's court.

The Word of the Lord.

Psalm 125

If you trust in God with your heart, you will be like Mount Zion,
which no one can ever move.
The hills surround the city of Jerusalem
just like God surrounded his people
and always will.
The wicked won't have any influence in the land God gives to
the good people,
and the good people won't have anything to do with the wicked.
Be kind and good, God, to those who are good
and to those whose hearts are good.
If you make a wrong turn off God's path, you'll end up with
the evildoers,
but peace will be with Israel.

A Reading from the Letter of James [2:1–10, 14–17]

Don't treat rich people any better than you treat poor people. And don't judge people by the type of clothing they wear. There is a special place in God's hearts for people who struggle. If you want to fulfill the law, don't bother trying to keep every little part of the law, because no one can do that. Instead follow this law: Love your neighbor as yourself.

If you say you have faith in your hearts, but nobody can tell by the way you act, what is the point of faith? If someone you know needs a warm coat, or some food, would you go up to them and say, "God loves you, be warm and don't be hungry anymore," instead of giving them a warm coat and good food?

If you just keep your faith inside of you, and it makes no difference to anyone else, I doubt that you have faith at all. It seems that your faith must be dead.

The Word of the Lord.

✠ *The Holy Gospel of Our Lord Jesus Christ According to Mark* [7:24–37]

Jesus was trying to have a quiet dinner at someone's house without anyone knowing about it. But that didn't happen. Instead a Greek woman whose daughter had suffered with an evil spirit found out where he was and came and fell at his feet. "Please make my daughter whole," she said. Jesus replied, "I've come to feed the children, not the dogs." (He was talking about the people of Israel being their children.) The woman came right back at him and said, "But the dogs are right under the table ready to eat the crumbs that the children throw off the table."

"Wow," Jesus said. "You are good and faithful. Your daughter has been healed." Sure enough, when she got home, she discovered it was true.

Jesus and his disciples got on the road again. A man who couldn't hear was brought over to him. Because he couldn't hear, he couldn't speak very well either. His friends wanted Jesus to make him hear. So Jesus took the man away from the crowds so they could be alone for a moment. He put his fingers in the man's ears, and then spit on his fingers and touched the man's tongue. He sighed, and looked up to heaven and said, "Open up!" All of a sudden the man could hear and speak clearly.

Jesus told them not to tell a soul about this. But the more he pleaded with them not to talk, the more people they talked to. They were totally amazed at the things Jesus could do in God's name and couldn't keep quiet about it.

The Gospel of the Lord.

Proper 19

A Reading from the Book of Proverbs [1:20–33]

Wisdom is like a woman who is yelling in the street, crying out on the busiest corner in town, at the entrance to the theater, "Will you be clueless forever, people? How long will you love making stupid jokes at others' expense and be totally in the dark?"

Listen to me.

I have called out to you even if you turn your head the other way. You have ignored me completely. Well, when catastrophe strikes you, I will laugh. I will mock you when you panic and your life is like a storm of distress and anguish. Then when you want me to listen to you I won't answer. You will look for me everywhere, but you won't find me. You didn't want any knowledge or wisdom then. So eat the fruit that you planted. And see how you like the taste of it. Being complacent will destroy you. But if you listen to me, Wisdom, you can be confident that you will live without fear of what's ahead.

The Word of the Lord.

Psalm 19 (see Proper 22, Year A, p. 192)

A Reading from the Letter of James [3:1–12]

Teachers are held to high standards, and they should be. So watch out if you want to become a teacher. All of us make mistakes, especially those of us who talk. Our tongues are little, and yet they can inspire great things or cause a lot of damage. Just like a spark can set a whole forest on fire, a tongue can do that, too. We can tame wild animals but we can't seem to tame our tongues. With those tongues we can praise God and then we can turn around and curse God's people. This really shouldn't happen. It's unnatural; can you get both fresh and nasty water at the same time from a spring? And can you get figs from a grapevine or olives from a fig tree?

The Word of the Lord.

✠ *The Holy Gospel of Our Lord Jesus Christ According to Mark* [8:27–38]

Jesus asked his disciples what people were saying about him. "Who do they think I am?"

"Some people think you might be John the Baptist or Elijah or a prophet," they replied.

"That's interesting," said Jesus. "Who do you think I am?" Peter said, "You are the Messiah, that's who you are." Jesus told him he was right, but not to tell anyone.

Jesus told his followers that soon he would suffer under the hands of the people in charge, that he would be rejected by them all and then killed. But that after three days he would come to life again. He didn't try to keep it a secret. Peter took him aside and jumped all over him for saying this. Jesus looked them right in the eye and turned to Peter and said, "Get behind me, Satan! We're not talking about the same thing. Your thinking is about what humans want. My thinking is about what God wants." Then Jesus gathered the crowd around him and his followers. "If any of you really want to follow me, you have to put your own wants aside, and walk with me carrying your cross. If you mainly want to save your life, you'll end up losing it. Those who lose the life they're living on account of me and God's message of love, will save it. After all, what's the point of having everything in the world you could want, but then losing your life? Don't be ashamed of me and what I've taught you, and I won't be ashamed of you when I return in glory with the angels at the end."

The Gospel of the Lord.

Proper 20

A Reading from the Book of Proverbs [31:10–31]

A good wife is hard to find. She is more valuable than diamonds or gold. Wise husbands trust their good wives. A good wife makes beautiful things with her hands, and cooks great food. She gets up early to make everything just right. She keeps herself in good shape so she can work hard and sell her wares. She opens her home to the poor and reaches out to those who need her. She keeps her household in warm clothes and sells beautiful clothing. She covers herself with strength and dignity and laughs at what's around the corner. She is wise and knows the right things to say. Her children love her and her husband couldn't be happier and prouder. She loves God and that makes her all the more beautiful.

The Word of the Lord.

Psalm 1 (see Seventh Sunday of Easter, Year B, p. 290)

A Reading from the Letter of James [3:13–4:3, 7–8a]

Who is the smart one? If you are gentle and good, your life is born of wisdom. But if you have envy and selfishness in your heart, don't bother bragging. That's not the way to be wise. In fact that will mean you've got all kinds of wickedness around you. Wisdom is peaceable, flexible, and full of mercy, without hypocrisy. Peacemakers will harvest righteousness.

Where do all these fights I keep hearing about come from? I think they come from the fight that is going on inside of you. You want things you don't need or can't have, and it causes conflict inside of you. You don't have what you need because you don't ask. Or because you ask wrong or for the wrong things, in order to just make yourself happy. Give yourself to God. Turn away from the devil, and he will leave you alone. Come closer to God and God will come closer to you.

The Word of the Lord.

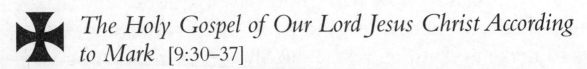

✠ *The Holy Gospel of Our Lord Jesus Christ According to Mark* [9:30–37]

Jesus was talking to his disciples, telling them that someone he trusted would give him over to the authorities; that they would kill him, and he would be raised three days later. The disciples didn't understand what he was talking about, and were afraid to ask him to explain it. When they got to where they were going, Jesus asked them, "I heard you arguing when we were walking. What were you arguing about?" They didn't want to tell him, because they'd been arguing about which one of them was the greatest disciple. Jesus decided to show them a lesson. He sat down, and said to them, "Whoever wants to be the first in line must be the last in line, and everyone's servant." Then he took a little child and held her on his lap and hugged her. He said to them, "If you welcome a child like this in my name, it's the same as welcoming me. And remember, if you welcome me, you welcome the one who sent me."

The Gospel of the Lord.

Proper 21

A Reading from the Book of Esther [7:1–6, 9–10]

The king and Haman were at a feast with Queen Esther. The king told Esther to tell him what her deepest desire was, and he would grant it to her. "Anything," he said. "Ask me anything." Then Queen Esther answered, "If I could have anything, and if it pleases you, I would like to ask for my life and the lives of my people. We have been treated badly, like slaves."

"Who has treated you badly?" asked the king. The queen pointed at Haman. And Haman was terrified. And they hung Haman for the way he treated Esther's people.

Someone in the king's court sent letters to all of Esther's people, that they were free. And after that day, they celebrated their freedom every year with feasting and gladness, sending gifts of food to each other and giving gifts to the poor.

The Word of the Lord.

Psalm 124 (see Proper 16, Year A, p. 174)

A Reading from the Letter of James [5:13–20]

Is someone in your group hurting? Pray for him. Is someone celebrating something wonderful that has happened to her? Sing songs of joy with her. Is anybody sick? Call the church leaders to pray with her and anoint her with oil in God's name. God will honor your faithful prayer. And God will forgive your sins. Confess your sins to each other, and pray for each other so you can move on with your lives and be whole again. The prayer of God's people is powerful and does wonders. Elijah was a human being like us, and remember, he prayed night and day that it would rain. It finally rained and things began to grow on the earth again.

My brothers and sisters, if anyone among you wanders from the truth and you can bring him back with you, you have done a good thing.

The Word of the Lord.

✠ *The Holy Gospel of Our Lord Jesus Christ According to Mark* [9:38–50]

John said to Jesus, "Teacher, we saw someone casting out demons in your name, and we tried to stop him, because he was not one of us." But Jesus said, "Do not stop him; for no one who does something wonderful in my name will be able soon afterward to speak evil of me. Whoever is not against us is for us. I'm telling you, whoever gives you a cup of water to drink because you bear the name of Christ will be honored. If anyone tries to keep someone with little faith from getting closer to me, it would be better if you were thrown into the sea. If your hand gets between someone and God, you should cut it off. It's not doing you any good. If it's your foot, cut it off. If your eye is the problem, poke it out, for it's better to be with God with one eye than not to be with God at all.

"Everyone is going to go through rough times, so prepare yourselves. And preserve what you have been given. Be at peace yourself and at peace with each other."

The Gospel of the Lord.

Proper 22

A Reading from the Book of Job [1:1; 2:1–10]

There was a really good man named Job who loved God. Satan was talking to God one day and he said he'd been on earth checking things out. God said, "Did you meet my good man, Job? There's no one better than Job." Satan said, "Well of course he's a good man. You've given him everything he could possibly want. Take it all away, make him sick and he'll curse you to your face." God said, "I don't think so. But go ahead; let's see what he'll do. Just make sure he's still alive."

So Satan left God and inflicted horrid sores on Job from the sole of his foot to the crown of his head. Job was so miserable he was scraping his sores and sat in ashes all day. Job's wife said to him, "You still love your God after all this? Curse God and die and you'll be out of your misery." But Job said to his wife, "You are foolish. Do you think I will just take the good God sends me and give up when things go bad?" And Job remained faithful and did not curse God.

The Word of the Lord.

Psalm 26

Tell me if I've honored you, God.
I've done my very best.
I have trusted you and still am faithful.
Examine my heart and my mind.
See the good that is in me.
I keep your love before my eyes
and I walk toward it faithfully.
I have stayed away from worthless people
And away from worthless things.

Examine my heart and my mind.
See the good that is in me.

I will wash my hands in innocence, God,
so that I may be clean when I worship you.
I sing loud songs of praise and thanksgiving
and remember all that you have done for me.

Examine my heart and my mind.
See the good that is in me.

God, I love being in your house
and soaking up your beautiful light.
Don't let me get swept away with sinners,
    or get beat up by hurtful people who plot evil schemes.

Examine my heart and my mind.
See the good that is in me.

I will always be my best for you, and do my best for you.
Redeem me and have pity on me.
I am grounded in you, God.
And I will tell everyone I know and see that you are my God.

Examine my heart and my mind.
See the good that is in me.

A Reading from the Letter to the Hebrews [1:1–4; 2:5–12]

A long time ago, God spoke to our mothers and fathers in lots of ways through the prophets, but now he has spoken to us through his Son, through whom the world was created. The Son reflects God's glory to us. He is the exact imprint of God's very being, and all things are held together by his powerful words. When he had completed his job of making us right with God, he sat down next to God on high, surrounded by angels. Angels do God's bidding, and are crowned with glory, but God has lifted the Son above them.

Jesus, while he was on earth, was a little lower than the angels, but now he is crowned with glory and by God's grace he has tasted death for us all. God, in bringing all his children to glory, made Jesus the pioneer of their salvation and he is perfect because of his sufferings. We all have one Father and Jesus is proud to call us his brothers and sisters.

The Word of the Lord.

✠ *The Holy Gospel of Our Lord Jesus Christ According to Mark* [10:2–16]

Some Pharisees came to test Jesus with this question: "Is it okay for a man to divorce his wife?" Jesus asked them, "What did Moses say about it?" They said, "Moses said a man could write a letter dismissing his wife, thereby divorcing her." Jesus said, "Moses wrote this because of your hard hearts. From the beginning of creation, God wanted us to live together faithfully and make new families together. So you don't put yourself first, but put your relationship with your loved one above your own interest. What God has joined together, no one should try to tear apart."

Then in the house the disciples asked him again about this. He said to them, "If you divorce your spouse to marry another spouse, you are committing adultery."

People were bringing little children to him in order that he might touch them and bless them. The disciples tried to shoo them away. But when Jesus saw this, he was upset and said to them, "Don't you dare try to keep these little ones from me. Let me hold them. The kingdom of God belongs to little ones just like these. If you aren't open to God's kingdom like a little child is open, you will never enter the kingdom." And he picked them up in his arms and laid his hands on the children and blessed them.

The Gospel of the Lord.

Proper 23

A Reading from the Book of Job [23:1–9, 16–17]

Job said, "Oh, I wish I knew where God was so we could talk together. I am full of things I'd like to say. I want to hear what God has to say to me. Would God tell me how great he is? I know God is reasonable and would listen.

"Where are you God? If I walk forward, you're not there. If I take a step back, I can't tell if you're there or not. If I turn to the left, I don't see you. If I turn to the right, you are nowhere in sight. God, you are wearing me down. I am terrified without you. If only I would just vanish in the darkness, and see nothing at all."

The Word of the Lord.

Psalm 22:1–15

My God, have you forgotten about me? Why have you left me all alone? Do you even hear my cry? Can you hear in my voice how distressed I am?

Don't be so far away, because trouble is so near
and there is no one else to help me.

I cry for you in the day, and I hear no answer from you.
During the night I cry out, and I cannot sleep.
I know that you are the Holy One,
the one all Israel praises.

Don't be so far away, because trouble is so near
and there is no one else to help me.

Those who came before me trusted you and you came to help them.

They cried out to you and you heard their voice.
They trusted in you and were not disappointed.

Don't be so far away, because trouble is so near
and there is no one else to help me.

As for me, I am a worm, not even human.
Everyone makes fun of me and hates me.
They laugh at me, saying:
Look what she gets for trusting in the Lord. If the Lord loves her,
let's see him rescue her.
Yet I know that you are the one who brought me to life
and kept me safe on my mother's breast.
I have been yours ever since I was born.
You were my God even when I was in my mother's body.

Don't be so far away, because trouble is so near
and there is no one else to help me.

It's like bulls are circling around me
and their jaws are wide open ready to eat me.
Like a roaring, hungry lion, they come after me.

Don't be so far away, because trouble is so near
and there is no one else to help me.

I am poured out like water out of a bottle;
all my bones are out of joint;
my heart is like wax that is melting.
My mouth is dried out and my tongue sticks to the roof
of my mouth;
I feel like you've laid me in my grave.

Don't be so far away, because trouble is so near
and there is no one else to help me.

A Reading from the Letter to the Hebrews [4:12–16]

God's Word is alive and acting in our lives. It is sharper than a double-edged sword and able to discover the intentions of our hearts. No one can hide from God. All of us are exposed and are accountable to God.

Thank God, we have a great high priest in Jesus, God's Son. Let us live up to what we believe. Jesus understands our weaknesses, and he understands us because he has been one of us, yet never built a barrier between himself and God like we have. Because of Jesus we can approach God and God's grace with boldness and receive mercy and help when we need it.

The Word of the Lord.

✠ *The Holy Gospel of Our Lord Jesus Christ According to Mark* [10:17–31]

As Jesus was about to hit the road, a man ran up and knelt before him, and asked him, "Good Teacher, what must I do to inherit eternal life?" Jesus said to him, "First of all, only God is good. Secondly, you already know what you should do. The commandments say 'Don't murder. Don't be unfaithful to your spouse, don't steal or lie. Don't cheat. Honor your parents.'" He said to him, "Teacher, I have done all those things since I was a kid." Jesus, looking at him, loved him, and said, "Okay. There's one more thing for you to do; go, sell what you own, and give the money to the poor, and you will have treasure in heaven. Then come and follow me." When the man heard this, he was shocked and went away upset, for he had many possessions and couldn't imagine giving them up. Not even for God.

Then Jesus looked around and said to his disciples, "It is so hard for those who have lots of things to enter into the kingdom of God!" And the disciples didn't quite understand what he meant. So Jesus said to them again, "Children, it's not easy to enter the kingdom of God! In fact, it is easier for a camel to go through the eye of a needle than for someone who is rich to enter the kingdom of God." They were confused and said to one another, "Well then, why should we bother if it's so difficult? How will people like us enter God's kingdom?" Jesus looked at them and said, "It's impossible for you, but not for God; for with God everything is possible."

Peter said, "Look, we have left everything we had to follow you." Jesus said, "I'm telling you, anyone who has left family or fields or dreams for my sake and for the sake of the Good News of God's love will receive a hundred times what you could want as well as a life that is eternal. Remember, I told you, many who are first will be last, and the last will be first. It will be completely upside down to what you might expect."

The Gospel of the Lord.

Proper 24

A Reading from the Book of Job [38:1–7, 34–41]

God spoke to Job from the middle of the whirlwind:

Who are you? How dare you question what I'm doing with no knowledge whatsoever? Get ready. Be a man. Because I have lots of questions for you, and I want you to answer me. Where were you when I laid the foundation of the earth? Tell me, who measured it and stretched out the land from sea to sea? Surely you know!

Who laid the cornerstone when the morning stars were singing together and all the beings that live in heaven were shouting for joy? Can you lift your voice to the clouds and have them rain down floods of water? Can you summon lightning bolts and have them come to you, saying, "Here we are?" Who puts wisdom in the deepest parts of people or introduces understanding to the mind? Do you know how many clouds there are? I do. Can you make the clouds spill over with water and nourish the dry, parched earth? I can. Can you hunt the prey for the lion, or satisfy hungry little lion cubs, when they crouch in their dens? Who provides food for the ravens, when their hungry little ones cry to God?

The Word of the Lord.

Psalm 104:1–9, 25, 37b

Let's bless God.
Deep in my heart I know how great you are, God.
And I can see you wear majesty and splendor like clothing.
You wrap yourself with light like a blanket around your shoulders
and spread out the heavens like a curtain across the sky.
You have built your home above the skies

and make the clouds your chariot,
and ride on the wings of the wind.

Deep in my heart I know how great you are, God.

You send the wind as your messengers to far ends of the earth
and use flames of fire as your servants.
You have built the world to be strong so that it will never move
an inch from side to side.
You covered it with the deep waters,
and mountains reach from the depths of the sea.

Deep in my heart I know how great you are, God.

You ordered the mountains to their places.
You have set boundaries for the mountains and valleys.
O God, everywhere I turn I see what you have created.
You've made all earth's creatures in your wisdom.

Deep in my heart I know how great you are, God.
Hallelujah!

A Reading from the Letter to the Hebrews [5:1–10]

Priests are called to offer prayers and praise and sacrifice to God on our behalf. Since they are sinful just like us, they confess their sins alongside us. It is a calling from God, not just a job anyone signs up for. Jesus didn't make himself a priest. He was appointed to the position by the Father who said, "You are my Son. You are a priest forever, working on behalf of the people." When Jesus walked the earth, he offered prayers for us. And cried to God with us and was heard by God because of his obedience to God. Jesus learned obedience through suffering. And when he was made perfect he became the source of salvation for all of us who listen to him and obey him.

The Word of the Lord.

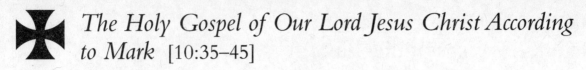

✠ *The Holy Gospel of Our Lord Jesus Christ According to Mark* [10:35–45]

James and John came up to Jesus and said, "We want to ask you to do something for us." Jesus said, "What would that be?" They said, "We would like to be seated right next to you in your glory, one of us on your right and one of us on your left." Jesus said to them, "You have no idea what you're asking for. Are you going to be able to drink the cup of suffering that I will drink, or be baptized with me?" They said, "Sure. We can do that." Jesus replied, "You will suffer as I will suffer, and you will be baptized as I am, but seating arrangements in heaven? Those are not my business. God will deal with that."

When the rest of the disciples heard what James and John wanted from Jesus, they were angry. Jesus tried to settle them down. "You've seen power plays among kings and rulers, haven't you? It shouldn't be like that with you. Whoever wants to be great must be a servant. Whoever wants to be first among you must be slave to all of you. The Son of Man did not come to be served, but to serve and to lay aside his life so that all of you could be free."

The Gospel of the Lord.

Proper 25

A Reading from the Book of Job [42:1–6, 10–17]

Job answered God, "Know that you can do whatever you want and nothing you want to do can be stopped. I didn't mean to offend you, not knowing what I was talking about. I didn't understand that things are too wonderful for me to know. I had heard of you but now my eyes have seen you. And I'm sorry for what I said and did." After all the trouble Job had been through, after the loss of his home and children and cattle, God restored what Job had lost. And Job had twice as much as he had before his troubles came. His friends and family came to be with him again. Job's latter days were more blessed than his younger days. He welcomed more children to his family and lived to be an old man, with a full rich life, having seen his children's children.

The Word of the Lord.

Psalm 13 (see Proper 8, Year A, p. 148)

A Reading from the Letter to the Hebrews [7:23–28]

Priests come and go, because they can't live forever. But Jesus will always be our priest, because he will never die. So for all time he will approach God for us. As a priest, Jesus doesn't have to offer God sacrifices; he already did that on the cross when he offered his own life. Jesus is the perfect priest for us, the priest God appointed.

The Word of the Lord.

✠ *The Holy Gospel of Our Lord Jesus Christ According to Mark* [10:46–52]

Jesus and his disciples were leaving Jericho with a large crowd. Bartimaeus was a blind man begging along the side of the road. When Bart heard Jesus of Nazareth was passing by, he shouted, "Jesus, Son of David, have mercy on me!" People tried to shush him, but he cried out even louder, "Son of David, have mercy on me!" Jesus stopped in his tracks and said, "Call him here." So they said to Bartimaeus, "You lucked out! Get up because Jesus is calling for you." So, throwing off his cloak, he leapt to his feet and came to Jesus. Jesus asked him, "What do you want me to do for you?" "My teacher," the blind man said, "let me see again. That's what I want." Jesus said to him, "Go, your faith has made you well." Immediately, he could see, and he became one of Jesus followers from that moment on.

The Gospel of the Lord.

Proper 26

A Reading from the Book of Ruth [1:1–18]

It hadn't rained for a long time and there was very little food in Judah. So a man took his wife, Naomi, and sons and daughters-in-law to live in Moab where there was some food. Then Naomi's husband died. Ten years later her sons both died, leaving behind their wives. Naomi heard that there was food enough in Judah again and wanted to return home. She took her two daughters-in-law, Orpah and Ruth, with her. When they got there, Naomi told them to go back to their own families where they might have a chance for a better life. "God bless you both," she said to them. She kissed them goodbye and they all hugged and cried together. "We won't leave you, Naomi," they said. We will stay with you because you are our family now." Naomi said, "But I can't provide you with husbands. Go on. Don't worry about me. It will be far better for you to say good-bye to me and start a new life." They all cried again. Orpah kissed Naomi goodbye and went to find her family. But Ruth didn't budge. "Go along with Orpah," said Naomi.

But Ruth said, "Don't make me leave you. Wherever you go, I will go. Your home will be my home. Your people will be my people and your God will be my God. I will die where you will die. May God grant me this." When Naomi was sure that Ruth meant it, she stopped begging her to go and lead a new life without her.

The Word of the Lord.

Psalm 146

Praise God!
As long as I'm alive I'm going to sing God's praises.
I'm not going to bother trusting in important people to help me.

I will trust in God who made everything there is.

There's nothing they can do compared to what God does.
They won't live any longer than I will, and their words die
with them.
No, I will trust in God who made everything there is,
who is faithful to us,
who sees that everyone gets justice and food.

I will trust in God who made everything there is.

God sets the prisoners free;
and makes blind people able to see.
God lifts up the chins of those who hang their heads,
watches out for people who are alone in a crowd,
and cares for orphans and widows who have no one.

God stops the wicked ways of people.
I will trust in God who made everything there is.
Praise God forever.

A Reading from the Letter to the Hebrews [9:11–14]

When Christ came as our high priest, he was able to enter God's holy place, not by offering a sacrifice of animals, but by offering his very life. Just think—if sacrifices of goats and bulls made people holy and acceptable, how much more will a pure lamb like Christ purify us!

The Word of the Lord.

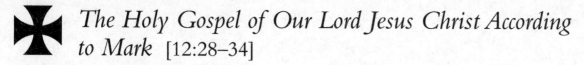

✠ *The Holy Gospel of Our Lord Jesus Christ According to Mark* [12:28–34]

A scribe had been listening to Jesus and the church leaders talking, and he was impressed with what Jesus had to say. So he asked Jesus, "Which commandment is the most important commandment?" Jesus answered, "This one: Hear O Israel, the Lord our God is one. You shall love the Lord your God with all your heart, with all your soul, with all your mind, and with all your strength. And the second most important is this: You shall love your neighbor as yourself. No other commandment is greater than these." The scribe said, "You are so right, teacher. These commandments are more important than any offering or sacrifice." Jesus was impressed and said, "You're not far from the kingdom of God. I can tell." After that, no one dared to ask Jesus any question.

The Gospel of the Lord.

Proper 27

A Reading from the Book of Ruth [3:1–5; 4:13–17]

Naomi said to her daughter-in-law Ruth, "I would feel much better if you had someone other than me in your life. You need some security. You know Boaz? He'll be down at the barn tonight working. Put your best clothes on and take a walk down to the barn and see what happens." Ruth said, "That's a good idea. I'll do it." Long story short, Boaz and Ruth got married and had a baby boy. People were happy for Ruth and Boaz, but also happy for Naomi, who now had a beautiful grandson to take care of and who might take care of her in her old age. His name was Obed. He grew up to become the father of Jesse, who was the father of King David.

The Word of the Lord.

Psalm 127

Unless God builds your house,
  there's no point in building it at all.
Unless God is watching over the city,
  there's no point in keeping watch.
Why do you get up so early in the morning and work hard until
  late at night,
and then wonder why you can't sleep? God will give you sleep
  because God loves you.
Children are God's gifts to you. They are as precious as arrows to
  a warrior.
If you want arrows or children, you'll be happy if you have a
  quiver full of them.
You can count on them to help you when enemies are at your door.

A Reading from the Letter to the Hebrews [9:24–28]

Christ has not entered the temple that human hands have made, but has entered heaven itself. And he is now in God's presence still working on our behalf. Unlike the priests in the temple who offer sacrifices time and time again, Christ has offered himself just once. And that was more than enough for all of us.

The Word of the Lord.

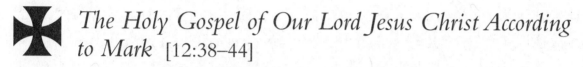

✠ *The Holy Gospel of Our Lord Jesus Christ According to Mark* [12:38–44]

Jesus was in the temple teaching, and said, "Watch out for those people who like to walk around in fancy robes and have the best seats in church or at dinner parties. They love the publicity they get when someone spots them in public. They pray long prayers, as long as people are listening to them. They take away from poor widows who don't have very much anyway."

Jesus watched people putting money into the temple treasury. Many rich people came and put in a great deal of money. Then a poor widow came and put in two little coins, which weren't worth very much. It was all she had. And she gave it to God. Jesus told his disciples about her, saying, "Some people can afford to give a lot because they have even more. But this woman, she gave her heart and all she had to God."

The Gospel of the Lord.

Proper 28

A Reading from the First Book of Samuel [1:4–20]

Elkanah had two wives whom he loved. His wife Penny had lots of children, but he especially loved Hannah, who had none. Penny used to remind Hannah of this all the time. Hannah would go to the temple to pray and cry as she begged God to send her children. Her husband worried about her because sometimes she would be so sad she wouldn't eat. He would say to her, "Why are you crying? Why are you so sad? You've got me. Aren't I better than ten sons?" That didn't make her feel any better.

One day Hannah was crying in the temple. Her prayer that day was for a son. She promised that if God sent her a son, she would dedicate him to God. She was crying so hard that no noise was coming out of her. Eli, the priest in the temple, thought she was drunk and told her to pull herself together and stop drinking. Hannah said, "No, sir. I haven't been drinking. I'm just hurting so badly and I've been pouring out my heart to God." Eli said, "Go in peace then, my dear. God will answer your prayer." That made Hannah feel better and she went back home.

It wasn't long before Hannah and Elkanah welcomed a baby boy into their family and they named him Samuel, which means, "I asked God for him."

The Word of the Lord.

The Song of Hannah [1 Samuel 2:1–10]

My heart is overjoyed and God has made me stronger than ever.
There is no Holy One like God.

Our God is a rock.

Humble yourself before the God of all knowledge.
Before God the strongest weapons are broken.
And the weakest are made strong.

Our God is a rock.

The ones who filled themselves are empty
and the hungry ones have more than they can eat.
Those who had no children are surrounded by happy little ones.
God makes poor and rich,
kills and brings to life again.
God raises up the poor from the dust,
and lifts the needy from the streets and brings them into the
palace to sit next to the king.

Our God is a rock.

God built the pillars of the earth that the world is set on.
God protects those who are faithful, but sends away the wicked.
God's thunder rumbles in the heavens,
and decides whom to strengthen.

Our God is a rock.

A Reading from the Letter to the Hebrews [10:11–14, 19–25]

Priests in the temple do their work day after day, offering the same sacrifices that never take away sin. But when Christ made the sacrifice of himself, it was for all people and for all time. Because of that sacrifice, we are confident that we can stand before God because Jesus is our great high priest. So let's approach God with true hearts, full of faith, being sprinkled clean with the pure water of baptism. We hold on tight to God's promises. Let's figure out how we can provoke each other to do good things for other people, and to love. We need to gather together often so that we can encourage each other as we see the Day of the Lord coming closer.

The Word of the Lord.

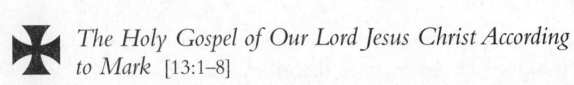

✠ *The Holy Gospel of Our Lord Jesus Christ According to Mark* [13:1–8]

Jesus walked out of the temple and one of his disciples said, "Can you believe how big that temple is! Look at the size of those stones!" Jesus said, "You mean these buildings here? I'm telling you, soon these stones will not be left standing; all will be thrown down." They got to the Mount of Olives where they could see the temple. When they were alone with him, Peter, James, John, and Andrew said, "When is this going to happen? What signs will there be?" Jesus said, "You'll need to watch out because all kinds of people will pretend to know the time and place. Wars will begin. But that won't be the end. That will be the beginning of the end. Nations will be fighting; there will be earthquakes and famines. Things will get worse before they get better. That will tell you something new is about to be born."

The Gospel of the Lord.

Proper 29

A Reading from the Second Book of Samuel [23:1–7]

These are David's last words. "The spirit of God speaks through me. I have God's own words on my tongue and here they are: 'The one who rules justly with people, and follows God, is like the morning light, like the sun rising in a clear blue sky, gleaming on the green grass below.' This is how I govern," says David. "God has made promises to me. Certainly God will help me.

"Those who don't follow God are like thorns that you can't pick up with your hand. You use the end of an iron bar to push them into the fire so they'll burn up on the spot."

The Word of the Lord.

Psalm 132:1–13

God, don't forget King David
and all he went through.
He swore he would follow you, saying,
I won't rest until I find a place for God to dwell,
until I build a house for God.
They heard that the ark, your dwelling, was in the fields
    and they found it and carried it home.

Let us all go to God's house,
and kneel before God in praise.

Come, God, into your resting place
where you are strong and true.
Let your priests wear righteousness for robes.
Let all your people sing their hearts out with joy.
For David's sake, remember your promise:
Your son will be king.

If your children follow me, and remember my promises, their
children will be kings forevermore.

Let us all go to God's house,
and kneel before God in praise.

A Reading from the Revelation to John [1:4b–8]

I send you grace and peace, from the one who is and who was and who is to come, and before all who are around his throne, and from Jesus Christ, ruler of all that is. To him who loves us more than we know and freed us from sin by his very lifeblood, and brought us together as a people to serve God. Look, he will come in the clouds and every single eye will see him, even those who put him to death, and they will be sorry for what they have done. That's how it will be.

The Lord God, who is and who was and who is to come, says, "I am the Alpha and the Omega, the beginning and the end. I am the Almighty."

The Word of the Lord.

✠ *The Holy Gospel of Our Lord Jesus Christ According to John* [18:33–37]

Then Pilate asked Jesus, "Are you the King of the Jews?" Jesus answered, "Do you ask this on your own, or did others tell you about me?" Pilate replied, "I am not a Jew, am I? I am a Roman. Your own people have handed you over to me. What have you done?" Jesus answered, "My kingdom is not from this world." Pilate asked him, "So you are a king, are you?" Jesus answered, "You say that I am a king. Everyone who belongs to the truth listens to my voice."

The Gospel of the Lord.

Year C

The First Sunday of Advent

A Reading from the Book of Jeremiah [33:4–16]

Soon I will make good on the promises I made to you. When I do, a branch will grow on David's family tree. This Branch will stand for justice and goodness in the land. Jerusalem will be safe from harm.

We will call this Branch: "The Lord is our righteousness."

The Word of the Lord.

Psalm 25:1–9 (see First Sunday in Lent, Year B, p. 257)

A Reading from the Second Letter of Paul to the Thessalonians [3:9–13]

There's no way we can thank God enough for the joy you bring into our lives. We pray constantly for you, hoping we can be face to face soon to encourage you. I pray God can find a way to let us come see you soon. May God increase your love for each other, and make it overflow into your lives. May God make your hearts strong until the time Jesus comes again.

The Word of the Lord.

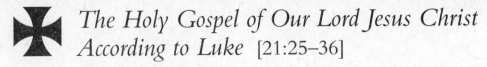

✠ *The Holy Gospel of Our Lord Jesus Christ*
According to Luke [21:25–36]

Jesus said, "At the end, there will be signs in the moon and stars and the sun. The people of the earth will be confused and overpowered by the sea and the waves. People will be scared to death at what is happening to God's world. Then the Son of Man will come in a cloud with power and glory. When you see these things take place, stand up tall and watch what happens, because that means your redemption is close."

Then he said this: "You know when the trees sprout leaves that means summer is near. When you see the signs I just told you about, you will know that the kingdom of God is near. I'm telling you, it's beginning to happen even as I speak. Heaven and earth will pass away, but the words I say to you will not.

"Watch out so your hearts are not weighted down with the worries of this life and that you are not caught unprepared like you've walked into a trap. Lots of people all over the world will be surprised by all this. But not you. I want you to be always on alert, praying that you have strength enough to escape what will happen and that you can stand up straight before the Son of Man."

The Gospel of the Lord.

The Second Sunday of Advent

A Reading from the Book of Baruch [5:1–9]

You don't need to wear your sadness like a jacket anymore, Jerusalem. Put on the beauty of God's glory instead and wear it forever. God will give you a robe of righteousness to wear. And a tiara glowing with God's goodness will be put on top of your head. God will show your beauty to everyone under the sun. And God will give you a new name, "Righteous Peace, Godly Glory." Stand up tall, Jerusalem. If you look to the east you will see all your children gathered because God called them together. They will rejoice that God has remembered them. Their enemies had taken them away, but God will bring them back to you as he promised like kings carried in glory on their royal thrones. God has ordered all the highest mountains to be lowered. And the valleys will be filled up to make the ground level. That way, Israel can walk back safely to where she belongs. The forests will provide shade for her at God's command. And God will be leading the parade back to Jerusalem with the light of his goodness that makes him glow from the inside.

The Word of the Lord.

Canticle 16: The Song of Zechariah [Luke 1:68–79]

Praise be to God; he's come to set his people free. God has sent us someone to save us, born in King David's family. The prophets from long ago promised that he would do this, that he would keep his people safe from their enemies. He said he'd be merciful and would remember the promise he made to our father Abraham, to set his people free. His people are free to worship him without fear. And they're holy and righteous in his sight now and forever. You, my little one, will be called God's prophet, because you will be making the way ready for God. You will tell the people about salvation, and the forgiveness of their sins. Our God is good and kind, and in the morning the dawn's bright light will break upon us and flood our darkness with glorious light, it will drown the shadow of death and make us walk on paths of peace.

A Reading from the Letter of Paul to the Philippians [1:3–11]

Every time you cross my mind, I thank God for you, and I think about you all the time! I am praying for you constantly. I know for sure that the one who started you off on this good path will get you where you belong by the time Jesus comes. I know that you hold me in your heart and you share in God's grace with me. It's helped me when I was in jail and defending myself in court. God knows how much I'd like to be with you.

Here's what I pray for you: that the love you share will overflow from your hearts, and that more and more you will know and have the wisdom to choose what is best. That way you can complete God's good work in you and be who Jesus meant for you to be to the glory of God.

The Word of the Lord.

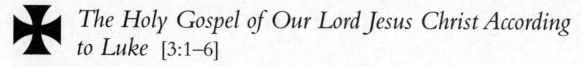

✠ *The Holy Gospel of Our Lord Jesus Christ According to Luke* [3:1–6]

When Tiberius had been emperor for fifteen years, and when Herod was the governor in Galilee, the Word of God came to John who lived in the wilderness. He wandered all over the region by the Jordan River, telling people to be baptized and wash themselves of their sin. The prophet Isaiah talked about him a long time ago: "I hear a voice crying out in the desert, 'Get ready for God to come. Straighten the paths. Build up the valleys and lower the mountaintops. Make the crooked places straight and the rocky roads smooth. Then everyone will see God's salvation.'"

The Gospel of the Lord.

The Third Sunday of Advent

A Reading from the Book of Zephaniah [3:14–20 or see Easter Vigil, Year A, p. 107]

Sing as loud as you can, O daughter Zion;
go ahead and shout, O Israel!
Rejoice and exult with all your heart,
O daughter Jerusalem!
God has taken away everything and everybody that could hurt you. God is right beside you and you don't have anything to be afraid of or worry about anymore.
God has won the day.
He will rejoice over you with gladness,
he will renew you in his love;
he will join you in singing loud and long.
God says: I will take care of the disasters,
and I will deal with the people who want to put you down.
I will save those who can't keep up with you
and gather the people on the fringes of your community,
and I will change their shame into praise and make their name famous all over the earth.
I will bring you home, and make you special among all the peoples of the earth.

The Word of the Lord.

Canticle 9 The First Song of Isaiah [Isaiah 12:2–6]
(see Easter Vigil, Year A, p. 103)

A Reading from the Letter of Paul to the Philippians [4:4–7]

Celebrate God. Always. Rejoice and let people see the smiles on your faces and the deep joy in your hearts. Be gentle with everyone. God is near. Don't let your worries overwhelm you.

Instead of worrying, take your concerns and prayer requests to God. And don't forget to thank him while you're at it. May God's peace, which is beyond our ability to understand, hold your hearts and minds close to Christ Jesus.

The Word of the Lord.

✠ *The Holy Gospel of Our Lord Jesus Christ According to Luke* [3:7–18]

Crowds of people came to the desert to be baptized by John the Baptist. Sometimes he would yell, "You are just a pile of snakes! If you want to turn your lives around, let me see you do it. Don't think just because Abraham was your ancestor you'll get away easy. God could turn these rocks into the children of Abraham. You're nothing special."

The crowds said, "What do you think we should do then?" John said, "If you have an extra coat, give it to someone who has no coat at all. If you have plenty of food, share it." Tax collectors, who used to cheat people, would come to be baptized. "What should we do, John?" John would say, "Don't collect more money from people than you should."

Soldiers would say, "And what about us? How do we turn our lives around?" John would tell them, "Don't squeeze money out of people just because you have power over them. Be satisfied with the money you earn."

John had filled the hearts of people full of hope. And they wondered if he might be the One they were waiting for to save them.

John made sure they knew that he was *not* the Messiah. "I just baptize you with water. The Messiah is much more powerful and will baptize you with the Holy Spirit and fire. He will make things right."

That was good news to people's ears and hearts.

The Gospel of the Lord.

The Fourth Sunday of Advent

A Reading from the Book of Micah [5:2–5a]

It's you, Bethlehem! You're the tiny town from which the leader of Israel will come. He comes from a distinguished and ancient family. His people have been wandering for a while, but they will come home soon. And then they will be well fed and cared for when their strong, good leader is with them. Then, they'll live in a safe place, because their leader will be honored all over the world as a peacemaker.

The Word of the Lord.

Canticle 15 The Song of Mary [Luke 1:46–55] (see The Third Sunday of Advent, Year A, p. 7)

A Reading from the Letter to the Hebrews [10:5–10]

When Christ came into the world, this is what he said: "God doesn't want sacrifices and offerings, instead God prepared a body for me to live in and do his will." God got rid of the sacrifices and offerings and replaced them with what Christ Jesus did. By God's will, you and I have been made okay in God's sight, through Jesus Christ's body, which he offered for our sake, once and for all.

The Word of the Lord.

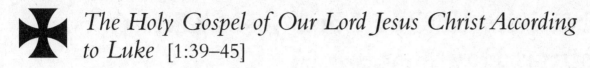

✠ *The Holy Gospel of Our Lord Jesus Christ According to Luke* [1:39–45]

Mary ran to see her cousin Elizabeth who lived in the hill country. When she cried out, "Elizabeth, it's so good to see you!" the baby in Elizabeth's belly jumped up and down.

Elizabeth all of a sudden was filled with the Holy Spirit and yelled, "You are so blessed, Mary! And the little one inside you is blessed as well. How God must love me to send the mother of my Lord to visit me. As soon as I heard your voice, this little guy inside me jumped up and down for joy. This is just as God said it would happen, and we are both so blessed to see things work out this way. God is good to us indeed."

The Gospel of the Lord.

The Nativity of Our Lord, Jesus Christ: Christmas Day (see Year A, p. 13)

Christmas 1 and 2 (see Year A, p. 16 and 20)

The First Sunday after the Epiphany: The Baptism of Our Lord

A Reading from the Book of Isaiah [43:1–7]

Here's what God who made you says: "Don't be afraid, for I hold you in my heart. I know exactly who you are. I have called you by name. You are mine. When you walk through deep water, I will be with you. When the water of the rivers rise, they won't overwhelm you. When the flames are lapping at your heels, you will not be burned. I am your God, the one who saves you. I will pay any price for you because you are precious to me, and I love you. Do not be afraid. I will gather all your people to me, everyone who bears my name. I created you to show my glory, and you do."

The Word of the Lord.

Psalm 29 (see Epiphany 1, Year A, p. 26)

A Reading from the Acts of the Apostles [8:14–17]

Word got back to the apostles in Jerusalem that the people of Samaria were open to God's Word. So Peter and John went to Samaria. They prayed for the people who had already been baptized that they might also receive the Holy Spirit. When Peter and John laid their hands on them, the Holy Spirit came and filled them up.

The Word of the Lord.

✠ *The Holy Gospel of Our Lord Jesus Christ According to Luke* [3:15–17, 21–22]

The people were buzzing with questions and ideas about John the Baptist, wondering if he might be the one they were waiting for, the Messiah. John knew what they wanted to know and answered them, "I just baptize with water. But the powerful one is coming who will baptize with the Holy Spirit. I am not half the man he is. He will turn things around and make them right." John baptized all the people and Jesus was baptized, too. As Jesus stood there praying, the clouds opened and the Holy Spirit flew down on top of him like a dove. A voice from heaven said, "You are my Son, and I love you. I am so very pleased with who you are."

The Gospel of the Lord.

The Second Sunday after the Epiphany

A Reading from the Book of Isaiah [62:1–5]

On behalf of Zion and Jerusalem, I will speak and not be silent until everyone can see that God has saved them. They will shine like a burning torch that no one can ignore. God will give them a new name. They will be like a tiara that God holds, a beautiful crown that God can't put down. No one will think you're lost and forgotten. In fact, God smiles when he thinks about you. God is absolutely delighted with you, as a young man is with his bride.

The Word of the Lord.

Psalm 36:5–10

Your love, God, is so enormous it reaches to the heavens,
    and your faithfulness to the clouds.
Your goodness is like the tallest mountains,
    your justice like the deepest seas.
You save both man and beast.

Keep up the good work, God.

How priceless is your love, O God!
Your people take shelter from the storm under the protection
    of your wings.
They feast upon the abundance of all you have to offer;
you invite them to drink from the river of your delights.

Keep up the good work, God.

You are the well of life that never runs dry,
    and in your light, we see light.
Continue your loving-kindness to those who love you
    and bless those whose hearts are true.

Keep up the good work, God.

A Reading from the First Letter of Paul to the Corinthians [12:1–11]

Here's the deal about the gifts that the Spirit gives. You know how easy it is to fall in love with things that have no life in them. But loving Jesus, and believing that he is your Lord, are things you can't even do unless the Holy Spirit moves you to. Cursing Jesus is *not* something the Spirit would ever cause you to do.

There are all kinds of gifts and ways to help people, ways to help the church, but they all come from the same Spirit. Each of us expresses God's Spirit in the way we share good things with each other. Some of us are very smart, some of us have faith that simply won't quit, some of us are good storytellers. Some people make you feel better when you're down just by being with you. Some have an idea of how things will work out, and others can tell who's lying and who isn't. Some people can speak right to people's hearts. All those gifts that support the work of the church are free gifts from the Spirit.

The Word of the Lord.

✠ *The Holy Gospel of Our Lord Jesus Christ According to John* [2:1–11]

On the third day, Jesus and his mother Mary and the disciples went to a wedding in a village called Cana. The party was fun until they ran out of wine. Mary told Jesus the wine was gone, like she wanted him to do something about it. And Jesus said to her, "I don't know that I should do anything at all about it, Mother. The time isn't right." His mother whispered to the servants, "Just do whatever he tells you."

Jesus thought more about it. The Jewish people washed themselves from huge stone water pots. And standing there were six stone water jars for the Jewish rites of purification, each holding twenty or thirty gallons. Jesus said to the guys in charge of the wine, "Fill those jars with water."

And they filled them up to the very top. He said to them, "Now take a cup of it to the wedding host." So they took it.

The host tasted it, and it wasn't water anymore. It was wine! The servants knew what had happened but the host wondered where this good wine had come from. "Everyone serves the good wine first, and then when everyone has had plenty to drink and they don't care how good the wine is, then you serve the regular wine. But you have kept the best wine until now! No one does that!"

This was a sign that God was working through Jesus. It was the very first sign, and people could see it and even drink it! It revealed who Jesus was and his disciples believed in him.

The Gospel of the Lord.

The Third Sunday after the Epiphany

A Reading from the Book of Nehemiah [8:1–3, 5–6, 8–10]

All the people of Israel were together in the town square. They told Ezra to bring the book of the Law of Moses, the book God had given them. Ezra read it aloud so all of them could hear. He kept reading from sunrise to noon. They couldn't get enough of it. And Ezra opened the book, and held it above his head for everyone to see. They all stood up and raised their hands. Ezra said, "Bless the Lord!" All the people shouted, "Amen! Amen!" lifting their hands over their head and waving them.

Then they quieted down, bowed their heads, and worshiped God with their faces to the ground. Ezra kept reading to them, and helped them understand what it meant for their lives.

People were crying because their hearts were so moved by the words they heard. And felt bad that they had never heard them before. "This is a very good and holy day," Ezra and the priests said. "Go home and celebrate. Share your food with those who have none. Don't be troubled by anything you heard, because God's joy is making you strong."

The Word of the Lord.

Psalm 19 (see Proper 22, Year A, p. 192)

A Reading from the First Letter of Paul to the Corinthians [12:12–31a]

Just like your body has lots of different parts but you have only one body, that's how it is with the Body of Christ, the Church. We were all baptized into one Spirit and into one Body—all of us, whether we're Jewish, or Greek, or slaves, or free. It's a good thing the foot can't say, "I guess I'm not part of your body because I'm not a hand." If all you had were eyes, but no ears, how could you hear? And what about being able to smell? We need all our parts, the ones we use all the time, and the ones we don't even think about. They're just as important.

Because we're all connected in the Body of Christ, if one of us suffers, we all suffer together. If someone is honored, we're all proud. In God's Church, there are different roles to play. Some are teachers, some preachers. Some are little helpers. Find your role and be your very best.

The Word of the Lord.

✠ *The Holy Gospel of Our Lord Jesus Christ According to Luke* [4:14–21]

Jesus came back from the desert filled with the power of the Spirit. Everyone was talking about him and they asked him to come teach them in their synagogues.

When he came to the synagogue in Nazareth, his hometown, he stood up to read the scroll of Isaiah that had been given to him. He found the part that read, "God has anointed me with his Holy Spirit and sent me to bring good news to people who need it most. I've been sent by God to put people back together whose hearts are broken, to let prisoners know they are free people, to release people from whatever is holding them back. To let them know that this time is God's time."

And he rolled up the scroll, gave it back to the attendant, and sat down. The people couldn't take their eyes off him. Then he said, "Today you have heard this scripture come true."

The Gospel of the Lord.

The Fourth Sunday after the Epiphany

A Reading from the Book of Jeremiah [1:4–10]

God told me this, "Even before you were a little baby inside your mother, I knew you were you. Before you were born, I made you special and holy. Way back then, I chose you as the one I wanted to talk to my people for me."

And I said to God, "But God, look at me; I'm just a boy. I can't be the one talking to your people for you!"

Then God said, "Don't say that. You are not 'just a boy!' You are MY boy and you'll go where I send you and say the words I will give you. Don't worry. You don't need to be afraid, because I will always be right there with you."

And then God touched my lips with his fingers and said, "There you go! I've just put my words in your mouth. And with those words you will lead nations and kings, pick some up and tear some down, destroy some and build new ones for me."

The Word of the Lord.

Psalm 71:1–6

I always run to you, God, when I'm in trouble.
Don't ever disappoint me.
In your goodness, rescue me.

Listen to me and make me whole.

Be my rock. Be a castle I can hide in.
Be strong for me.

Listen to me and make me whole.

Rescue me from people who want to hurt me.
You are my hope, O God.
I have always believed in you, ever since I was little.

Even before I was born, you've been strong for me.
I will always, always praise you.

Listen to me and make me whole.

A Reading from the First Letter of Paul to the Corinthians [13:1–13]

It doesn't matter how many beautiful words I use, if I don't have love in my heart I might as well be a noisy gong. So what if I'm the smartest person in the world, or if I have so much faith that I can move mountains? If I don't have love, I am nothing. I can give away all that I have to the poor, but if I have no love in my heart, I am worthless.

Love is patient; love is kind; love is not envious or full of itself or rude. It does not insist on getting its own way all the time; it is not irritable or resentful; it is not happy when something goes wrong for someone else. It can handle a lot. It believes all things, hopes all things, endures all things. Love never ends. Words and knowing things will end, but not love. We can't know everything right now, but we will someday. When I was little, I spoke like a little kid, I thought like a little kid. When I grew older, I acted wiser. Right now we can't see everything clearly, but someday, we'll see God face-to-face and we will know him fully just as he knows every bit of us. And now faith, hope, and love remain, these three; and the greatest of all of them is love.

The Word of the Lord.

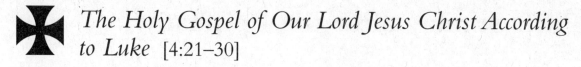

✠ *The Holy Gospel of Our Lord Jesus Christ According to Luke* [4:21–30]

After Jesus read from the prophet Isaiah at the synagogue in his hometown of Nazareth, he told people, "What you just heard has come true today right before your eyes and in your ears." Everyone was so impressed with him and the beautiful things he said. Then they started saying, "Wait a minute. Isn't that Joseph and Mary's boy? Who does he think he is?"

Jesus said, "I know you want me to do here the things you've heard I did in Capernaum. But, just like the prophets, I know I won't be accepted in my hometown. The truth is, there were a lot of things Elijah could have done in his home country, but God sent him to a different place to do God's work. Just as Elijah went out of Israel do to his best work, God is sending me to the people beyond your borders to do mine."

That's when their rage exploded. They didn't want to hear that Jesus was taking the Good News outside their little group. They chased him out of the synagogue, right out of town, and up the highest hill so they could throw him off the cliff. But Jesus was able to make his way through the crowd unharmed, and kept on walking.

The Gospel of the Lord.

The Fifth Sunday after the Epiphany

A Reading from the Book of Isaiah [6:1–8, 9–13]

The year that King Uzziah died, I saw a vision of God sitting on a throne, way up high. The hem of the robe he wore filled the whole temple. Angels were all around him. Each of them had six wings, two to cover their faces, two to cover their feet, and two to fly with. They were calling back and forth to each other, "Holy, holy, holy is the Lord of hosts. The whole earth is full of his glory." The doorways shook at their voices, and the place filled with smoke.

I was scared. "I am doomed," I cried. "For I'm a sinful person with unclean lips and yet I have seen the King, the Lord of hosts, with my very eyes."

Then one of the angels flew over to me, holding a burning hot coal with a pair of tongs that he'd just taken from the altar in the temple. He touched my mouth with it and said, "Now that this has touched your lips, you're not sinful anymore."

Then I heard God speak, "Who can I get to do my work for me? Who should I send?"

I spoke up and said, "I'm the one you can send, God. Here I am. Send me."

Then God said, "Go and say this to the people: Keep listening, everyone, but you're not going to get it. Keep looking even though you won't see. Stop up your ears and close your eyes and turn off your brain. Then turn and be healed."

"How long should I say that, God?" I asked.

God said, "Until I send everyone far away and their land is completely empty. When everything is burned to the ground, there will be a tiny holy seed in the stump of the last tree that was cut down."

The Word of the Lord.

Psalm 138 (see Proper 5, Year B, p. 300)

A Reading from the First Letter of Paul to the Corinthians [15:1–11]
(see Easter Day, Year B, p. 277)

✠ *The Holy Gospel of Our Lord Jesus Christ According to Luke* [5:1–11]

Jesus was standing by the lake, and the people were crowding around him to hear what he had to say. He got into a boat that belonged to Simon and asked him to push out into the lake. Then he sat down in the boat and started teaching the people on the shore.

When he was done talking, he said to Simon, "Let's go out into the deeper water and see what we can catch with your nets." Simon said, "Jesus, we fished there all night long and didn't catch a thing. But, if you want, we'll do that and I'll let down the nets." Was Simon surprised when they caught so many fish they didn't know what to do with them! Their nets began to break they were so full of fish.

Simon signaled the other boat to come help them. They filled up both boats so full of fish that they began to sink. When Simon saw that, he fell on his knees in front of Jesus and said, "You are so holy, I don't think I should even be near you. You know, Jesus, I am really sinful. I don't think I can take all this holiness."

But Jesus said to Simon, "Do not be afraid; from now on I will show you how to catch people and bring them to God." They brought their boats in to shore, and then Simon and his partners, James and John, left everything behind and followed Jesus.

The Gospel of the Lord.

The Sixth Sunday after the Epiphany

A Reading from the Book of Jeremiah [17:5–10]

God says, "You're heading for nothing but trouble if you trust in people who think they know everything, but turn their hearts away from God. You'll be like a shrub in the desert, waiting for some rain. It'll be like you're living in the salt flats, which blind your eyes and have no hope of shade.

"But if you trust God, you'll be like a tree planted by water, sending your roots deep into the soil next to the stream. You won't have to worry about the heat. Your leaves will always stay green. Even in drought, you'll grow lots of good fruit.

"Your heart can lead you in the wrong direction, and you might not even realize it. I know your heart," God says. "I can see what's really going on inside your heart and I will give you what you need."

The Word of the Lord.

Psalm 1 (see The Seventh Sunday of Easter, Year B, p. 290)

A Reading from the First Letter of Paul to the Corinthians [15:12–20]

If you believe that Christ was raised from the dead, how can you let people think there is no such thing as resurrection? If Jesus wasn't raised from the dead, then there is no point in doing what we're doing, and nothing that we've said is true. And if we believe what's not true, then we're pretty pathetic, aren't we?

But the fact is, Christ *has* been raised from the dead, and is alive, the first of many who will live again.

The Word of the Lord.

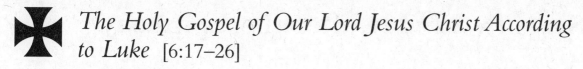

✠ *The Holy Gospel of Our Lord Jesus Christ According to Luke* [6:17–26]

Lots of people from all over the country surrounded Jesus to hear what he had to say and to be healed of their diseases and released from their troubles.

Jesus looked his disciples in the eye and said,

"You are blessed when you think you have nothing, because you really have the kingdom of God.

"You are blessed when you are hungry for something better, because you will be filled.

"You are blessed when you are crying now, because later you won't be able to stop laughing.

"I know it's hard when people hate you, exclude you, make fun of you because of me. Don't feel too bad, because you're in excellent company. That's how the greatest prophets were treated too.

"Don't think you've got it made because you have lots of money; that might be all you have.

"Don't think you've got it made because you've stuffed yourself with good food; hunger will catch up with you later.

"And don't think that if you're laughing now, the fun will never end. Because it will. And soon you'll be crying.

"If people can only say nice things about you, maybe you're not pushing them hard enough. Don't just do what feels good. People love it, but that's not what you were called to do."

The Gospel of the Lord.

The Seventh Sunday after the Epiphany

A Reading from the Book of Genesis [45:3–11, 15]

Joseph's brothers had sold him as a slave to the Egyptians many years ago. They thought he was probably dead by now. But Joseph had become an important man in Egypt, helping the government give out grain to people from the region when there was little to eat. The brothers travelled from their home to Egypt to see if they could find food for their families. Little did they know, they would have to ask for help from their brother Joseph. Joseph's brothers, whom he hadn't seen for many years, were standing in front of him. They didn't recognize him. He said to them, "Look, it's me, Joseph. Is my father still alive?" His brothers could hardly talk; they were so shocked to see him.

"Come closer," Joseph said. "I am your brother, Joseph, the one you sold into slavery so many years ago. But God turned that into a good thing, so I've forgiven you. I work for the Pharaoh and am in charge of getting grain to people who need it during this famine. Go home and tell our father that I'm alive, that God has blessed me by making me very important here in Egypt. Bring him here, along with your families and flocks. I will provide for you here, because I've got plenty of food."

And he kissed all his brothers and they cried together for a long time; and after that, they talked long into the night.

The Word of the Lord.

Psalm 37:1–12, 41–42

Don't give wicked people a second thought,
 or wish you could be clever like they are.

They will fade very soon and shrivel up like a weed you pull
from the lawn.

Trust in God. Walk God's Way and do good for others.
And you will have nothing to worry about.

Trust in God, and do good;
so you will live in the land, and enjoy security.
Spend your time in God's company,
and God will give you want you need and want.

Trust in God. Walk God's Way and do good for others.
And you will have nothing to worry about.

Choose to walk in God's direction.
Trust God, and watch what God does.
God will turn a bright light on everything you do and
highlight the justice of your cause.
In the meantime, calm yourself, and just be in God's company.
Wait patiently and don't worry about what people think or what
others do.

Trust in God. Walk God's Way and do good for others.
And you will have nothing to worry about.

Don't bother getting angry, and give up trying to be right
all the time.
Do not worry—it only leads to trouble.
If you're on God's side, you will be blessed in many ways.
But if you're wicked, you will be totally lost.
God will help you walk this path, and keep you safe when you
run into trouble.

Trust in God. Walk God's Way and do good for others.
And you will have nothing to worry about.

A Reading from the First Letter of Paul to the Corinthians [15:35–38, 42–50]

People ask, "But how can dead people be brought back to life? What kind of body will they have? How does all that work?" Silly questions. All things move toward life. A seed in the ground dies, until it is brought to life in the spring and grows into something you can eat. Same thing with our bodies; they will die, but will be raised in glory. Our physical bodies will die, but our spiritual bodies will be raised. First, we are made from the dust of the earth, but when God raises us we will be heavenly and reflect God's shining face.

What I am saying, brothers and sisters, is this: We will be changed from flesh and blood, and will receive God's kingdom in bodies that will never die.

The Word of the Lord.

✠ *The Holy Gospel of Our Lord Jesus Christ According to Luke* [6:27–38]

Everyone, listen to me. I'm telling you to love your enemies. Be good to people who hate you. If they throw curses at you, throw blessings back. Pray for them. If they punch you in the face, don't punch back, but shame them by offering your other cheek to hit. Give your coat to someone who asks, and food to beggars. Treat people the way you would want them to treat you and you can't go wrong.

I know it's hard. If it were easy, everyone would do it. If you love only people who are good to you, what would be special about that? That's simple. "Love your enemies, do good, give from your heart and expect nothing in return." That's how God works. Follow God's example.

Do not judge, and you will not be judged; do not condemn, and you will not be condemned. Forgive, and you will be forgiven; give, and you will find that you have so much more to give. You won't believe how many ways God will bless you if you love as God loves, and give as God gives.

The Gospel of the Lord.

The Eighth Sunday after the Epiphany

A Reading from the Book of Sirach [27:4–7]

When you use a filter, you keep what you want and let the rest fall away.

That's what happens when someone speaks. Filter what people say. You will find their faults.

A kiln tests the pots that someone has made, whether or not they'll withstand the fire.

You will know someone by what he says and how he says it.

You can tell a tree by the fruit that grows on its branches.

What you say is the fruit of your thoughts.

So listen carefully to what people have to say, and test their words to see if they are true.

The Word of the Lord.

Psalm 92:1–4, 11–14

It's a good thing to thank you, God, and sing your praises.
To shout first thing in the morning how deep your love is
and how your faithfulness hugs us at night.
It is good to pick up a harp and tambourine and drum and sing
beautiful songs about you.
You make me happy, God. I watch what you do and I can't keep
the joy inside me.
It's a good thing to thank you, God, and sing your praises.

I've seen you turn away my enemies.
I've heard you call my name and I walk away from those who
want to hurt me.
Good things and good people will grow big and beautiful like
palm trees in the desert.
It's a good thing to thank you, God, and sing your praises.

They are planted in God's house.
They will never outlive their usefulness.
They will always be full of life and ready for the next season.
It's a good thing to thank you, God, and sing your praises.

A Reading from the First Letter of Paul to the Corinthians [15:51–58]

Here is a mystery for you. Not all of us will die. But we'll all be changed in the twinkling of an eye, when the trumpet sounds at the end. We will all be changed and have bodies that will never die. Death will finally be defeated. Sin destroys, and so does death. The law fuels sin's power. Thanks be to God that Jesus came and won the battle with sin and death!

So my dear friends, keep one foot in front of the other, no matter how hard it is to keep moving; I'm telling you, you are not working for nothing. You are working for God who has already won the battle for you.

The Word of the Lord.

✠ *The Holy Gospel of Our Lord Jesus Christ According to Luke* [6:39–49]

Jesus said this, "How can blind people lead other blind people? Won't they both fall into a pit they can't see? If you're a student, you need to listen to your teacher, who knows more than you do. Why is it that you notice a little tiny speck in someone else's eye, but can't see that you've got a big wooden log in your own eye? First, get the log out of your own eye before helping others get the specks out of theirs. In other words, get your life together before you try to fix anyone else's life.

"Good trees bear good fruit. Bad trees can't bear good fruit. You know someone's heart by the way they act. And by the words they speak.

"Don't bother calling me Lord, if you're not going to listen to what I say and do what I tell you to do. That would be like building a house without putting it on a foundation. When the river busts out over its banks, the water washes it away. A good foundation will keep your house strong."

The Gospel of the Lord.

The Last Sunday after the Epiphany

A Reading from the Book of Exodus [34:29–35]

When Moses came down from Mount Sinai with the tablets on which the commandments were written, he didn't know that the skin of his face was all lit up with God's glory. When Aaron and everybody saw Moses's face they were afraid to get close to him. Moses called out their names and then they realized it was him and there was nothing to worry about. Then everybody gathered around Moses to hear what God had said to him. After Moses was done talking, he covered his face with a cloth. After that, whenever Moses went to talk to God, he would take the cloth off his face, and then put it back on when he talked to the people. So the people could tell when Moses had been talking to God and that what he was telling them was straight from God's mouth.

The Word of the Lord.

Psalm 99 (see Proper 24, Year A, p. 200)

A Reading from the Second Letter of Paul to the Corinthians [3:12—4:2]

We have a lot of hope in our hearts, which helps us be strong and act strong. We don't need to hide our faces with a cloth like Moses did. When some people hear God's Word, they put a cloth over their minds, but when they are open to what God has to say, that cloth is removed.

Wherever the Spirit of the Lord is, there is freedom. God's Spirit is turning those of us who face God little by little into God's image. We are being transformed into the same image from one degree of glory to another. We don't lose heart because God's Spirit and mercy are carrying us in the job we've been given to do. We are honest and have nothing to hide. And we are willing to be tested in the sight of God and everyone.

The Word of the Lord.

✠ *The Holy Gospel of Our Lord Jesus Christ According to Luke* [9:28–36]

Eight days after Peter said he believed Jesus was the Messiah, Jesus took Peter and John and James up to the mountain to pray. While Jesus was praying, his face started to glow and it changed right in front of them. His clothes were dazzling white. All of a sudden, Moses and Elijah were there on the mountain, talking to Jesus! They were talking about what was going to happen to Jesus in Jerusalem. Just as Moses and Elijah were getting ready to go, Peter said to Jesus, "I've got a great idea. Let's never leave this place. This is awesome. I'll make houses for each of you so we can stay here forever." Peter was so excited he didn't know what he was talking about. While he was saying this, a cloud came all around them and they were really scared. Then they heard a voice from the cloud. "This is my Son," the voice said. "Listen to him." After the voice had spoken, Jesus was alone again. They said nothing to anyone about what they had seen.

The Gospel of the Lord.

Ash Wednesday (see Year A, p. 54)

The First Sunday in Lent

A Reading from the Book of Deuteronomy [26:1–11]

When you finally get to the place God has given you and settle down there, harvest some grain, put some in a basket and take it to God's house. Give it to the priest there and tell him that God has brought you to your ancestors' land. The priest will set it before the altar.

Then tell him your story. "My great-grandfather was a wanderer. He went to Egypt as an immigrant, and stayed there for generations. His family grew and grew, and the Egyptians treated them like slaves. When we cried out for help, God brought us out of Egypt, into this place, which is beautiful and flowing with milk and honey. So now, I offer to God the best of what God has given me."

Then throw a party in honor of God, and invite your neighbors who are immigrants to your land and the priests as well. Be thankful and mindful of all that God has given you.

The Word of the Lord.

Psalm 91:1–2, 9–16

God is a shelter where we can hide from the storm,
the shadow where we can be safe from the hot sun.
Here's what I say: "God, I know I can always trust you.
I run to you and grab on to you when I need you."

When I call God's name, God answers.
God is beside me when I'm in trouble.

If you make God the house you live in,
nothing bad can happen to you.
God will assign angels to you, to follow you, to keep you close.
They will hold you in their arms, and watch your back.

When I call God's name, God answers.
God is beside me when I'm in trouble.

Nothing can hurt you—not lions, not snakes.
In fact, lions and snakes will be scared of you!
God will say, "I will protect that one there, because I know she loves me.
I will rescue her from trouble, because she knows my Name and knows how to use it.
When she calls out my Name I will answer. I will be with her in trouble. I will bring her back to a place where she can be proud of herself, and not frightened.
I will reward her with a good long life, and show her what real living is all about."

When I call God's name, God answers.
God is beside me when I'm in trouble.

A Reading from the Letter of Paul to the Romans [10:8b–13]

Moses said, "The Word is so close to you, it's on your lips and inside your heart." He meant the word of faith. By saying out loud that Jesus is Lord, and believing it in your heart—you're saved. Make those words real in your life. Welcome God's work in your heart and your life and God will be there for you, making your life new. God promises that he'll be there for everyone who wants God in his or her life. It doesn't matter who you are. You ask God into your heart, you ask God to save you; you're already made right with God.

The Word of the Lord.

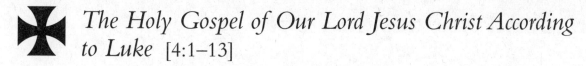

✠ *The Holy Gospel of Our Lord Jesus Christ According to Luke* [4:1–13]

After he was baptized, Jesus was full of the Holy Spirit. The Spirit led him out into the wilderness, where he spent forty days to learn some lessons before he began his ministry. He didn't eat anything during that time, and after forty days he was really, really hungry. The devil started talking to him: "You could turn this rock into some bread if you were really the Son of God, you know." Jesus told him, "The scriptures tell me that bread is not the only thing that'll keep me going." That stumped the devil. Then the devil showed him all the kingdoms in the entire world. He said, "I'll give you all the riches and power in the world, if you worship me instead of God. Everything you see will be yours." Jesus thought about it, when suddenly the devil and Jesus were in Jerusalem at the temple. The devil dared Jesus to jump off the top of the temple, because scripture says, "God will send angels to protect you and catch you when you fall." Jesus had had enough. "Scripture also says, don't push God. Don't make God pass your test."

That was it for the devil. He had no more tests in him. So he left Jesus alone, for now.

The Gospel of the Lord.

The Second Sunday in Lent

A Reading from the Book of Genesis [15:1–12, 17–18]

Abram had a vision in which God talked to him. "Don't be afraid, Abram. I will be your shield. You stick by me and you will have a great reward." Abram said, "What kind of reward? I have no children to carry on my name. So a slave born in my house is my only heir." And the Word of God came to him and said, "You will have your very own son." God took him outside and told him to look up at the skies. "Count the stars, if you can, Abram; that's how many children you will have." And Abram believed him.

God said, "I'm the one who took you far away from your home and brought you to this place. This is all yours, from the great river of Egypt to the great river Euphrates."

The Word of the Lord.

Psalm 27

God, your light shines in my life and makes it worth living.
I rely on you. No one scares me.
When people want to see me fall on my face,
I watch them stumble and fall instead.
No matter how many bullies team up against me, my heart will
 be strong and I won't be afraid.
And even if a war breaks out all around me, I will trust in you to
 save me.

God's light shines in my life and makes it worth living.

I have only one thing to ask you, God: "Can I live with you
 forever?"
To see your beautiful face, and to be with you where you live
 would be awesome.

You always keep me safe when I know I'm in trouble.
You take me to a safe place that no one knows about,
when the floodwaters come. You pick me up and put me high upon a rock.

God's light shines in my life and makes it worth living.

When my face is drooping, you lift up my head in front of those who make fun of me.
Because you do these things for me, I couldn't be any happier.
I can't stop singing and making music that praises you.

God's light shines in my life and makes it worth living.

Listen to me, God. And then answer me.
I heard you whisper to my heart—come find me.
And that's what I'm doing, looking for you.
So don't hide from me, God.
Don't turn the other way when I come.

God's light shines in my life and makes it worth living.

You have always helped me. So don't leave me now. I count on you.
Even if everyone who loves me leaves me, you will be with me.
So show me your way, God. Lead me in a clear direction.

God's light shines in my life and makes it worth living.

Don't let me walk into their traps.
I know some people lie about me, and want to see bad things come my way.

God's light shines in my life and makes it worth living.

I don't know what would happen if I didn't believe in your goodness!
So calm down and wait for God. "Be strong," I tell myself,

"and God will make things right and comfort your restless heart." Wait patiently. Wait for the God you trust.

God's light shines in my life and makes it worth living.

A Reading from the Letter of Paul to the Philippians [3:17–4:1]

You are my brothers and sisters, and I want you to imitate me. Follow my example. Don't live as if the cross of Christ does not matter. Some people do. They live to eat the best food and make fools of themselves at parties and embarrass their families. Their minds are in the gutter. Your mind should be with God. God sent Jesus to transform you into something so special to God's heart that reflects God's glory. Be firm about living in God's ways, my brothers and sisters. You are my pride and joy.

The Word of the Lord.

✠ *The Holy Gospel of Our Lord Jesus Christ According to Luke* [13:31–35]

Some church lawyers came to Jesus to warn him about King Herod. "Herod wants to kill you. You'd better watch your back." Jesus replied, "You tell that fox that I will cast out demons and cure people's ills today and tomorrow and then, on the third day, I'll be done. Jerusalem, O Jerusalem. You are the city that kills its prophets and stones those who are sent to you to give you warning. I wish I could hide all your children as a hen protects her chicks under her wings, but you won't let me. One day, you will see me and shout, 'Blessed is the one who comes in the name of the Lord.'"

The Gospel of the Lord.

The Third Sunday in Lent

A Reading from the Book of Exodus [3:1–15]
(see Proper 17, Year A, p. xxx)

Psalm 63:1–8

O God, you are my God. And I am eager to find you.
I'm thirsty for you, just as if I was in the middle of the desert without water.
I have had a glimpse of your power and glory.
Your kindness to me is better than life itself. And I will tell everyone how wonderful you are.
I will raise my hands above my head and shout your praises.

O God, you are my God. And I am eager to find you.

My soul is happy deep down like I've had a very good meal,
and my lips are happy to talk about you.
I think about you before I go to sleep at night, and at those times when I wake up.

O God, you are my God. And I am anxious to find you.

You have been my helper all along. And I can rest under the shadow of your wings.
My soul clings to you and your right hand won't ever let me go.

O God, you are my God. And I am ready to find you.

A Reading from the First Letter of Paul to the Corinthians [10:1–13]

You know, our ancestors came through the wilderness on their journey, through the cloud, through the sea, and ate and drank together until they made it to their new land. But not all of them made it. Some of them even started worshipping other gods, even though God himself had saved them. We must not follow their example and turn the wrong direction. We must not put God to the test by using other people or whining without end. Life is hard for everyone. And if you think you're standing, be careful you don't fall like others have. God is faithful. And even if you're being tested yourself, God will help you endure whatever it is you're going through.

The Word of the Lord.

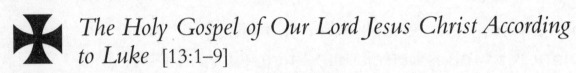

✠ *The Holy Gospel of Our Lord Jesus Christ According to Luke* [13:1–9]

Jesus heard about some people who had been murdered. He asked his disciples if these people were bad people because of what happened to them. Then he answered his own question: "No, they weren't, but you'd best change your ways so you won't end up like them. And then there were people who died because a tower of bricks fell on them. Did that happen because they were sinful?" Jesus asked. "No. It doesn't work like that. But pay attention and turn your lives around for the good anyway."

Then he told them this story: "A man had a fig tree that didn't produce any figs for three years in a row. He told the gardener to cut the tree down. 'Why should I waste the soil on this tree anyway?' The gardener said, 'I think we should give it another chance. Let's see if it will grow us some figs next year. If not, then go ahead and cut it down.'

"You've got a chance to turn your ways around," says Jesus. "Take that chance and do something productive with your lives."

The Gospel of the Lord.

The Fourth Sunday in Lent

A Reading from the Book of Joshua [5:9–12]

The LORD said to Joshua, "Today's the day I'm going to leave the disgrace of Egypt behind. Right here. Right now. And we'll call this place Gilgal to mark where it happened."

While the Israelites were camped there, they kept Passover in the evening on the fourteenth day of the month in the plains of Jericho. That very next day, they ate what the land produced along with bread and grain. God stopped providing them with manna each day. That's the year they ate the crops of the land they lived in, the land of Canaan.

The Word of the Lord.

Psalm 32 (see The First Sunday in Lent, Year A, p. 58)

A Reading from the Second Letter of Paul to the Corinthians [5:16–21]

From now on, we will see people the way God sees them. We knew Jesus from a human point of view, but now we know him as God has always known him—as a new creation. If any of us belongs to Christ, we are a new creation, too. God has made everything new. We are now right with God because of what Jesus did, and God asks us to help others become right with God, too. Jesus came into this sinful world to find us and bring us back in line with God's purpose.

The Word of the Lord.

✠ *The Holy Gospel of Our Lord Jesus Christ According to Luke* [15:1–3, 11b–32]

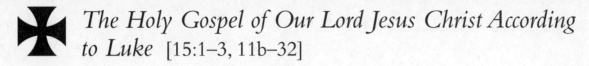

Sinners who wanted to hear what he had to say constantly surrounded Jesus. That made the authorities grumble and say, "Look at this guy—eating with sinners. It even looks as if he likes them!"

So Jesus told them this story: "Once there was a man who had two sons. The younger one asked his father for his inheritance early. So the father divided his property and gave it to his sons. The younger son packed up everything he had along with the money and hit the road. He wasted his money on things that don't last. When he'd spent everything, he found himself with no money, no food, no job, and no family. He found work slopping pigs. He'd have been happy to eat the food the pigs were eating. It hit him one day that his father's servants were a lot better off than he was. He decided to go back home, tell his father he was sorry, and ask to become his servant. So he went home. When he was still a ways from home, his father could see him in the distance and his heart was overjoyed. He ran to his son, hugged him tight, and kissed his face.

"Then the son said to him, 'Father, I have made wreck of myself. I am no longer worthy to be called your son.' But the father said to his servants, 'Go get the best robe you can find for my son and put rings on his fingers and shoes on his sore feet. Let's have a feast and celebrate. Because I thought my son was dead, but he's alive. He was lost to me, and now he's been found.'

"The older son came back from the field, and heard music and dancing. A servant told him that his brother had come back so his father was throwing a big party to celebrate. That made the older son really angry and he refused to go see his brother. The father tried to talk him into coming into the party. The son said, 'I have been here working hard for you all these years, never giving you any trouble and you've never given me any party. Then this son who ran away from you, who has thrown away good money comes back, you go all out for him.' Then the father said to him, 'Son, you are always with me, and all that is mine is yours. But we had to celebrate, because this brother of yours was dead and has come to life; he was lost and has been found.'"

The Gospel of the Lord.

The Fifth Sunday in Lent

A Reading from the Book of Isaiah [43:16–21]

God, who carved a path for us to walk through the sea,
who saved us from the chariots and horses and all the warriors
and armies,
says this to us,

"Don't get stuck on the way things were.
Don't rehearse them over and over again in your head.
I am about to do something completely new.
It's happening all around you. Can you see it?
I am making roads in the wilderness and rivers in the desert.
The animals who run wild will bow down to me—even the
ostriches and the coyotes.
I give my people in the desert water to drink.
They are people I formed for myself, so that I might hear
their praise."

Psalm 126 (see The Third Sunday of Advent, Year B, p. 224)

A Reading from the Letter of Paul to the Philippians [3:4b–14]
(see Proper 22, Year A, p. 194)

✠ *The Holy Gospel of Our Lord Jesus Christ According to John* [12:1–8]

Six days before Passover, Jesus and his disciples were in Bethany, where Lazarus and his sisters lived. (Jesus had raised Lazarus from the dead, remember?) Martha put on a lovely dinner for them. After supper, Mary brought out some very expensive perfumed oil and massaged Jesus feet with it. Then she wiped them dry with her hair. The whole house was full of the fragrance. Judas Iscariot, one of the disciples, the one who was going to betray Jesus to the authorities, ruined the moment by saying, "I can't believe you didn't sell this perfume and give money to the poor." It's not like Judas cared at all about the poor. He said that because he was a thief. He was the treasurer of the disciples and used to steal from the money they had set aside.

Jesus said, "Back off. Leave her alone. She honors me with this beautiful perfume and her care of me. She bought that perfume to prepare me for my burial. You always have the opportunity to help poor people. You won't always have me here with you in the flesh."

The Gospel of the Lord.

The Sunday of the Passion: Palm Sunday

At the Liturgy of the Palms

The Holy Gospel of Our Lord Jesus Christ According to Luke [19:28–40]

After teaching people with stories in Jericho, Jesus went to Jerusalem with his disciples. When they were near the Mount of Olives, he sent two of them into the village, saying, "Go and find a donkey that's never been ridden. Untie it and bring it to me. Don't worry about anyone wanting to know what you're doing. If they ask, just say, 'The Lord needs it.'" And they brought the donkey to Jesus, set their cloaks on it, and Jesus sat on it. He rode through the crowds, who kept laying down their coats on the road for a path. The crowds praised God and sang with loud voices, "Blessed are you, the king who comes in the name of the Lord. Peace in heaven, and glory in the highest heaven."

Some authorities in the crowd asked Jesus to tell his followers to stop the racket and the singing. Jesus said, "There's no point. If they stop singing, the stones along the road would shout out."

The Gospel of the Lord.

At the Liturgy of the Word

A Reading from the Book of Isaiah [50:4–9a]
(see Palm Sunday, Year A, p. 79)

A Reading from the Letter of Paul to the Philippians [2:5–11]
(see Palm Sunday, Year A, p. 81)

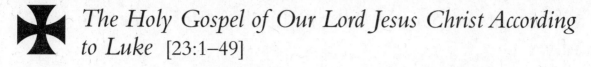

✠ *The Holy Gospel of Our Lord Jesus Christ According to Luke* [23:1–49]

Jesus had been arrested and brought before Pilate the governor. People accused him of crimes against the government and saying that he was the Messiah, and a king. Pilate asked him, "So, are you the king of the Jews?" Jesus answered, "You say so." After Pilate questioned Jesus, he turned to the crowds and said, "I see no reason to condemn this man and hold him against his will." The crowds insisted that Jesus be held, saying, "He is stirring up the people with his teaching throughout the whole countryside."

Pilate decided to send him over to Herod, who questioned him for a long time, with people accusing him the whole time. Herod and his soldiers made fun of Jesus and sent him back to Pilate.

Pilate then called the crowd together and said, "You've accused this man and yet I don't find him guilty of any of your charges. Neither has Herod. He certainly doesn't deserve the death penalty. So I will simply beat him and release him."

Then they all shouted out together, "We don't want Jesus released. Release somebody else if you want to release somebody!"

Pilate tried to talk them into letting him set Jesus free; but they kept shouting, "Nail him to a cross!" A third time he said to them, "Why, what on earth has he done wrong? I have found no reason to sentence him to death." But the people kept shouting that they wanted Jesus to die, and finally Pilate gave in. He released a murderer named Barabbas, and handed Jesus over to die.

They made a wooden cross and forced Jesus to carry it himself to the place where they would have him die. At one point, someone from the crowd carried it for him because Jesus was so weak. Lots of people followed behind Jesus, crying very loudly.

Two criminals were put to death with Jesus at the place they called "The Skull." Jesus said out loud, "Father, forgive these people for doing this." Even while he was on the cross, people made fun of Jesus. "Why can't he save himself if he is the Messiah? What a phony." One of the criminals said to Jesus, "Remember me in your kingdom." Jesus replied, "Oh, I will. In fact, today you will be with me in Paradise."

Before Jesus died, he cried out, "Take my spirit into your loving arms, Father." And then he breathed one last time. The sun went dark. There was a Roman soldier at Jesus' feet who was convinced that Jesus was innocent, and praised God even as Jesus died. Jesus' friends were watching from a distance, including many women who had been following him.

The Gospel of the Lord.

Maundy Thursday (see Maundy Thursday, Year A, p. 83)

Good Friday (see Good Friday, Year A, p. 86)

The Great Vigil of Easter

(see The Great Vigil of Easter, Year A, p. 94)

Easter Day

A Reading from the Acts of the Apostles [10:34–43]
(see First Sunday after the Epiphany, Year A, p. 27)

Psalm 118:1–2, 14–24 (see Easter, Year A, p. 110)

A Reading from the First Letter of Paul to the Corinthians [15:19–26]

Don't think think our hope is just for the life we are living now. That would be a real waste and people should feel sorry for us. But Christ has actually been raised from the dead. And since we die because we're human, the resurrection will also come through a human. We will all be made alive in Christ. When he returns, those who belong to Christ will be raised. Then the end will come. All will pass away—every authority and power on earth. All his enemies will be defeated. The last enemy to be defeated is death.

The Word of the Lord.

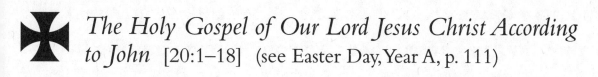

✠ *The Holy Gospel of Our Lord Jesus Christ According to John* [20:1–18] (see Easter Day, Year A, p. 111)

The Second Sunday of Easter

A Reading from the Acts of the Apostles [5:27–32]

The apostles had been arrested and the temple police brought them before the council. The high priest told them, "Did you forget we gave you strict orders NOT to teach in Jesus' name? Yet now all of Jerusalem is filled with your teaching and you are determined to make us responsible for his death." Peter spoke up, as Peter always did, saying, "Sorry. We have to obey God rather than you or any human authority. Our God raised Jesus, whom you killed. He is now at God's right hand so that he might hand out forgiveness all around. This is what we've witnessed. The Holy Spirit, whom God gave us, is our witness as well."

The Word of the Lord.

Psalm 118:14–29

I hear people singing in their homes, and claiming victory. God
has triumphed!
I will live to shout about the work God has accomplished today.
Sometimes I am punished, but I get back up and try again.
When God opens his doors to me, the doors to good things, I
will walk right through them.
Thanks for inviting me in, God.

Today our God has acted. Let everyone rejoice and be happy.

The stone that the builders threw out because they didn't like it,
is now the cornerstone that the whole building is built upon.
It's all because of what God has done for us, and we are amazed.

Today our God has acted. Let everyone rejoice and be happy.

A Reading from the Revelation to John [1:4–8]
(see Proper 29, Year B, p. 366)

✠ *The Holy Gospel of Our Lord Jesus Christ According to John* [20:19–31] (see the Second Sunday of Easter, Year A, p. 114)

The Third Sunday of Easter

A Reading from the Acts of the Apostles [9:1–6]

A man named Saul was determined to get rid of those who followed Jesus, even if he had to kill them. He was on his way to get permission to enter the synagogues in Damascus, where he was going to flush out any Jesus-followers and bring them as prisoners to Jerusalem. On his way a bright light from heaven stunned him and he fell to the ground. Then he heard a voice that said, "Saul, why are you doing this to me? Why are you torturing me?" Saul had no idea who was talking to him. He asked, "Who are you?" The reply came, "I am Jesus, whom you are persecuting. Get up right now, go into the city, and you will be told what's going to happen next and what you are supposed to do."

The Word of the Lord.

Psalm 30 (see The Great Vigil of Easter, Year A, p. 105)

A Reading from the Revelation to John [5:11–14]

I looked around and heard the voices of thousands and thousands of angels and animals and others singing at the top of their lungs around God's throne:

> "Worthy is the Lamb that was slaughtered
> to receive power and wealth and wisdom and might
> and honor and glory and blessing!"

Then I heard every creature in heaven and on earth and under the earth and in the sea, singing,

"To the one seated on the throne and to the Lamb
be blessing and honor and glory and might forever and ever!"
And the four living creatures said, "Amen!"

And all fell down and worshiped God.

The Word of the Lord.

✠ *The Holy Gospel of Our Lord Jesus Christ According to John* [21:1–19]

Some of the disciples were by the Sea of Tiberias. Peter said he was going fishing, and took the others with him. They spent the whole night fishing, but couldn't seem to catch any fish at all.

Just after daybreak, Jesus showed up and stood on the beach, but the disciples couldn't tell it was him. Jesus said to them, "You haven't got any fish, have you?" They answered him, "No." He said to them, "Try this. Cast the net to the right side of the boat, and you will find some." So they followed Jesus' suggestion, and now they couldn't even haul them in the boat, they had so many. Then somebody realized it was Jesus who'd been talking. When Peter heard that it was the Lord, he jumped into the sea and the other disciples followed him in their boat with the net full of fish.

When they got to shore, they saw a charcoal fire there, with fish on it, and bread. Jesus said to them, "Bring some of the fish that you have just caught. We'll cook them up and have some breakfast." So Peter went aboard and hauled the net ashore, full of large fish, a hundred fifty-three of them. You'd think that many fish would tear the net, but the net was just fine. Jesus said to them, "Come and have some breakfast." None of them had to ask Jesus who he was because now they all knew it was Jesus himself. Jesus passed the bread and the fish all around, and everyone ate.

This was the third time Jesus had appeared to his disciples after he was raised from the dead.

When they had finished breakfast, Jesus said to Peter, "Do you love me, Peter?" Peter said to him, "Yes, Lord, you know that I love you." Jesus said to him, "Feed my lambs." A second time Jesus asked to him, "Do you love me?" Peter said to him, "Yes, Lord, you know that I love you." Jesus said to him, "Take care of my sheep." A third time Jesus said, "Do you love me?" Peter felt hurt because he had to ask the third time, "Do you love me?" And he finally said, "Lord, you know everything; you know that I love you." Jesus said to him, "Feed my sheep. You know, Peter, when you were younger you were able to do whatever you wanted, but when you are an old man, someone will bind you and take you to places you don't want to go." Peter was confused. Jesus was giving him a hint about what Peter's life was going to be like at the end. Finally Jesus said to Peter, "Follow me."

The Gospel of the Lord.

The Fourth Sunday of Easter

A Reading from the Acts of the Apostles [9:36–43]

Dorcas was a disciple who was devoted to being kind and doing good things for people in Joppa, but she got sick and died. They prepared her for burial and laid her in a room upstairs. Two of her friends brought Peter to the house where she was. People were gathered together, remembering Dorcas, and crying. Peter sent them all outside and kneeled down to pray. Turning to her body he said, "Get up." She opened her eyes, looked at Peter, and sat up. He gave her his hand and helped her up. He called everyone back in to the room to show them she was alive. News spread about this and many people came to believe in the Lord.

The Word of the Lord.

Psalm 23 (see The Fourth Sunday in Lent, Year A, p. 70)

A Reading from the Revelation to John [7:9–17]

In front of me, there were so many people in white robes with palm branches that I couldn't count them all. They came from every country, and spoke every language, as they stood before the throne of God and the Lamb of God. They were crying in a loud voice, saying,

> "God is the one who saves us."

Everyone in heaven—the angels, the elders, the creatures—fell on their faces and worshiped God, singing,

> "Amen! Blessing and glory and wisdom
> and thanksgiving and honor
> and power and might
> be to our God forever and ever! Amen."

Someone asked me, "Who are all these people dressed in white robes?" Then he said, "I know who they are—they are people who've been made clean by the Lamb of God. That's why they worship God night and day. Never again will they be hungry or thirsty, or get sunburned. The Lamb of God will be their shepherd and guide them to springs of the water of life. And God will wipe their tears away."

The Word of the Lord.

✠ *The Holy Gospel of Our Lord Jesus Christ According to John* [10:22–30]

Jesus was in the temple with people gathered around him. Somebody asked him, "So how long are you going to keep us in suspense? Just tell us already if you are the Messiah or not." Jesus answered, "But I have told you, and you don't believe me. Everything I do in my Father's name shows you that I am the Messiah. You don't believe because you don't belong to me. Those who belong to me hear my voice and know who I am. I know them and they follow me. I give them life that never ends. No one can take them away from me. The Father has given me these sheep. The Father and I are working on this together."

The Gospel of the Lord.

The Fifth Sunday of Easter

A Reading from the Acts of the Apostles [11:1–18]

The followers of Jesus heard that "outsiders" had heard God's Word and believed it. When Peter went to Jerusalem, some of the believers who'd always done things a certain way criticized him for letting these people into their circle. "They're not like us," they said. "Why did you sit and eat with those people?"

Peter told them this story: "I had a vision while I was praying. A sheet came down from heaven and landed in front of me. It had different kinds of animals on it. A voice said, 'Kill the animals and eat.' But I said, 'I'm not doing that. Some of these animals are unclean and according to God's law I can't and won't eat them. I have always followed that law.' Then the voice said to me, 'You shouldn't call unclean what God has made clean.' Three times that vision happened. And then the sheet with the animals went away.

"At that moment, three men came to my door. The Spirit whispered to me to go with them. We went to somebody's house and this man told us that an angel had been in his house saying, 'Find Peter and bring him here. He has wonderful news for you that will give you and your whole family new life.' I started telling them the Good News of God in Jesus, and as I talked the Holy Spirit was poured out on them, just like it had been poured on us. I remember Jesus telling us about being baptized with the Holy Spirit.

"Then I thought, well if God gave them the Holy Spirit just like God gave us the Holy Spirit, who am I to keep them out of the circle of believers?"

That convinced the people who were criticizing Peter. They all praised God and said, "Wow. God gives everyone a new life in Christ, even people we consider outsiders. Even people who are not like us."

The Word of the Lord.

Psalm 148

Praise God!
Praise God from down below and praise God from up above.
Praise him from the mountaintops.
All you angels, praise God.
Everyone in heaven, praise God.
Praise God, sun and moon and all the shining stars.
Praise God, you clouds and the rain that is in them.
God created you and gave you your assignments.

Praise God from down below
and praise God from up above.

Praise God from the earth,
you sea monsters and everything in the deep seas,
fire and hail, snow and frost,
stormy wind: you all follow God's command.
Mountains and all hills,
fruit trees and all cedars!
Wild animals and cows that moo,
spiders and snakes and birds that soar.

Praise God from down below
and praise God from up above.

Kings of the earth and all peoples,
people who make the news,
young men and women alike,
old people, and little kids together!
All of you praise God's name.
Let's praise God's name together.

Praise God from down below
and praise God from up above.

A Reading from the Revelation to John [21:1–6]

Everything I saw was brand new: a new heaven, a new earth. I saw a brand new Jerusalem coming down from heaven, all shiny and beautiful. I heard a voice saying, "God belongs with the people. God sets up housekeeping where they live. The people belong to God. God wipes their tears dry and has wiped out death. No one needs to cry or be in pain any longer. That old life is gone and I am making everything new. I am the Alpha and the Omega, the beginning and the end. If you're thirsty, I will give you water from the spring of life as my gift to you."

The Word of the Lord.

✠ *The Holy Gospel of Our Lord Jesus Christ According to John* [13:31–35]

When they were together for their last supper and Judas had already left the house to betray Jesus, Jesus said, "God has been glorified in me now. My dear, dear friends, I will only be here with you a little longer. You will miss me, but as I have said before, I'm going where you can't come. Here is your assignment: Love each other. Just as I love you, love each other that way. People will be able to tell you are my followers if they can see that you love each other."

The Gospel of the Lord.

The Sixth Sunday of Easter

A Reading from the Acts of the Apostles [16:9–15]

Paul had a dream one night. He dreamed about a man far away in Macedonia saying to him, "When are you coming to come over to Macedonia? We need your help. Come see us soon."

Paul woke up and took that as a sign that God wanted us to go to Macedonia and tell the people God's Good News.

So the next thing we knew we were all on a boat and we sailed a long time across the sea until we got to Macedonia. We stayed with those good people for a few days. On Sunday we went down to the river to a place where people liked to pray. There were lots of women who wanted to hear what we had to say. One nice lady named Lydia really liked what we were telling her about God's love and wanted to be baptized right then and there. All of the people in her family were baptized with her. Afterwards she was so happy she wanted us to stay with her for a few days longer. We said, "No, thank you very much, but we need to get on the road." But she wouldn't take no for an answer. So we gave in and stayed at her house and had a very nice time.

The Word of the Lord.

Psalm 67

God, be good to us and give us your blessing.
Let us see your shining face and smile on us.
We want people all over the world to know the good things
    you do,
how you keep us safe and smile on us.

God, be good to us and give us your blessing.

We want people all over to praise you.
Everyone should praise you.
All people can be glad and sing happy songs because you treat everyone the same
and guide people to do good things.

God, be good to us and give us your blessing.

May the crops grow so that we have plenty of food to eat
and plenty of food to share.
God, be good to us and give us your blessing.
May everyone, everywhere, bless you back.

God, be good to us and give us your blessing.

Let us see your shining face and smile on us.

A Reading from the Revelation to John [21:10, 22–22:5]

God's angel swept me away to the highest mountain to show me the city of Jerusalem being lowered from heaven. I could tell it was Jerusalem, but it didn't have the temple in it because God himself is Jerusalem's temple. The city was glowing with the glory of God, so it didn't need the sun or the moon to brighten it. It shone so bright all the world would be able to see by its light. It was pure, nothing unclean about it. Only good people with kind hearts could enter it. The angel showed me the river flowing with the water of life itself, flowing from the throne of God, right down the middle of the city. On either bank of the river was the tree of life with twelve kinds of fruit. And each leaf could heal an entire nation. In that city, people would be able to see God's face and God's name would be written on their foreheads. It would always be daylight, and they would never need any light but God forever.

The Word of the Lord.

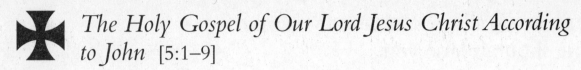

✠ *The Holy Gospel of Our Lord Jesus Christ According to John* [5:1–9]

Everyone was in Jerusalem for a Jewish festival. Jesus was there and he walked by a pool of water by the Sheep Gate. People who couldn't walk or see would lie around the water, waiting for a cure. Jesus came across a man there who had been lying there, sick, for thirty-eight years. Jesus said, "Do you want to get better? Do you want a better life for yourself?" The sick man said, "Yes, I do. But there's no one to help me get to the place where I might be cured, down by the water. I try, but I'm so slow other people crowd me out."

Jesus told him to stand up right then and there, pick up the bed he'd been lying on so no one would trip over it, and walk out of there. The minute Jesus said that, the man was made whole again. He picked up his bed and began to walk for the first time in thirty-eight years. And, by the way, that day was a Sabbath day.

The Gospel of the Lord.

The Seventh Sunday of Easter

A Reading from the Acts of the Apostles [16:16–34]

We were on our way to a church in Philippi with our friends Paul and Silas, when we ran into a slave girl, who had a spirit of fortune telling inside of her. The people who owned her made a lot of money from her fortunes. Every time she saw us she ran after us crying, "You are slaves of God, aren't you, and you tell people about a better way to live." Paul got annoyed at her and turned to her and said, "I don't know what is possessing you, but I order it to come out in the name of Jesus Christ." And the spirit left her.

The people who owned her were angry because she couldn't tell fortunes anymore, and if she couldn't tell fortunes, then they couldn't make money. They grabbed Paul and Silas and took them to the police. When they came before the judge, the men said, "These two are pests. They are Jews, not Romans, and are trying to change our ways." The crowds around them chimed in and started attacking Paul and Silas. The judges handed out clubs to beat them with. After they got beat up, they were thrown in prison. Their feet were in chains, and they were in the most secure cell there was.

At midnight, Paul and Silas were praying and started singing hymns to God. The other prisoners were listening to them. Suddenly there was an earthquake that opened all the prison doors and knocked the chains off everyone's feet. The jailer, who was in charge of watching them, saw the prison doors wide open; he knew he'd be blamed that the prisoners were free. He took out his sword and was about to kill himself with it, rather than face the judge's punishment. But Paul yelled at him, "Stop! Don't do it! We're all here! There's no reason to hurt yourself."

The jailer threw himself at Paul and Silas's feet, shaking like a leaf. He took them outside the jail and said, "Tell me, what do I need to do to be saved?" They said, "Just believe in Jesus and you'll be saved along with everyone at your house." At the jailer's house they told the people there about God and how God loved them and sent Jesus to them. The jailer washed them up, and cared for their wounds. And then Paul and Silas baptized everyone in the house. They all had a big meal and rejoiced together that they had all become believers in God's love.

The Word of the Lord.

Psalm 97

You are god of everything, God.
Let all the world be happy.
Let all the islands in all the seas be glad.

Rejoice, those of you who know and love God.
Be thankful that God is God.

There may be clouds and darkness all around you,
but your throne sits on top of goodness and justice.
Fire goes before you and scares off your enemies.
Your lightning lights up the night sky and everyone is afraid.

Rejoice, those of you who know and love God.
Be thankful that God is God.

The mountains melt just like they were made of wax when you
are near.
The heavens cry out so everyone can hear, "God is good!
Check out God's glory!"
There's no point in worshipping statues or any god but our God.

All the cities in Judah listen to you, God, and are made glad by
your goodness and wisdom.

Rejoice, those of you who know and love God.
Be thankful that God is God.

For you are so far above any of us,
above anything we used to think were gods.
You love it when we turn our back on evil.
You protect your people and keep them out of harm's way.
Those of us who try to be good and do good are like lights to
the world.

Rejoice, those of you who know and love God.
Be thankful that God is God.

A Reading from the Revelation to John [22:12–14, 16–17, 20–21]

I will be with you again very soon. And you will all be paid in full. I'm like the first and last letter of the alphabet, the beginning and the end. Blessed are you whose robes are as clean as your lives. My name is Jesus and I will send my very own messenger with this message for the churches: I am the root of the tree of life and a descendent of King David. I am the bright morning star. Let everyone come to me. Especially you thirsty ones and take the water of life as your gift.

Amen, I say. Come Lord Jesus! And may the grace that Lord Jesus offers be with us all. Amen.

The Word of the Lord.

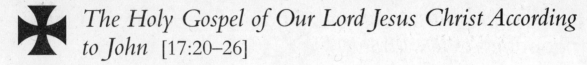

✠ *The Holy Gospel of Our Lord Jesus Christ According to John* [17:20–26]

Jesus prayed for his disciples. And then he prayed for all of us who believe because the disciples told other people about Jesus. "Father," Jesus said, "You and I are one. May these people also be one with us so that the whole world will believe in your love for them. Let me be with them, Father, because I love them and they need me. I have told them everything I know about you and the love that you have for them. Let them feel that love."

The Gospel of the Lord.

Day of Pentecost

A Reading from the Acts of the Apostles [2:1–20] (see Day of Pentecost, Year A, p. 130)

Psalm 104:25–35, 37 (see Day of Pentecost, Year A, p. 131)

A Reading from the Letter of Paul to the Romans [8:14–17]

If you follow where the Spirit of God leads you, you are children of God! God doesn't want you to slip back into your old ways of being scared, because now you have a new way of being. You are children of God, which means you can depend on God like a child can depend on its father. The Spirit helps us live as children whom God recognizes, and will always claim as his own. Just know that if you are suffering now because you love God, you will also be made holy because you love God.

The Word of the Lord.

✠ *The Holy Gospel of Our Lord Jesus Christ According to John* [14:8–17, 25–27]

Philip said, "Jesus, just show us the Father and we'll stop bugging you about him and we'll be happy." Jesus couldn't believe it. "What? You've been with me for years now, and you still don't know me? I keep telling you, whoever has seen me, *has* seen the Father. The Father and I are one, and we work together. I haven't just made up words on my own—they're the Father's words. Please believe me. If you do, you'll be able to do great things in God's name, too. I will be going to the Father soon. I will do whatever you ask in my name to further God's kingdom. Ask me! I will do it!

"If you love me, show me by doing the things I told you to do. I will ask the Father to send you someone else who will be with your forever: the Spirit of Truth. Not everyone will be able to understand that. But you will know the Spirit, because she'll be inside of you, and part of everything that you're doing.

"I've tried to teach you as much as I could. But the Holy Spirit, who will follow me, will teach you everything you need to know, and help you remember what I've asked you to do.

"As I leave, I give you my peace. Please, don't be troubled and anxious. Don't let your hearts be afraid."

The Gospel of the Lord.

Trinity Sunday

A Reading from the Book of Proverbs [8:1–4, 22–31]

Wisdom is calling to me. What does she want me to understand? Wisdom is like a lady who stands on the busiest sidewalk where everyone can see her, and cries out, "My name is Wisdom. Listen to me. Before he made anything else, God made me. Long before he made you, or the oceans, or the mountains, or the soil in the fields. I was there when he pieced together the heavens, and the shores on the edges of the waters. I have always been beside him since then. I have rejoiced in his creation and delighted when he made you. Listen to me. My name is Wisdom."

The Word of the Lord.

Psalm 8 (see Trinity, Year A, p. 134)

A Reading from the Letter of Paul to the Romans [5:1–5]

Our faith brings us peace with God. Because of our faith, we know in our hearts that we have a connection to God and God's grace. It is awesome to think that we will share in God's glory! Because of that, the ways we suffer for Jesus are awesome, too. May those troubles make us stronger and better people. And those troubles help to grow hope inside of us. Our hope is strong because God's Spirit has poured God's love into our wide open hearts.

The Word of the Lord.

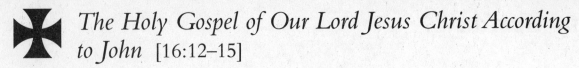

✠ *The Holy Gospel of Our Lord Jesus Christ According to John* [16:12–15]

Jesus said to the disciples, "There is so much more that I want to tell you and teach you, but it's just too much for you right now. When the Spirit of truth comes, she will guide you into all the truth and help you see what needs to happen. The Spirit is working with the Father and me, not just on her own. The Spirit will honor me and what I've said. And all I've said is what the Father has given me to say."

The Gospel of the Lord.

Proper 1 (see The Sixth Sunday after the Epiphany, Year C, p. 388)

Proper 2 (see The Seventh Sunday after the Epiphany, Year C, p. 390)

Proper 3 (see The Eighth Sunday after the Epiphany, Year C, p. 394)

Proper 4

A Reading from the First Book of Kings [18:20–39]

The king got the prophets together at Mount Carmel. Elijah said to the people, "How can you keep your feet in two different parades at the same time? If God is your God, follow him. If Baal is your god, then go with him. But decide already!"

The people had nothing to say about that. Elijah said, "Come over here, everybody," and they did. Elijah saw that the altar they'd built to worship God had been destroyed, so he put it back together again. He took twelve stones, because there were twelve tribes of Israel, and he built another altar. Then he dug a trench around the altar, put wood on the top of it and a bull on the top of the wood. Then he doused the whole thing with water. Then he doused it again. He told them to do it a third time and this time to fill the trench with water, too. They were going to offer the bull to God.

When the whole altar and wood were soaking wet, Elijah said, "O God of Abraham, Isaac, and Jacob, let everyone today know you are God and that I work for you. Answer me, God, so that all these people will turn their hearts over to you."

And God threw fire from the heavens on the altar, and even though everything was as wet as it could be, the wood, the stones, the dust, and even the water went up in flames!

"WOW!" exclaimed the people. They fell on the ground and worshipped God, convinced that the Lord who had made this happen was their God.

The Word of the Lord.

Psalm 96 (see Christmas Day, Year A, p. 13)

A Reading from the Letter of Paul to the Galatians [1:1–12]

Here's another letter from Paul:

Hi everybody. With this letter I send God's peace and grace to all of you. Now you know that God chose me for this job; I didn't pick it for myself. You need to listen to me. I can't believe that you are leaving God and God's teachings behind. What happened? You know the truth. Don't let your heads be turned by someone who thinks they know better.

Does it make me popular to say this? No. But who do I want to please? People or God? I choose God. And I want you to choose God, too. If I wanted to be popular, believe me I wouldn't be doing this job.

I didn't make up the Good News of God's goodness in Jesus. Jesus came to me and told me himself!

The Word of the Lord.

✠ *The Holy Gospel of Our Lord Jesus Christ According to Luke* [7:1–10]

When Jesus was done preaching in the countryside, he came to a town called Capernaum. A highly decorated Roman soldier lived there. Someone who worked for him was very sick and going to die. When the soldier heard about Jesus and his healing power, he had some people from Jesus' church beg Jesus to come and heal his dying friend. They said, "Jesus, you've got to help him. He's a good guy, even if he is a Roman, Jesus. He is kind to us. He even built our church for us!"

So Jesus went with them to go heal this dying man. As they were on their way, they were met by the soldier's people who sent this message from the soldier: "Don't bother coming any further. I am not worthy to have you at my house. That's why I didn't come to meet you myself. I believe that if you just say the word, your word is so powerful my friend will be healed. I understand power, because I am a powerful man myself, in charge of many soldiers. I know you have God's power, and God's power is in your word."

Jesus couldn't believe how much faith this man had in him! He turned to the people who had gathered around him and said, "Wow, did you hear what he just said? I haven't heard faith like that among my people who know God!"

The soldier's people went home after giving Jesus their message and they found the dying man perfectly healthy again.

The Gospel of the Lord.

Proper 5

A Reading from the First Book of Kings [17:8–16]

It had not rained for a very long time, and food was scarce in the land. God's Word came to Elijah, "Go live in Zarephath, in a foreign land. Find a widow there who will feed you." So Elijah went and found a widow who was picking up sticks for her fire. "Could you bring me some water, please?" Elijah asked her. When she went to find some water for him, he said, "And bring me some bread too." She told him, "I'm sorry, I don't have any bread. All I have is a little bit of grain in a jar, and a tiny bit of oil in a jug. I'm going to put a fire together, make something from the grain for my son and me to eat before we die of starvation."

Elijah told her not to be afraid. "Go, do what you had planned, but first make me a little cake and then something for you and your son. God told me that you would not run out of grain or oil and that it's finally going to rain."

She believed him and did what he said. And the three of them ate well for many days. The jar always had grain enough for them. And the jug of oil filled up each time she emptied it. It happened just like Elijah said God had told him it would.

The Word of the Lord.

Psalm 146 (see Proper 26, Year B, p. 358)

A Reading from the Letter of Paul to the Galatians [1:11–24]

Paul says in his letter:

I'm not making any of this up, you know. The Good News of God's love was revealed to me by Jesus Christ himself. I'm sure you've heard about me in my former life. How I was killing

Christians and trying to destroy God's church. I was a rising star, in fact, because of the awful things I was doing.

But God before I was born decided to use me and introduced me to Jesus, his Son. My assignment was to go to the outsiders, the Gentiles, to tell them the Good News. I didn't meet with anybody about it, or get permission from the apostles in Jerusalem. I went to Arabia for a while, and then came back to Damascus. Finally after three years I went to visit Peter and met James, who is Jesus' brother.

I went to the churches in the outlying areas, and they'd heard about what I used to do to Christians so naturally they were a little nervous. But they praised God that my life had been turned around and now I am proclaiming the faith I tried to destroy.

The Word of the Lord.

✠ *The Holy Gospel of Our Lord Jesus Christ According to Luke* [7:11–17]

Jesus came to a town called Nain along with a large group of followers. As they were walking into the gate of the town, a group was carrying out the body of a man who had died. He was his mother's only son, and now she was all alone. Jesus' heart ached for her and he said, "Please don't cry." Those carrying the body stood still as Jesus came and touched it and said, "Young man, get up!" And the dead man sat up and started talking. Jesus gave him back to his mother. Everyone was paralyzed with fear. Then they praised God, saying, "A great prophet is here with us. God is good." The news about Jesus spread throughout the countryside.

The Gospel of the Lord.

Proper 6

A Reading from the First Book of Kings [21:1–10, 15–21a]

Naboth had a vineyard next to King Ahab's palace. The king wanted Naboth's land so he could grow vegetables close to his palace. "I'll give you some better land or money for it. You decide."

Naboth told Ahab, "But this is my family's land. We've always lived here. I'm not getting rid of it at any price." The king was not happy, and sulked for days. The queen was tired of the king moping. "Who's the king here anyway? I'll get you that vineyard. Don't you worry."

So she wrote letters in the king's name and sealed them with his seal. The letters said, "Bring Naboth in on these charges: You have cursed God and the king. And then stone him to death." The queen told the king, "The vineyard is yours. Naboth is dead."

Elijah, a prophet of God, heard about this. God told him to confront the king about what happened to Naboth. Elijah told the king, "You have done horrible things in God's sight. You will pay for this."

The Word of the Lord.

Psalm 5:1–8

Listen to me, God!
Listen to me cry and whine, my King and my God.
Every morning I wake up and turn my eyes to you and
    start talking.
And then I wait and watch to see what you will do.
Make the path I need to follow straight.

I know you're not a god who loves wickedness.
Evil plots go nowhere with you.
And people who are too full of themselves can just keep walking and talking
because you don't want to hear them.

Make the path I need to follow straight.

You turn away people who lie, and are violent and hurtful.
But you invite me right into your house, because you are more than loving toward me.
I will bow down in awe of you.
Lead me in the right way.
Lead me right through the middle of my enemies.

Make the path I need to follow straight.

A Reading from the Letter of Paul to the Galatians [2:15–21]

You and I grew up in the Jewish faith. We know now that it's not the law that counts, but faith in Jesus Christ. It's like we've died to the law, but now live to God. We've been crucified with Christ, and now Christ lives in me. I live by faith in Jesus, who loved me and gave his life for me. The grace of God is everything.

The Word of the Lord.

✠ *The Holy Gospel of Our Lord Jesus Christ According to Luke* [7:36–8:3]

One of the Pharisees invited Jesus to dinner at his house. A woman from the city who had a bad reputation found out Jesus was there. She came to the house with a jar of perfumed ointment. She knelt down, crying, and bathed his feet with her tears and dried them with her long hair. Then she kissed his feet and anointed them with the ointment. When the Pharisee saw this he thought to himself, "Who does she think he is? If Jesus was really a prophet, he would know what kind of woman is touching him." Jesus said, "Here's what I have to say about that, Simon."

And Simon said, "Go ahead. Teacher, tell me."

"Two people owed a man money. One owed five hundred dollars, the other owed him fifty. When neither of them could pay up, he cancelled both of their debts. Now who do you think would be most grateful?" Simon answered, "Well, I guess the one who owed the most."

Jesus said, "That's right." Jesus turned to the woman at his feet and said to Simon, "Do you see this woman? I came into your house, and you gave me no water for my feet, but she has bathed my feet with her tears and dried them with her hair. You gave me no kiss to greet me. But she has not stopped kissing my feet. I'm telling you, her sins, which I realize were many, have been forgiven. And she has shown great love."

Jesus said to the woman, "Your sins are forgiven."

The people eating at the table with Jesus said to each other, "Who does he think he is, forgiving sins like that?"

Jesus said to the woman, "Your faith is awesome. Go in peace."

And Jesus walked through the cities and villages of the countryside, bringing with him the Good News of God's kingdom. His twelve disciples were with him, as well as some women whom he had healed: Mary Magdalene, from whom Jesus released seven demons; Joanna; and Susanna. There were many other women who funded Jesus' ministry out of the resources God had given them.

The Gospel of the Lord.

Proper 7

A Reading from the First Book of Kings [19:1–4, 8–15a]

Ahab told Jezebel that all the prophets except for Elijah had been killed. Jezebel sent a message to Elijah that said, "That's what I'm going to do to you by this time tomorrow." Elijah fled for his life. Going into the wilderness, he crawled under a broom tree. He prayed to God and said, "I'm done, God. Just let me die, because I am worthless." He fell asleep under the tree. An angel woke him up and said, "You'd better get up and eat something or you won't be able to go on." Elijah turned to see a cake and water right there next to him. So he got up and ate and drank. God's angel came a second time, touched him, and said, "Get up and eat, you need your strength for the journey ahead of you." He got up, and ate and drank. It took him forty days and nights to get to Horeb, where he expected to talk to God. He spent the night in a cave.

Then the word of God came to him, saying, "What are you doing here, Elijah?" He answered, "Well, as you know, I've worked hard for you, God. But the people aren't listening and they even want to kill me. I don't know what to do."

Elijah got a message that he should stand on the mountain, because God was about to pass by. The wind kicked up, and it was so strong it was breaking rocks into pieces. God was not in the wind. Then there was an earthquake, but God wasn't in the earthquake. And then a fire, but God wasn't in the fire. Then it was dead silent. When Elijah heard that silence, he put his coat over his face and went to the entrance of the cave. A voice said, "Tell me now, Elijah. What are you doing here?"

He answered, "Well, as you know I've worked hard for you, God. But the people aren't listening and they even want to kill me. I just don't know what to do."

God said to him, "Go. Go home a different way."

The Word of the Lord.

Psalm 42

I am like a deer who longs for flowing streams;
that's how my soul longs for you, O God.
My soul is thirsty for you.

You are the living God.
When can I see your face?

I've done nothing but cry big, heavy tears day and night;
people around me wonder where you are.
They ask me, where is your God now?
In my mind I go over the times I remember when you were with me as my heart aches,
all those times when I went with the crowds to your house to praise you.

You are the living God.
When can I see your face?

I tell myself I shouldn't be so sad. "Why," I say to myself, "Why do you feel like this?"
Remember your hope in God. You will praise him again. He is your help.
I feel so heavy and tired. I will try to remember you, God.
I feel overwhelmed, like water rushing through canyons.
I feel like I might disappear in the rapids.

You are the living God.
When can I see your face?

But I know that God grants his loving-kindness to me all day long and sings to me in the night.
I ask, "God, have you forgotten me? Why would you do that?
Why can I not stand up to my enemies?"

You are the living God.
When can I see your face?

They break my bones and mock me to my face.
They make fun of me all day long, and ask, "So, where is your God now?"
Why does my heart feel so heavy and restless?
I trust God and thank God for being my help and my God.

You are the living God.
When can I see your face?

Psalm 43

I need you to be on my side, God.
Defend me from people who lie about me.
The only strength in me comes from you.
Why have you pushed me away?
Why do I let these people get to me?
I need to see your light in front of me, and have your truth inside me
so they can lead me to the place you live.
When I get to your house, I will go straight to the altar to praise you.
I will pick up my harp and play musical thanks to you, God.
I need to calm down.
And I need my heart to lighten up.
I will remind myself to trust in God
who looks me in the face and helps me.
Thanks in advance, God.

A Reading from the Letter of Paul to the Galatians [3:23–25; 4:4–7]
(see Christmas 1, Year A, p. xxx)

✠ *The Holy Gospel of Our Lord Jesus Christ According to Luke* [8:26–39]

Jesus and his disciples met a man who had some demons. He didn't wear any clothes and he lived in the cemetery. He had seizures and he was kept bound in chains, but he would break out and go into the wilds. He recognized Jesus and he fell down before him and shouted as loud as he could, "Jesus, Son of the Most High God, don't torment me!" Jesus asked him what his name was. He said, "Legion" (because there were a *lot* of demons in him). Jesus commanded the unclean spirits to leave the man. The spirits begged Jesus not to send them away.

On the hillside there was a herd of pigs. The demons said, "Send us into these pigs instead." So that's what Jesus did. They left the man and entered the pigs. Then the pigs rushed into the lake and were drowned. The people who owned the pigs went to tell people what had happened. They found the man clothed and in his right mind. Everyone was afraid. And they asked Jesus to leave. So he got into the boat and sailed away. The man Jesus had healed asked him to stay with him, but Jesus told him to go back to his home and tell everyone what God had done for him. So he proclaimed throughout the city what Jesus had done.

The Gospel of the Lord.

Proper 8

A Reading from the Second Book of Kings [2:1–2, 6–14]

God was planning on taking Elijah up to heaven by a whirlwind. Elijah and Elisha were walking together, when Elijah said, "You stay here, because God wants me to continue on my own." But Elisha said, "What? I'm not leaving you."

Then Elijah said, "Stay here; for now God is sending me to the Jordan." But Elisha said, "Forget it. I'm not leaving you. Let's go to the Jordan." They started walking and fifty of the prophets went to see what was going to happen. They saw Elijah take off his cloak and roll it up and hit the water with it, and the water moved so that they could walk on dry land right through the middle of the river. (Just like the Israelites did in the Red Sea!)

On the other side of the river, Elijah said to Elisha, "Before God takes me, tell me what I can do for you." Elisha said, "The only thing I ask for is twice the amount of Holy Spirit that God has given you. That's what I want." Elijah said, "That's a hard thing to give you! If you see me as God takes me to heaven, then you'll get what you ask for."

As they kept walking and talking, a chariot and horses made of fire came between the two of them, and Elijah went up into heaven in a whirlwind. Elisha kept watching and crying out, "Father, father! The chariots of Israel and its horsemen!" He saw it all. And, when Elijah was gone, he tore the clothes he was wearing and began to cry.

He picked up Elijah's clothes, and stood on the bank of the Jordan River. Then he took the coat and struck the water with it, saying, "Where is the God Elijah believed in?" As he struck the water, it was parted to one side and the other, and Elisha walked through the river to the other side.

The Word of the Lord.

Psalm 77:1–2, 11–20

I will cry out loud to God;
I will cry out loud, and God will hear me.
When I was in trouble, I went looking for God;
I stayed up all night wondering, praying, looking for God.
I couldn't find anything to make myself feel better.
I will remember things God has done
and think about the stories of how God helped people
long ago.

I will cry out loud to God;
I will cry out loud, and God will hear me.

I tell myself, God's way is holy.
Who is greater than you, God?
You are the God who works wonders
and have shown your power to all the people.

I will cry out loud to God;
I will cry out loud, and God will hear me.

You were strong enough to save the children of Jacob
and Joseph
and bring them back to you.
The water in the oceans saw you, God;
the waters saw you and shuddered in fear.
the very deepest waters were shaken.

I will cry out loud to God;
I will cry out loud, and God will hear me.

The clouds overflowed with water;
the skies thundered;
your arrows flashed across the heavens.
The sound of your thunder was in the whirlwind;

lightning lit up the whole world;
the earth itself trembled and shook.

I will cry out loud to God;
I will cry out loud, and God will hear me.

You walked on the sea,
and followed a path in the oceans;
yet no one could see your footsteps.
You led your people like a flock of sheep
by the hand of Moses and Aaron.

I will cry out loud to God;
I will cry out loud, and God will hear me.

A Reading from the Letter of Paul to the Galatians [5:1, 13–25]

Christ set us free so that we would live free. So, don't ever give in to slavery again. You were made for freedom, brothers and sisters. But don't use that freedom to just do whatever it is you want to do. Instead, become slaves to each other because of love for each other. The entire law is in this one sentence, "Love your neighbor as yourself." Don't take bites out of each other so that there is nothing left of you.

Live by the Spirit, not your own flesh. The Spirit will not steer you wrong. But your own desires might—arguments, jealousy, envy, being drunk, and things like that. If those things are what your life is all about, you might not be part of God's kingdom.

But if you live by the Spirit, here are the things we'll notice about you—love, joy, peace, and patience. You'll be kind and generous and faithful, and be able to control yourself. Become more and more like Jesus, and less and less about your own desires. If you live by the Spirit, let yourself be guided by the Spirit.

The Word of the Lord.

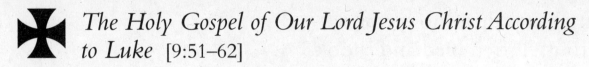

✠ *The Holy Gospel of Our Lord Jesus Christ According to Luke* [9:51–62]

Jesus got more focused the closer he got to Jerusalem. He sent some messengers ahead of himself into a Samaritan village to get things ready. But the villagers wanted to have nothing to do with him because he was so intent on going to Jerusalem. James and John saw this, and said, "So do you want us to destroy them for you, Jesus?" Jesus said, "No. Please, no." And then they moved on to another village instead.

As they travelled, someone said to Jesus, "I will follow you, Jesus, wherever you go." Jesus said to him, "Foxes have holes to sleep in. Birds build nests. But I have no place to call my own. Are you sure this is the life you want?" To another person, Jesus said, "Follow me." But that person replied, "I've got lots of things to do first, and then I'll follow you. Let me wait until my father has died." Jesus told him to let the dead bury their own dead. "I'm calling you to proclaim the kingdom of God. Isn't that important work?" Jesus said, "You've got to commit to me fully, or the kingdom of God might not be for you."

The Gospel of the Lord.

Proper 9

A Reading from the Second Book of Kings [5:1–14]
(see Epiphany 6, Year B, p. 245)

Psalm 30 (see Easter Vigil, p. 105)

A Reading from the Letter of Paul to the Galatians [6:1–16]

My friends, if there's somebody in your church who keeps doing something wrong, you need to talk to him or her and see if you can help that person do better. But be gentle! Watch that you don't get sucked into hurting others. Help each other—that's what Jesus would have you do. Don't be too full of yourselves. Don't kid yourselves. God knows what you're doing. You get what you give. If you plant the seeds of hurt, you'll just grow more hurt. If you plant good things, the Holy Spirit will grow eternal life inside you.

Don't get tired of doing the right thing. In the end, it will make all the difference. Don't give up. Whenever you can, work for the good of everybody, especially those who are your brothers and sisters in the faith.

I'm writing this in really, really big letters so you know it's important. People who say their way is the only way to do things are just trying to look good themselves. And they are trying to get out of the hard part of following Jesus. They want to win you over so that it looks like they won the contest.

But this is not a game! And there is nothing to "win" except Jesus and his love for us. God's new way of life, God's new world is the only thing that matters. Keep that in mind. God grant you peace and mercy!

The Word of the Lord.

✠ *The Holy Gospel of Our Lord Jesus Christ According to Luke* [10:1–11, 16–20]

Jesus picked seventy people and sent them two by two to all the towns where he was planning on going. He told them, "People are ready to hear what you have to say about God, but there are not enough people willing to say it. Pray that God will find more people willing to go out there and talk about God. Get going, people!

"I know it's a little like sending lambs into the pack of wolves. Pack lightly. Don't take too much with you. Don't stop on the road to talk. Whenever you are invited into someone's house, bring God's peace with you. If they don't want God's peace, you'll know it and don't push it. Stay with people for a while if they give you a room. Accept the food and drink they offer you. Don't be too anxious to move on to the next place.

"If people welcome you, cure the sick in their town and tell them that God's kingdom is near. But if they don't want you there, leave. But before you go, tell them again that God's kingdom is very close, whether they want to hear that or not.

"Whoever listens to you is listening to me; whoever rejects you, rejects the one who sent you."

The seventy who'd gone out eventually came back, all excited. "Jesus," they said, "Even the demons listened to us when we used your name. It was awesome." Jesus replied, "You haven't seen anything yet! I've seen Satan fall right out of heaven. I have given you all kinds of power over evil. Nothing will hurt you. But that's nothing. What really matters is that God knows your names and has them written in his book in heaven."

The Gospel of the Lord.

Proper 10

A Reading from the Book of Amos [7:7–17]

Here's what I saw:

God was standing by a wall built with a plumb line. (A plumb line is string with a weight on the end to show you when a wall is straight up and down.) And God said to me, "What do you see, Amos?" I said, "I see a plumb line." God said, "I'm putting a plumb line in the middle of my people to see if they measure up. I'm not turning the other way anymore. Their worship places are history. They'll go into exile."

So the priest at Bethel went to the king of Israel to say, "Amos is plotting against you. He says God is angry at you."

The priest told Amos to get out of town and not come back. Amos said, "I'm not a prophet. I raise cattle. God grabbed me and dropped me here to tell you something, that's all. And he told me to tell you all that you will soon be scattered, and taken away to live in another land."

The Word of the Lord.

Psalm 82

God gathered all the other gods together and asked them,
How long are you going to be on the side of the evil people?
Treat the poor fairly.
Defend those who are helpless
and those who have the most need.

Come save us, God!
Be the powerful God we know you are
and show everyone who is God.

Rescue weak people and people who have no homes from
people who have no heart.
Be fair to the poor.
You don't know anything.
You close your eyes while the earth shakes so you don't have to
see what's going on.
I, the Most High God, am the father of all of you.
But you will die just like everyone else, including the most
powerful kings.

Come save us, God!
Be the powerful God we know you are and show everyone who is God.

A Reading from the Letter of Paul to the Colossians [1:1–14]

Everyone gather round. I just received a letter from Paul and Timothy. Here is what they have to say:

Hello, good people of Colossae. I hope God is blessing you with all kinds of good things, like grace and peace and love.

Timothy and I pray for you every single day and we always thank God for you. You are doing such an awesome job. We hear good things about your faith and how you show love for each other.

I can tell the Good News you heard about God's love is growing inside you. You seem to really get the point of God's grace for everyone.

You've got a great preacher in Epaphras. And you connect God's love for you to the love you show for others. I know that God is very, very pleased. Keep up the great work! As you learn more and more about God and God's love, we pray that your faith grows stronger each day. And that God gives you patience to get through the tough times, because I know it's not always easy.

What a wonderful gift it is to share this joy with you and with all God's people around the world. It's like we used to live with our eyes closed, not knowing what we were doing or where we were going. But now, God has come into our hearts and opened our eyes for us. We can see Jesus now, who has given us a whole new life.

Gotta go—keep up the good work. Pray for us.

Love, Paul and Timothy

The Word of the Lord.

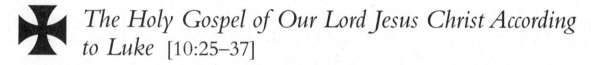

✠ *The Holy Gospel of Our Lord Jesus Christ According to Luke* [10:25–37]

A lawyer came to test Jesus. "Teacher," he said, "What do I need to do to have eternal life?" Jesus said, "What does the law say?" The man said, "Love God with all your heart, soul, mind, and strength and love your neighbor as yourself." Jesus said, "Well, there you go. You've got your answer. Do it and you'll have eternal life."

But, the lawyer said, "And who exactly is my neighbor?" Jesus told him this story:

A man was walking to Jerusalem when he got mugged and was left to die. A priest was coming down that road. When he saw him lying on the road, he walked around him. And a Levite did the same thing. But a Samaritan (an outsider) came near and right away gave him first aid, put him on his mule, took him to a motel, and took care of him there. The next day he gave some money to the innkeeper, because he had to leave for the day. He said, "Take care of him, and when I come back, I'll repay you for whatever extra expenses there were."

"Now," Jesus said, "of those three men, who do you think was a neighbor to the man who had been beaten up?" The lawyer said, "The man who showed him mercy was the neighbor." Jesus said, "Then that's what you should do."

The Gospel of the Lord.

Proper 11

A Reading from the Book of Amos [8:1–12]

There was a basket of fruit in front of me. God reminded me that we were entering a new season.

"Things are going to change for my people," said God. "The singing they've done in the temple will turn into wailing over those who have died.

"Pay attention, those of you who walk over the homeless people and take food out of the mouths of the hungry. Don't be so anxious to make money. I was proud to be Jacob's God, but you people disgust me.

"Your parties will turn into funeral receptions. The sun will go dark during the day. Your crops will dry up. You will be desperate for my word, but you may not be able to hear it."

The Word of the Lord.

Psalm 52

You big bully. You think you are such a big guy when you
hurt people
and make fun of people who trust in God.

As for me, I'm gonna trust in God's kindness.

You make up ways to trick people so they look stupid.
If I used words you use, I'd be in big trouble around my house.

As for me, I'm gonna trust in God's kindness.

You like to cut people into little pieces with your tongue.
You must really love being bad. And I don't think you even know
how to tell the truth!

As for me, I'm gonna trust in God's kindness.

You make me so angry that I wish you would go away forever
so I would never have to see your face or hear your voice again.

As for me, I'm gonna trust in God's kindness.

Sometimes I imagine that I'm the one laughing at you for
being stupid.
But I know that's not how God wants anyone to act.
I would rather imagine myself as an olive tree growing in a
beautiful courtyard in God's house.

As for me, I'm gonna trust in God's kindness.

I will always trust in God's mercy and kindness.
That's the better way to live.
I give thanks to you, God, and I will tell everyone about the great
things you have done for me.

As for me, I'm gonna trust in God's kindness.

A Reading from the Letter of Paul to the Colossians [1:15–28]

When we see Christ Jesus, we are looking at a picture of God whom we cannot see. In him everything in heaven and on earth were created, even the invisible things. Because of him, all things hold together. He is the head of the church body. He is the beginning, and was the first from the dead. In Christ Jesus all the fullness of God has found a home, and through him God has made peace with all things, on earth and in heaven.

You were once angry at God, going in the wrong direction, and doing wrong things, but now Christ has brought you back, and offers you to God as holy. Keep the faith. Stay steady on the right road now.

For your sake, I will put up with all that I have to suffer. And I endure for the sake of the church. God commissioned me to make God's Word fully known to you, to reveal the mystery to everyone. Christ is the hope of glory. And we proclaim him, and teach you, so that you may mature in Christ.

The Word of the Lord.

✠ *The Holy Gospel of Our Lord Jesus Christ According to Luke* [10:38–42]

Jesus stopped again at Mary and Martha's house. Martha was busy cooking dinner and cleaning up, but her sister Mary was sitting at Jesus' feet listening to him talk. That did *not* make Martha happy. She came to Jesus and said, "Doesn't it bother you that Mary is letting me do all the work by myself? Make her get up and help me." Jesus answered her, "Martha, calm down. So many things are making you crazy. But you really only need one thing. Mary has made the right choice."

The Gospel of the Lord.

Proper 12

A Reading from the Book of Hosea [1:2–10]

God said to Hosea, "Marry a woman who will be unfaithful to you, because that's what Israel is doing in their relationship with me and you'll see what it feels like." Hosea married Gomer. They had two sons and a daughter together, who only reminded them that the children of Israel did not behave as children of God should. Yet the numbers of the people of Israel grew to be like the sand of the sea. And even though God had said to them, "You are not my people," (because he was so disappointed in them), he knew he'd promised to call them the children of the living God.

The Word of the Lord.

Psalm 85 (see the Second Sunday of Advent, Year B, p. 221)

A Reading from the Letter of Paul to the Colossians [2:6–15]

You have received Christ Jesus, so live your lives in him. Plant the roots of your faith and let them grow in him. May your hearts be overflowing with thanksgiving. Don't let anyone sweet talk you out of your faith. Because in Christ Jesus God is fully alive, and you have become fully alive in Christ, who is the head of every ruler. In him you have been sealed to his death and resurrection. You have been raised with him in faith. Before you had committed yourself to God, you were living a life going in the opposite direction of God. God brought you to life, erasing all that kept you from God. All the charges he had against you, he nailed to the cross. They're gone.

The Word of the Lord.

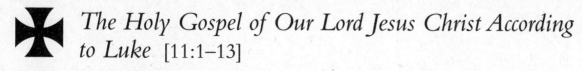

✠ *The Holy Gospel of Our Lord Jesus Christ According to Luke* [11:1–13]

When Jesus finished praying, one of the disciples asked him, "Jesus, would you teach us to pray? John the Baptist taught his disciples how to pray." So Jesus said, "When you pray, say, 'Father, your name is holy. Bring your kingdom closer and closer. Give us what we need each day. Forgive what we do to harm our relationship with you and with others. Help us to forgive others when they harm us. Please don't let our faith be tested.'" Jesus said, "If you go to a friend's house at midnight, wanting to borrow three loaves of bread, would he say, 'Go away and stop bothering me? I'm not getting up for you for any reason.' No, a friend will hear what you need and try to help you. Don't be afraid to ask God for what you want, or to look for what you need. Be bold and knock on God's door! God will open it for you. If you ask, you'll receive. If you seek, you'll find. God loves you and wants to give you good gifts. He won't give you a snake if you've asked for a fish, or drop a scorpion in your basket when you really wanted an egg."

The Gospel of the Lord.

Proper 13

A Reading from the Book of Hosea [11:1–11]

This is what God says:

When you were little, I loved you so much. I brought you out of Egypt where they didn't treat you well. But the more I ran after you sometimes, the further you ran away. It's like you loved others more than you love me. But I'm the one who taught you to walk. I picked you up and held you tight when you were scared, but you didn't know how special that was. I led you in the right direction. I bent down to feed you. You might as well go back to those who hurt you now. You'll be sorry. You seem to insist on turning away from me. You are breaking my heart. How can I give you up? I can't hate you; I can only love you. And I'm not a person; I am God, but still my heart melts when you are around. I will be patient and wait until you come back to me. I can't be angry for long. Someday, when you grow up, you will come back to me.

The Word of the Lord.

Psalm 107:1–9, 43

I can't say this often enough.
We have you to thank for everything good we have, God. You are so good.

God is really good. God's kindness never ends.

You look for ways to be good to us, and you are always calling us to yourself.
We run away, wander in the desert, and forget about you,

then we wonder why we're thirsty and hungry, like there's a big hole in us.

God is really good. God's kindness never ends.

When we come whining to you because we're hungry and thirsty,
you feed us and give us water to drink.
You listen to us and hug us because you love us.

God is really good. God's kindness never ends.

You pick us up by the scruff of the neck and plop us on the right path.
You place our feet on the ground and then nudge us in the right direction.
Again and again.

God is really good. God's kindness never ends.

Thirsty people will have plenty of water
and empty hearts and stomachs will be filled with good things.
You really should think about all that God has done for you.

God is really good. God's kindness never ends.

A Reading from the Letter of Paul to the Colossians [3:1–11]

If you really mean it when you say you love Jesus, your life had better show it. You don't have to be like everyone else—you can make your own choices. Because you belong to God, you can live a life that God would be proud of.

So, don't do things that make you a small, bitter person. Don't make fun of people because it makes other people laugh. Don't use somebody to get your own way. Don't take all the good things for yourself and give the leftovers to the others. Share! Think of other people.

Don't use bad words. That just makes you look like you're not smart enough to be clever. You need to stop hurting other people; watch your tongue, don't mock other people, and you've got to do something about that temper of yours.

Don't lie. God doesn't lie to you.

When you can't remember the right way to act, stop and think about what is kind and loving and think about the way God treats you.

Live your new life, no matter who you are, like you belong to God. Because you do.

The Word of the Lord.

✠ *The Holy Gospel of Our Lord Jesus Christ According to Luke* [12:13–21]

Somebody standing around said to Jesus, "Hey, tell my brother he has to divide up the family inheritance with me." (His dad had died and left the house and all his stuff to one of his boys.) Jesus said, "Why would you think I should tell you or your brother what to do?"

And then he said. "You've got to watch out, or greed will get you. If you're not careful, you'll just keep wanting more and more and more stuff. You think you'll get enough; but you'll find you never have enough. And that's no life to live, with this hole inside your heart that can't be filled up.

"Let me tell you this story: There was a rich man who owned a farm that produced lots and lots of corn. He looked out over his field and said, "What am I going do with all that corn? I don't have room for all that grain! Here's what I'll do. I will tear down the barns I've got and build even bigger ones. That'll be enough room for my grain, and maybe some extra room for storage of all my stuff. Then I can relax and say to myself, 'Self, you have it made. You've got everything you need. Eat, drink and be merry! Nothing to worry about.'"

But God knew better. God knew all that grain and the buildings and his stuff were eating him up inside. And that he would never have enough. He thought he'd have a good life, but it turned out that good life was having him! All those things aren't going to make you happy and being rich doesn't give you peace of mind. It's only when you've got God in your heart that you can say you are rich.

The Gospel of the Lord.

Proper 14

A Reading from the Book of Isaiah [1:1, 10–20]

Isaiah had a vision about what was to come. He shouted, "Listen to God, people! God doesn't want empty gestures or gifts he doesn't need. God says, 'Don't bring me any goats or sheep. Don't bother going to my temple. Douse the incense. I don't want to hear your hymns or listen to you speak on your holy days. They are too much for me to bear. And I'm tired of it. Your hands are full of blood and I can't stand looking at them when you reach out to me. Wash yourselves; make yourselves clean; turn yourselves around. Stop the evil and learn how to do good. Be just. Lift up those who are oppressed. Be there for orphans and widows who have no one to help them. Then, we'll talk about our relationship. Your sin will no longer stain your soul. Your life will be good but if you turn away from me, your life will be full of violence.' Listen to what God is saying, people."

The Word of the Lord.

Psalm 50:1–8, 23–24

You have spoken, God.
You talk to the earth from sunup to sundown.

The heavens point to God's goodness.

You show us your glory and will not be silent.
Wherever you go, you are surrounded by a raging storm
and a flame leads you.
You gather the people: Come here, you who have made promises
with me.

The heavens point to God's goodness.

God says: Listen to me, people. I am your God.
It's not your fancy sacrifices that tug at my heart.
It's your sacrifice of thanksgiving that honors me.
And if you walk the way I show you,
I will show you salvation.

The heavens point to God's goodness.

A Reading from the Letter to the Hebrews [11:1–3, 8–16]

Having faith is choosing to believe in something you can't see, but hope for. Our ancestors walked with faith. With faith, we know that the Word of God created the world, and made things visible that were invisible. It was faith that moved Abraham to obey God and set out on a trip, not knowing where he would end up. Faith helped him dream of a city designed by God. Faith helped him father a child that God promised. And because of this one person's faith, many people were born, as many as the stars in the heavens, or as the grains of sand on the shore.

Faith doesn't mean you'll receive the promise, but that you can see it from a distance. You might be wandering, looking for home, but you know that you have a home. You have a heavenly home, where God is prepared to welcome you. All of these died in faith without having received the promises, but from a distance they saw and greeted them. They confessed that they were strangers and foreigners on the earth, for people who speak in this way make it clear that they are seeking a homeland. If they had been thinking of the land that they had left behind, they would have had opportunity to return. But as it is, they want a better country, that is, a heavenly one. Therefore God is not ashamed to be called their God; God has prepared a city for them.

The Word of the Lord.

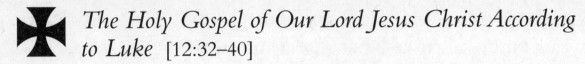

✠ *The Holy Gospel of Our Lord Jesus Christ According to Luke* [12:32–40]

Jesus told his disciples, again, not to be afraid. He reminded them that God really wanted to give them God's kingdom. "Give away what you own. Give to those who need what you have. Build up your wealth in heaven, where no one can touch it. Watch what you value; it will always claim your heart. Be ready and alert. You never know what is coming or what will be required of you. Always be ready for God and God's goodness to break into your life."

The Gospel of the Lord.

Proper 15

A Reading from the Book of Isaiah [5:1–7]

Here's a song and a story for my loved one:

My loved one had a vineyard, in a beautiful spot, just right for growing grapes. He dug it up and cleared the rocks from it, and planted excellent vines. He expected grapes, but got wild grapes that he didn't plant. I'm not sure what he could have done better. What do you think, people of Jerusalem? I did all I could. Here's what I will do: I'm going to break down its wall and let the animals eat what they want and trample what they will. I'm not bothering to prune or hoe. The thorns will overtake the vines. There's no point in sending rain down on them either.

The vineyard, you see, is the house of Israel and Judah. God expected justice but saw violence. God wanted righteousness but heard crying instead.

The Word of the Lord.

Psalm 80:1–2, 8–18

Shepherd of Israel, leading the people like a flock of sheep,
hear us. Shine brightly in front of us, you who are seated with
 the angels.

Stir up your strength and help us.

You brought a vine out of Egypt;
 you cleared the land and planted it.
You prepared the ground for it;
 it took root and filled the land.

Stir up your strength and help us.

The mountains were covered by its shadow
    and the towering cedar trees by its boughs.
This vine stretched to the sea and its branches reached the river.
Why have you broken down its wall,
    so that all who walk by pluck off its grapes?
The wild boar of the forest has chomped on it,
    and the beasts of the field are picking away at it.

Stir up your strength and help us.

Turn now, God, look down from heaven;
Look at this vine and tend it.
Take care of this precious vine that you have planted.
Let your hand guide and care for us
so that we will never turn away from you.

Stir up your strength and help us.

Give us life again, so we can say your name aloud once more.
We will never turn away from you again.
Make us whole, God.
Let us see your shining face, and we shall be saved.

Stir up your strength. We need your help.

A Reading from the Letter of Paul to the Hebrews [11:29–12:2]

Faith helped the people walk through the Red Sea like it was dry land. Faith brought down the walls of Jericho after they'd been circled for seven days. Rahab was saved by faith because she helped the spies and didn't give them away. What more can I say? I could go on and on about how faith conquered kingdoms, obtained promises, shut the mouths of lions, quenched fire, and sent enemies away screaming.

Some people with faith have been tortured, thrown in jail, sawn in two. Some wandered around in deserts and caves and holes in the ground. And God honored them for their faith. God has made them perfect and given them to us as examples.

We walk through a cloud of these faithful witnesses each day. As we walk, let's lay down everything that holds us back, along with the sin that clings to us like dirt. In fact, let's not walk, let's run on the path that is in front of us, with Jesus who has run this way ahead of us. He is the perfect example of faith. He endured the cross and its shame, and is now sitting with God.

The Word of the Lord.

✠ *The Holy Gospel of Our Lord Jesus Christ According to Luke* [12:49–56]

Jesus said, "I have come to set the world on fire, and I wish it were ready to be ignited. I am so ready to begin this new thing God is doing. It is hard for me to hold back. Don't think I've come to make your life easy and peaceful. I'm here to shake things up instead. Things will get ugly before they get better. Families will be divided because they cannot agree on me or how to act or how to worship God. You know how you look to the sky to see what the weather might be like tomorrow? Why don't you look around you and see what is happening around you here on earth too, and figure out what tomorrow will bring."

The Gospel of the Lord.

Proper 16

A Reading from the Book of Jeremiah [1:4–10] (see the Fourth Sunday after the Epiphany, Year C, p. 383)

Psalm 71:1–6 (see the Fourth Sunday after the Epiphany 4, Year C, p. 383)

A Reading from the Letter of Paul to the Hebrews [12:18–29]

You have come to the city of the living God. It's not a place you can touch. There is no blazing fire or storm or a sound of a trumpet, like the Israelites saw when Moses was talking to God on the mountain. More angels live in this city than you can count, and they are all praising God. In this city are the spirits of those who have gone before who have been made perfect. And Jesus, who is the one who has worked out a new agreement between God and us, is here also.

This city, this kingdom, cannot be shaken. Let's be thankful for that, and worship God. Our God is working to clear things out, ready for a new beginning. Our God is on fire!

The Word of the Lord.

✠ *The Holy Gospel of Our Lord Jesus Christ According to Luke* [13:10–17]

Jesus was teaching on the Sabbath in a synagogue. A woman who had been crippled by pain for eighteen years came in. Jesus called her over when he saw her and said, "Woman, be free. Stand up straight. You are cured." He laid his hands on her, and she immediately stood up straight and began praising God. The leader of the synagogue was furious that Jesus had cured somebody on the Sabbath (that was against the law). He said to the crowd, "God said we work on six days and not on the seventh day, which is the Sabbath. Those other six days are when you should come for healing."

Jesus looked at him and said, "What a hypocrite! If your donkey needs water on the Sabbath, don't you go untie it and lead it to drink? That's working on the Sabbath. Shouldn't this woman, who has suffered for eighteen long years, and is a daughter of Abraham, be set free from her pain on the Sabbath day?" When people heard this, they were ashamed of themselves. The entire crowd rejoiced at the wonderful things they saw Jesus doing.

The Gospel of the Lord.

Proper 17

A Reading from the Book of Jeremiah [2:4–13]

Listen to what God is saying, everyone:

Why did your ancestors leave me, and go for worthless things instead?
Why did they become worthless themselves?

They forgot that I brought them out of Egypt and led them in the wilderness, through deep darkness to the other side. I settled them in a beautiful land full of fruit and good things to eat. Then they began to destroy the land, and trash the relationship we had together. Even their leaders turned away from me. They exchanged my love for things that don't matter. I will hold you accountable for this; I will hold your children accountable. I want the heavens to see what you've done and be shocked and disgusted with you.

Not only have you abandoned me completely, and turned away from the fountain of living water that I offer, you have dug pits, which are cracked and can hold no water for you at all.

The Word of the Lord.

Psalm 81:1, 10–16

Sing as loudly and as long as you can.
Sing with joy in your hearts
and shout to the God of Jacob.

"Listen to me, people," says God.

I am your God,
who brought you out of the land of Egypt and said,
"Open your mouth wide and I will fill it."

"Listen to me, people," says God.

But people wouldn't listen to me and they wouldn't obey.
So I let them do what they wanted.
They were stubborn and stupid, and they made my heart ache.
Oh, I wish they would listen to me and walk my way.
I will turn away their enemies from them, and I will feed them
with the finest wheat
and delight their tongues with honey from the rock.

"Listen to me, people," says God.

A Reading from the Letter to the Hebrews [13:1–8, 15–16]

Here's what Paul has to say in his letter to us:

Keep on loving each other like you do. But remember to pay attention to people you *don't* know because sometimes they are messengers from God and you don't even know it! Don't forget about people who are locked up in prison. Imagine what it would be like to be them—not getting to do whatever you want, and not having your friends or family around. Everyone who is married needs to be faithful to his or her husband or wife, because that's what God expects. Don't be so greedy, wanting more money or things than you actually need. Try being happy with what you've got and not being afraid.

Watch the good things your leaders in church do and try to be faithful like they are. Jesus Christ is always the same and always, always there for you. Don't forget that.

And when you offer yourself to God, when you praise God, do it in Jesus' name. Remember that God especially likes it when you share with other people and do good in the world.

The Word of the Lord.

✠ *The Holy Gospel of Our Lord Jesus Christ According to Luke* [14:1, 7–14]

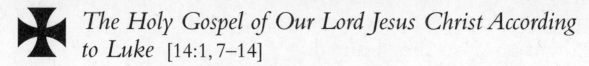

Jesus was invited by a leader of the Pharisees to come to dinner at his house on the Sabbath, so they were watching him closely. Jesus watched how, as people came into dinner, they would choose to sit in the places of honor. So he told them this: "When you are invited to a wedding feast, don't sit at the place of honor. Because someone even more distinguished than you might walk in and you'll be sitting in the place intended for them. How embarrassing. Then the host will reseat you at the furthest place in the room. It makes more sense to choose to sit in the furthest, lowest place, and have the host come to you and say, 'Please, let's get you a better seat.' Then you will honored in front of everyone. Believe me, those who put themselves first, will find themselves humbled. And those who choose to be humble, will find themselves exalted."

Turning to his host, Jesus said, "When you give a dinner, don't just invite your friends or rich relatives who will return the favor. Instead, invite the poor, those who can't walk or can't see. They won't have the means to repay you, but you will be blessed. God will know and will repay you."

The Gospel of the Lord.

Proper 18

A Reading from the Book of Jeremiah [18:1–11]

The word that came to Jeremiah from God: "Go down to the potter's house, and we'll talk there."

So I went down to the potter's house, and there he was working at his wheel. The jar he was making of clay was ruined in the potter's hand, and he reworked it into another jar. Then God's Word came to me. "Can't I rework you, House of Israel, just as this potter has reworked his clay? You are clay in my hands. You know I can destroy what I've made and I've made everything. I can shape something that will bring disaster on you. Or I could reshape it and bring you blessing. I want you to say to the people of Judah and Jerusalem, 'Pay attention, people. I am shaping a plan right now for you. All of you had better turn from the evil things you are doing, and change your ways and the things you do.'

The Word of the Lord.

Psalm 139:1–5, 12–17

(see the Second Sunday after the Epiphany, Year B, p. 233)

A Reading from the Letter of Paul to Philemon [1:1–21]

I am Paul, a prisoner of Christ Jesus, and this letter is from Timothy and me.

To Philemon, our dear friend and co-worker, to the church that meets in your house, we send along our wishes for God's grace and peace.

We always remember to pray for you. We thank God because we hear of the love you have for each other and your strong faith in Jesus. I pray that you share your faith and that the seeds you plant take hold. Your love warms my heart, and gives me courage. You have refreshed the hearts of many, my brother.

You know, I could make you do what I want (because I'm that important!), but I would rather appeal to you on the basis of love. I am old, and still the prisoner of Jesus. I'm asking you on behalf of Onesimus, whom I've grown close to while I was in prison. I'm sending him back to you. I hate to see him go, but this makes more sense. Please treat him as a beloved brother, not as a slave. If you consider me your partner, welcome him as you would welcome me. If he owes you anything, let me know, and I'll pay up. Please do this for me. I am confident that you will do this kindness for me. It does my heart good knowing that you will do this kindness for me.

The Word of the Lord.

✠ *The Holy Gospel of Our Lord Jesus Christ According to Luke* [14:25–33]

Jesus turned to the large crowds who were following him and said, "If you aren't willing to give up your family, and even your life itself, don't bother being my disciples. If you want to follow me, you have to carry your cross. I just want you to know what's ahead so you can make plans. If you were going to build a garage, you'd figure out the cost first, wouldn't you? You'd want to know if you had enough money to complete the project. How embarrassing it is to start something you can't finish just because you hadn't done your research. If you were a king and going to war, you'd figure out whether your army was big enough and equipped with what was needed to oppose the enemy, right? And if you didn't have what it takes, you would send out someone to work out a peaceful agreement and avoid the battle altogether.

None of you can be my disciples, if you don't give up everything you own.

The Gospel of the Lord.

Proper 19

A Reading from the Book of Jeremiah [4:11–12, 22–28]

God says this to the people of Jerusalem:

I will cause a strong hot wind to blow in judgment against you. You are foolish, stupid people. You know all about doing evil, but have no idea how to do good. I looked down on earth, and it was a wasteland. And the heavens had no light. The mountains were shaking and the hills were moving back and forth. The people had deserted the earth. The orchards were now deserts and the cities were in ruins. I will not destroy you completely. The earth will mourn. The heavens will dress in black and sorrow. I mean it. I will not turn back.

The Word of the Lord.

Psalm 14 (see Proper 12, Year B, p. 321)

A Reading from The First Letter of Paul to Timothy [1:12–17]

I am so grateful that Jesus has given me strength and put me to work for him, even though I fought him and his believers for years, and I made sure they suffered. I was ignorant of God's grace then. But now, God's grace and faith and love have been poured all over me. I know this for sure, that Christ Jesus came into this world for us sinners. And believe me, I'm the biggest sinner of them all. Jesus made me an example; if God can love me and forgive me, you know God can forgive and love anyone! To you, God, King, awesome and only God, I give you honor and glory forever. Amen.

The Word of the Lord.

✠ *The Holy Gospel of Our Lord Jesus Christ According to Luke* [15:1–10]

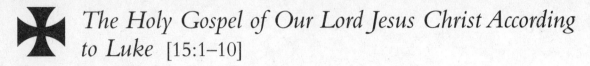

The tax collectors and sinners were coming close to Jesus to listen to him. The Pharisees and other leaders were grumbling, saying, "Look at him; eating and talking with all those sinners." So he told them this story:

There was a man who had one hundred sheep, and he loved each one of them. One of them got lost, so he left the ninety-nine in the wilderness to search for the lost one. He looked and looked, calling his name. Finally he found it, and put it on his shoulders and was relieved and happy. When he got home, he had a party with his friends and neighbors and said, "Be happy for me. I finally found that one sheep of mine that was lost." That's how it is in heaven, when one sinner turns from his ways and joins the ninety-nine who had never strayed.

If you had ten silver coins and lost one, wouldn't you keep your lamp lit all night, and sweep the entire house, looking under everything for that last coin? Then you would tell everyone you know how awful you felt when that coin was lost, and how happy you are now that it's found. The angels in heaven party all night over one sinner who changes his ways and turns to God.

The Gospel of the Lord.

Proper 20

A Reading from the Book of Jeremiah [8:18–9:1]

God says, "I have nothing to be happy about. I'm drowning in grief and my heart is sick.

> I can hear my people.
> They've been worshipping other gods and they make me angry."
> They say, 'We've harvested, summer is over, and still we are not saved.'
> I ache for my hurting people.
> Is there nothing to help my people?
> No doctor to cure them, no treatment for their wounds?
> Why have they not been healed?
> My head is a spring of water, and my eyes are fountains of tears
> I cry day and night for my poor people.

Psalm 79:1–9

God, those who hate you have walked into your temple and ruined it.
They have marched through Jerusalem and turned it into rubble.
They have left your servants in the street for the birds to pick at
or in the fields for the animals to enjoy.

How long will you be angry with us, God?
How long will your fury blaze like fire?

They have shed blood like it was water throughout the city of Jerusalem
and there is no one left to bury the dead.

Now we are being shamed
And mocked by everyone who sees us.

How long will you be angry with us, God?
How long will your fury blaze like fire?

Turn to those who hate you and let them taste your
  anger instead.
They're the ones who are trying to destroy you like they
  destroy Jerusalem.
Forget the wrong we have done.
We are scraping the bottom here, and we are miserable.
Please show us your compassionate side soon.
Help us, O God our Savior, for the glory of your Name;
  we beg you to deliver us and forgive us our sins, for your
  Name's sake.

How long will you be angry with us, God?
How long will your fury blaze like fire?

A Reading from The First Letter of Paul to Timothy [2:1–7]

First off, I want you to pray for everyone, especially those in authority, so that we can live a peaceful life with the people around us. God will be pleased because God wants everyone to be saved. There's only one God and one person who gave himself for all of us—Jesus. That's the truth and that's why God appointed me his messenger, so I could make sure the truth gets to everyone.

The Word of the Lord.

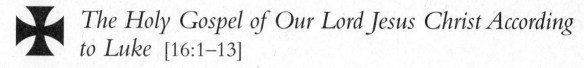

✠ *The Holy Gospel of Our Lord Jesus Christ According to Luke* [16:1–13]

Jesus told his disciples this story:

There was a rich man who learned that his manager was not handling his property honestly. So he hauled him in, and said, "I don't like what I'm hearing about you. I want an investigation of what you've been doing. You can't be my manager anymore." The manager said to himself, "What am I going to do without this job? I'm not strong enough for construction work, but I'm too proud to beg. I know—I'll sweet-talk the people who owe my master money, so that after I'm fired, they'll give me work." So, that's what he did. And his master applauded the manager even though he was dishonest, because he was crafty. We don't need to be dishonest, but we need to be at least as creative as the dishonest people are.

If you are honest with little things, you'll be honest in big things. Just like faith. If you are faithful with what belongs to someone else, perhaps you will be faithful with your own. Nobody can serve two masters. You'll hate one or the other. It's like that with God and wealth—you've got to choose between them, which one you're going to build your life around.

The Gospel of the Lord.

Proper 21

A Reading from the Book of Jeremiah [32:1–3a, 6–15]

I bought the field from my cousin, gave him the money for it, and took the deed of purchase to Baruch. With many witnesses I told Baruch to take the deeds and put them in a safe place, because they would need to last for a long time. God himself said that we will be in this land a long time, so we might as well start buying houses and fields and vineyards and settle down.

The Word of the Lord.

Psalm 91:1–6, 14–16

God is a shelter where we can hide from the storm,
The shadow where we can be safe from the hot sun.
Here's what I say: "God, I know I can always trust you.
I run to you and grab on to you when I need you."

When I call God's name, God answers.
God is beside me when I'm in trouble.

If you run to God, and actually live with God all around you,
nothing bad can happen to you.
God will assign angels to you, to follow you, to keep
you close.
They will hold you in their arms, and watch your back.

When I call God's name, God answers.
God is beside me when I'm in trouble.

Nothing can hurt you—not lions, not snakes. In fact, lions and
snakes will be scared of you!
God will say, "I will protect that one there, because I know he
loves me.

I will rescue him from trouble, because he knows my Name and
knows how to use it.
When he calls out my Name, I will answer.
I will be with him in trouble.
I will bring him back to a place where he can be proud of
himself, and not scared.
I will reward him with a good long life,
and show him what real living is all about."

When I call God's name, God answers.
God is beside me when I'm in trouble.

A Reading from the First Letter of Paul to Timothy [6:6–19]

We brought nothing into this world when we were born, and we can take nothing out of it with us when we die. Enough food and clothing should make us happy. If you want to be rich, though, it is very easy to fall into temptation and get trapped into things that can destroy you. The love of money is the cause of all kinds of evil. Some rich people forget about their faith and sometimes cause themselves no end of trouble.

Best to forget about pursuing lots of money. Instead go after faith and love, endurance and gentleness. It's a fight for sure, but it's a good fight. Grip eternal life, because that's what God has called you to and what you have made known to your friends. Keep God's commandments until Jesus Christ returns in God's good time. Right now he is surrounded by an unapproachable light, which no one has ever seen. He is Lord of all lords, and we praise him. If you know people who are rich, tell them not to trust their riches, because wealth is uncertain. And tell them not to think too much of themselves, just because they have money. Instead they should rely on God, who provides us with everything we need. Rich people can do good and be rich in good works and generous. If they can do that, they will have a great foundation for the future and be able to embrace the life that really *is* life.

The Word of the Lord.

✠ *The Holy Gospel of Our Lord Jesus Christ According to Luke* [16:19–31]

Jesus told a story about a rich man who loved to wear fancy purple clothes and eat lots of great food. Right outside his door was a poor man named Lazarus, who was covered with sores that never healed. The dogs would even come and lick his sores. Lazarus would have been happy to eat whatever fell off the rich man's table. The poor man died and was carried by the angels and placed in the arms of Father Abraham. The rich man died and was buried. His soul went into torment, and he was really tormented when he looked up and saw Abraham holding Lazarus in his arms. He called out, "Father Abraham, have mercy on me, and send Lazarus with a drop of water on his finger to come and cool my tongue with it. I am in agony." Abraham said, "You received good things in your lifetime, and Lazarus had nothing but misery when he was alive. How ironic that now he is in comfort and you are the one in agony. It's too late."

"Then, I beg you to send him to warn my brothers so they won't end up here." Abraham said, "They have warning enough. They should listen to Moses and the prophets." "I know they won't listen," said the rich man. "But if someone from the dead comes, I bet they'll listen and change their ways."

Abraham said, "If they ignore Moses and the prophets, no one from the dead will convince them either."

The Gospel of the Lord.

Proper 22

A Reading from the Book of Lamentations [1:1–6]

It makes me so sad to see an empty city that was once full of people. This city is like a widow who once was married to a powerful man. She is like a princess who has become a housekeeper. She is like someone who cries herself to sleep with no one to comfort her. All of her friends have dumped her. The nation of Judah is suffering now with no one to comfort her people. No one comes to the temple anymore for festivals. Her children grieve together instead of play together. Her enemies are thriving. She is paying for the wrong she has done. Her best young men have become like deer looking for pasture with no success, and running away from those who are pursuing them, having no strength left in their legs.

The Word of the Lord.

Psalm 137

Sometimes I feel so far away from home.
Because I *am* far away from home.
It makes me cry to think of what my life used to be like.
I used to play happy music on my harp
but I've given that up altogether and just chucked my harp
in the bushes.

Pray for the peace of Jerusalem.

The people who took me far from my home
know I can play the harp and sing,
and they have asked to hear my songs from home.
But how can I do that?
How can I sing a happy song about God's love

when I don't live anywhere around God anymore
and I don't even know where God is?

Pray for the peace of Jerusalem.

I don't want to forget Jerusalem, my home,
and I don't want to forget how to play beautiful music.
If I forget how to sing,
I might as well just glue my tongue to the roof of my mouth
and forget all the good things I knew back home.

Pray for the peace of Jerusalem.

God, do you remember when Jerusalem was strong
even when we thought we were doomed?
Babylon, you faraway land where I am held,
you will get paid back for what you've taken from us.

Pray for the peace of Jerusalem.

A Reading from the Second Letter of Paul to Timothy [1:1–14]

Hey Timothy! You just got another letter from Paul. Read what he has to say:

Dear Timothy, my special boy,

I hope you feel all the grace, mercy, and peace that God our Father has to offer.

I never stop thanking God for you. I remember you cried when I left last time. And I can't wait to see you again. It makes me so happy to know that you truly believe in God, just as your grandmother Lois taught you and your mom, too. It's like they passed down their own faith to you! You have to pay attention to your faith, though, and keep it burning hot, just like a fire. Remember that you can't be a coward, because God put power inside you just as God put in love and self-discipline.

I'm writing this letter to you from prison. I hope you are not ashamed to know me. I landed here in prison not for doing something that would hurt someone, but because I was talking about Jesus, even though they didn't want me to. And I hope you'll do the same.

If you do, you'll have to rely on God's grace. It's the only thing that keeps me going. Following Jesus is a holy calling, but it sure isn't easy. God's grace is all around me. In fact, it was around before Jesus even showed up! I don't know why, but God appointed me to be his messenger and teacher. And I suffer because of it. But it's all good. Because it's all for God and I trust in him more than I've ever trusted in anything before.

Hang on to what I taught you. And hold on tight to the faith and love that are yours in Christ Jesus. Faith and love are treasures that God has given you, and the Holy Spirit, who lives inside of you, will help you carry on.

Gotta go.

Love ya, Paul

✠ *The Holy Gospel of Our Lord Jesus Christ According to Luke* [17:5–10]

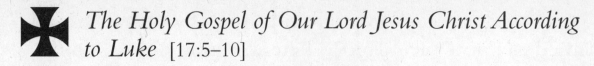

The apostles said to Jesus, "Give us more faith. We want more faith!" And they started chanting, "More faith. More faith. More faith."

Jesus replied, "If you only knew how little faith you actually need—as much as this tiny seed—and you could do anything! You could talk to this tree and tell it to go jump in the lake, and it would.

"Which one of you would say to your slave who has just come in from plowing or tending sheep in the field, 'Forget about getting me my dinner. Come over here and sit down.'?

"Would you not rather say to him, 'Bring me some good food and something good to drink, and afterwards you can sit and feed yourself'?

"Do you thank the slave for doing what was commanded? Isn't that his job? So you also, when you have done all that you were ordered to do, say, 'Aw, it was nothing. I only did what I was supposed to do!'"

The Gospel of the Lord.

Proper 23

A Reading from the Book of Jeremiah [29:1–7]

Here's what the letter said that Jeremiah sent to his friends who had been kidnapped and taken to Babylon to live:

Go ahead and build houses. Plant your gardens to enjoy what grows in them. Fall in love and get married. Have kids and let your kids give you beautiful grandbabies. I know you'd rather be back home in Jerusalem. I know that. But make the best of what you have and where you are. Bloom where you are planted! Ask God to bless Babylon and you will share in the blessing.

The Word of the Lord.

Psalm 66:1–11

Let's make some noise everyone!
Sing loud and long because God is good.
Tell God this: "*You*, God, are the best."
And those who don't like you shrivel up when you are around.
Come on, people. Let's make some noise and praise God.

The earth itself worships you and every plant and animal on it
does too.
Come here, and see how God is good.
We'll show you what God is doing with us.
Come on, people. Let's make some noise and praise God.

You dried up the waters, God, and dried out a path through
the river for us to walk.
It's awesome how you can watch over everyone and care
for everybody.
I don't know how you do it, but I'm sure glad you do.
Come on, people. Let's make some noise and praise God.

You make our lives strong and keep us from tripping over our own feet.
Life can be hard and sometimes it feels like a test we don't want to take.
Sometimes it feels like an obstacle course
And yet you help us make it through to the end.

Come on, people. Let's make some noise and praise God.

First, there's a fire that burns everything up because we can't find water to put it out.
And then, it rains so much it floods.
But finally you bring us to a place in the cool grass
where we can lie down and feel the warm, happy sun on our faces.

Come on, people. Let's make some noise and praise God.

A Reading from the Second Letter of Paul to Timothy [2:3–15]

My dear friend Timothy, I keep telling you that Jesus Christ is alive. I know people don't want to hear that. They don't know what it means, or how to deal with it. In fact, that's why they've thrown me in prison. I will be okay, though. I'll keep talking about Jesus because I have to. I have to let people know about God's Good News. God loves us and will be with us all the way. Keep telling people this. And tell them to quit arguing about stupid things. I can't believe the things people fight about, can you?

Be the best you can be—the person God made you to be. So that God can be proud of whom you've become.

The Word of the Lord.

✠ *The Holy Gospel of Our Lord Jesus Christ According to Luke* [17:11–19]

On his way to Jerusalem, Jesus walked into a village. Ten people who had a horrible ugly skin disease walked his way. They didn't come close to Jesus though, because they didn't want him to catch their disease. So they shouted to him, "Jesus, have mercy on us. Look, this disease is eating us alive!"

Jesus yelled back, "Go check in with your priests like you're supposed to and see what they have to say." (That's what you were supposed to do so the priest could see that you were healed and ready to be around people again.) So they went, and sure enough, they were healed and the priests said they were okay again.

One of them, seeing that his skin was clear and knowing it didn't hurt anymore, turned around before he went to the priests and ran to Jesus' feet and threw himself on the ground in front of Jesus. "THANK YOU! THANK YOU! THANK YOU! I can't thank you enough, Jesus." This man was from Samaria, meaning he wasn't like the others. "Wait a minute," Jesus said. "Weren't ten of you cured? Where's everyone else? I mean, REALLY, you're the only one who could be bothered to thank God that he's cured? And you're not even one of God's special ones."

Jesus knelt down and helped the man to his feet. "Go," Jesus said. "Have a good life. Your body is healed and your faith has made you strong and whole again."

The Gospel of the Lord.

Proper 24

A Reading from the Book of Jeremiah [31:27–34]

"One of these days," says God, "I will fill Israel and Judah with more people and animals. Just as I've seen them destroyed, I will make sure they build up and establish new growth. When that day comes, people will be responsible for their own actions. They won't be able to blame their parents for the wrong they themselves are doing. They will be accountable to me. I'll draw up a new agreement with my people. It won't be like the agreement I made with your fathers, when I had to take them by the hand and lead them out of Egypt. They broke that agreement. I will put my law inside of them, and write it on their hearts. I will be their God and they'll be my people. They won't even have to teach each other about me, because all of them will know me! Even the little kids. I will forget all that was wrong between us, and start all over again."

The Word of the Lord.

Psalm 119:97–104

I love everything you've told us, God.
I think all day long about what I've learned.
I'm a better person for listening to you,
and I'll pay attention to your word for the rest of my life.

Your words are like honey on my lips.

I study what you have said and I'm smarter than all my teachers.
Because I follow your way, I am wiser than the wisest old woman.

Your words are like honey on my lips.

Your word keeps me from going in the wrong
direction.

You have taught me well, so I don't have a problem following
your ways.
Your words are like honey on my lips.

Because of your wonderful laws, I am a better person,
and I won't settle for anything less from now on.
Your words are like honey on my lips.

A Reading from the Second Letter of Paul to Timothy [3:14–4:5]

Timothy, keep doing what you've been doing and believing what you've always believed. Keep on reading God's Word because it will make you ready for the work God has given you to do. Speak up about God's Good News. Talk about it whenever you can, wherever you can, to whomever you can. There will be the day when people will make up their own good news and not bother with God's Good News. But you—stay strong as you carry out your ministry.

The Word of the Lord.

✠ *The Holy Gospel of Our Lord Jesus Christ According to Luke* [18:1–8]

Jesus told his disciples a parable about always praying and never giving up. He said, "In a certain city there was a judge who didn't care about God or anybody, just did whatever he wanted. A widow kept coming to him saying, 'I demand justice!' For a while he refused; but later he said to himself, 'This woman is wearing me out. I don't give a hoot about her, but to shut her up I'm going to give her what she wants.'" Jesus said, "Won't God grant justice those who cry to him day and night? Won't God be on your side right away? I wonder, when the Son of Man comes, will he find faith on earth?"

The Gospel of the Lord.

Proper 25

A Reading from the Book of Joel [2:23–32]

You special people of God, you've got every reason to be happy. Your God has poured down lots of rain just when you needed it. You will harvest plenty of grain this year and lots and lots of wine and oil. You remember all those years you fought the locusts and grasshoppers that destroyed what you were growing? Well, now you've got plenty of food and grain. You will know for sure that I am with you no matter what and that I am really your God. And after this abundant harvest of yours, I will share my Spirit with everybody. Your sons and daughters will be able to see how things can work out, the old guys will dream dreams and the young ones will be able to see their way into the future. Even the lowliest of the lowly will feel my Spirit, too. Everyone will see signs that I am God and it won't necessarily be pretty. But if you trust me and ask me to help you, you won't need to worry about anything.

The Word of the Lord.

Psalm 65

God, you deserve all of our praise, all the time. Everywhere.
Everyone comes to you with their problems
and tells you where they've gone wrong.
When we sin, those sins become stronger than we are
but you are even bigger and stronger than them.
Those who come close to you are happy;
To live close to your heart is like living in a beautiful house.

God, you deserve all of our praise, all the time. Everywhere.

When we walk close to you, you show us beautiful scenery along the way.
We hope to always walk with you
to the ends of the earth,
to the edges of the faraway seas.
You are so strong, you hold the mountains in place.
You make the oceans be silent and calm down the waves.
You put quiet in the noisy hearts of people.

God, you deserve all of our praise, all the time.
Everywhere.

Everyone in the world can see your work when they look up to the skies.
You teach the sun a song to sing when it comes up in the morning
and a lullaby to go to sleep with at night.
You bring the rains that we need from the heavens.
You are a river full of water.
You make the grain grow that we eat and bless the earth so that it grows our food.

God, you deserve all of our praise, all the time.
Everywhere.

Every year wears a crown on its head because you've blessed it.
And everywhere you walk, flowers appear.
May the deserts have plenty of grass for our cattle to eat
and when we look at the mountains, may they make our hearts happy.
May the meadows be covered with lots of little leaping lambs.
May all the earth sing happy songs.

God, you deserve all of our praise, all the time.
Everywhere.

A Reading from the Second Letter of Paul to Timothy [4:6–8, 16–18]

Paul writes in his letter to Timothy:

I feel like a cup that someone's poured all the water out of. There's just not much left of me, I'm afraid. It's time for me to go. I have fought the fight. I have crossed the finish line of the race. I still have my faith in God. I know God has only good things in store for me.

It made me sad when no one stood up for me when I needed them in court. But God was standing up for me. God gave me strength and put words in my mouth that everyone could understand.

God loves you, people. And God sent you his Son Jesus to prove it.

Because God was with me, I didn't get thrown to the lions. I know that God will always be there for me when I need him. Thank you, God. Amen.

The Word of the Lord.

✠ *The Holy Gospel of Our Lord Jesus Christ According to Luke* [18:9–14]

Jesus told this story to some people who thought they were better than everyone else:

There were two guys in church. One of them was somebody everybody respected. The other was one nobody really liked. The first guy was praying out loud so everyone could hear him. "Thank you God for making me so special. I really wouldn't want to be anyone else, especially not somebody who steals, or who is dirty, or like that other guy in the corner over there. I follow all your rules, just like you want me to. That's why I'm so special."

Then there was the guy in the other corner. He knew people didn't like him and he felt bad about the poor choices he'd made that hurt other people. He was so sad he couldn't even lift up his head. He put his hand over his heart and said, "God, you know I mess up my life and the lives of other people all the time. Help me. Please help me."

Which one do you think God would rather hear from? I think it was the man who knew he needed God's help and asked for it.

If you think too much of yourself, people, God won't be that impressed with you. There's no point in thinking you're so special. There's always room for improvement, so let God help you.

The Gospel of the Lord.

Proper 26

A Reading from the Book of Habakkuk [1:1–4; 2:1–4]

How long do I have to cry out for you before you will listen to me, God? If I'm screaming that someone is hurting me, you'll come save me, won't you? All I can see is violence and destruction. The law has no meaning anymore and justice is there for no one. The good people are completely surrounded by the bad. I keep watch where I'm assigned to stand. I keep watch for you, God, to see how you will answer for this. Finally, God answered me and said, "Write this vision down plainly so everyone can see. There is a vision. Wait for it. In the hearts of proud people, things aren't right. But good people live by their faith."

The Word of the Lord.

Psalm 119:137–144

You are so good, God, and you always make good decisions.
I get so angry sometimes because other people forget you and
    what you say,
and then they turn against me.
I hold what you've said very close to my heart.
It is near to me and I never forget it.

You are so good, God, and you always make good decisions.

I'm nothing special, and I probably don't matter
but I do not forget your commandments.
Your justice will last forever
    and your law is the truth.

You are so good, God, and you always make good decisions.

Even when I'm in trouble and I think I can't breathe,
your commandments give me hope.
I know what you want will always be the right thing to do.
Help me to understand this and obey, that I might live
a good life.

You are so good, God, and you always make good decisions.

A Reading from the Second Letter of Paul to the Thessalonians [1:1–4, 11–12]

Here's a letter from Paul, Silvanus, and Timothy:

To the church of the Thessalonians in God our Father and the Lord Jesus Christ,

We send God's grace and peace along with this letter, brother and sisters. We thank God that your faith is growing so fast and so deep, and that the love you have for each other is growing, too. We brag about you to the other churches because of how strong you are in God even though you are going through such tough times. We will always pray that God gives you power and strength and that Jesus' name will be glorified in you.

The Word of the Lord.

✠ *The Holy Gospel of Our Lord Jesus Christ According to Luke* [19:1–10]

A man named Zacchaeus was a rich man who collected taxes. He was trying to see Jesus as he made his way through the streets of Jericho, but there were so many people there, and he was too short to see over the top of them. He climbed up a tree so he could get a glimpse of Jesus. When Jesus got to the tree where Zacchaeus was, he stopped and said, "Zacchaeus, what're you doing up in that tree? Get down from there. Let's go to your house and have dinner." That made Zacchaeus very happy, and he was thrilled to have Jesus come to his home. But people who watched this started to grumble, "Did you see that Jesus is going to eat with the sinners again?"

On the way to his house, Zacchaeus stopped and said, "Jesus, I'm going to give half of everything I own away to the poor. And the people I've cheated I will repay four times as much as I took from them." Jesus smiled and said, "This is really a great day for you, Zacchaeus. You are turning your life around. The Son of Man came to find the lost and save them."

The Gospel of the Lord.

Proper 27

A Reading from the Book of Haggai [1:15b–2:9]

God told a prophet named Haggai to speak to the people who had been dragged away from their homes to live in a strange land:

Are there any people who remember the good old days?

How do things look to you now? Things seem pretty bad, don't they?

But don't worry. Find the courage that is deep inside you because your God is with you! Just as God promised to be with you always and brought you out of Egypt. Don't be afraid, God's Spirit is inside of you.

"Pretty soon, I'll make this all better. I will shake everything up, and when I'm done shaking, this place will be a palace. Everything belongs to me," God says. "And I'll make your lives better than you could ever imagine. Better than they used to be. Don't be afraid. It will happen."

The Word of the Lord.

Psalm 145:1–5, 18–21

I will always sing your praises, God. You are the one in charge.
Every day I wake up and say, "God, you're the best.
Your greatness is as great as any greatness can be."
All the old people tell stories to the young ones about how great
you are.

Every day I wake up and say, "God, you're the best."

I look at the stars and the sunsets and the mountains and the trees and I am reminded of how great you are.

You are not just great and powerful. You are good, too.
And you're loving and kind.

Every day I wake up and say, "God, you're the best."

You listen to those who pray to you. And even answer our prayers.
You, O Lord, take good care of those who love you, and those who don't love you yet need to rethink their lives.

Every day I wake up and say, "God, you're the best."

A Reading from the Second Letter of Paul to the Thessalonians
[2:1–5, 13–17]

Remember when Jesus said he'd come back to us and gather us all around to be with him? Well, don't be worried about what others say that day will be like. That day will come, but not until things get better. A lot of bad things happen in the world, you know that already.

We always thank God for you because you believe in God and act like you are God's children! God called you to be his people, and will reward you with the glory God has given Jesus.

So keep on believing even when it's hard to believe. Don't forget what we taught you. May God who loves you and promises peace and puts hope in your heart comfort you when you're scared. May God make you strong so that you can go on believing and live the way God wants you to live.

The Word of the Lord.

✠ *The Holy Gospel of Our Lord Jesus Christ According to Luke* [20:27–38]

Some people, who didn't believe in life after death, found Jesus and asked him this trick question, "So, Jesus, you're a teacher. Moses taught us if a man's brother dies and leaves a wife but no children, he should marry her and have some children with her. So, what if there are seven brothers in all, and each one dies after having married that woman and still there are no children. When the woman finally dies, whose wife is she anyway? Who is her husband in heaven, since she had been married to all seven of them?"

Jesus said, "You know what? People marry each other on earth, but after they die everything is different. They are children of a NEW life. People who die are raised, but God isn't concerned about dead people but about living people. For to God all of them ARE alive."

What do you think about that?

The Gospel of the Lord.

Proper 28

A Reading from the Book of Isaiah [65:17–25]

I am ready to create a new heaven and a new earth.
What's in the past will stay in the past.
But be glad and rejoice forever in the new thing I'm creating.

Jerusalem will not be a city of pain, but full of joy. There will be no more crying there. All the children will grow up strong and live long and happy lives. People will build houses for their own families and plant vineyards and harvest excellent fruit. They will get to live their own lives. I will bless them. I will hear their prayers before they even pray. Wolves and lambs will eat side by side, and lions and ox will share their dinner. On my holy mountain, all will be peace, says God.

The Word of the Lord.

Canticle 9 (see The Great Vigil of Easter, Year A, p. 103)

A Reading from the Second Letter of Paul to the Thessalonians [3:6–13]

I'm telling you, dear ones, you must stay away from those believers who do absolutely nothing to further God's kingdom. That's not what they learned from us. We know that *you* know how to conduct yourselves because you have watched us. When we were with you we paid our own way. We worked night and day so that we wouldn't be a burden to you. We did this so we could set an example for you. Here's what I think—if you don't want to work, you shouldn't expect to eat. Those of you who aren't working need to get off your rear ends and earn your own living! Brother and sisters, don't give up on doing the right thing. Ever.

The Word of the Lord.

✠ *The Holy Gospel of Our Lord Jesus Christ According to Luke* [21:5–19]

When some were speaking about the temple, how it was decorated with beautiful things dedicated to God, Jesus said, "As for these things that you see, the days will come when not one stone will be left upon another; all will be thrown down." They asked Jesus, "How will we know when this is about to happen?" Jesus told them, "Lots of people will try to predict when the end will be. Don't listen to them. Just know that things are going to get worse before they get better. There will be wars, and earthquakes, famines, and plagues. All will signal the end. But before that happens, you will be arrested and brought to the authorities because you believe in me. This is your opportunity to speak up. Don't worry about what you will say, because I will give you the words and wisdom you need that will amaze your opponents. I'm sorry to tell you that you'll be betrayed, you will be hated, and some of you will be put to death because of my name. But you will have lost nothing, not a hair on your head. Because by holding on to your faith and to me, you will gain your souls."

The Gospel of the Lord.

Proper 29

A Reading from the Book of Jeremiah [23:1–6]

"You shepherds who destroy and scatter my sheep will have to answer to me," says God. "If you have not cared for them, I will hold you accountable for your evil doings. Then I will round up those sheep that are left, and bring them back to their fold and they will be fruitful and multiply. I will find new shepherds who will take care of them, so they won't need to be afraid anymore, or upset, or go missing."

"One of these days," says God, "Someone will come who will be a wise king like David, who will treat all people fairly. Then Judah will be saved and Israel will be safe. And everyone will say, 'God is our righteousness.'"

The Word of the Lord.

Canticle 16 (see The Second Sunday of Advent, Year C, p. 369)

A Reading from the Letter of Paul to the Colossians [1:11–20]

I pray that God will make you strong with God's very own power. I pray that you are ready to handle everything that happens with patience, all the while giving thanks to God. God has allowed you to share the gifts he has given the saints. God has rescued you from the power of darkness and surrounded you with the kingdom of his beloved Son, in whom all our sins are forgiven.

When we see Jesus Christ we are looking at the image of God whom we cannot see. He is the very first, and in him, everything there is was created—the things we can see and the things we cannot see. He holds everything together. He is the head of the body called the church. He is the beginning of the new creation, and leads us to that new creation. In him all of God's being was pleased to dwell. Through him God holds all things in his loving arms, by making peace through Jesus' lifeblood on the cross.

The Word of the Lord.

✠ *The Holy Gospel of Our Lord Jesus Christ According to Luke* [23:33–43]

When they came to the place they call The Skull, they nailed Jesus to a wooden cross and left him there to die. There were criminals with him, one on his right and one on his left. Jesus said, "Father, forgive them because they don't know what they're doing." The soldiers drew straws to see who got to keep his clothes. Some people stood there to watch him die, but the leaders who put him there said, "If he's the Savior, why can't he save himself? Some Messiah he is!" The soldiers mocked him, too, giving him sour wine to drink, saying, "If you are the King of the Jews, save yourself." There was a sign over his head that read, "This is the King of the Jews."

One of the criminals hanging there with him made fun of him. But the other defended Jesus, saying, "If I were you I'd shut up. You and I are getting what we deserve, but this man Jesus has done nothing wrong. Leave him alone." Then he said to Jesus, "Remember me when you come into your kingdom." And Jesus said, "For sure you will be with me today in Paradise."

The Gospel of the Lord.

Scripture Index